GREEK ATHLETES AND ATHLETICS

Olympia: vaulted entrance to the Stadium

GREEK ATHLETES
AND
ATHLETICS

H. A. HARRIS
Professor of Classics at St. David's College, Lampeter

With an introduction by
THE MARQUESS OF EXETER
Chairman of the British Olympic Association

GREENWOOD PRESS, PUBLISHERS
WESTPORT, CONNECTICUT

Library of Congress Cataloging in Publication Data

Harris, Harold Arthur.
  Greek athletes and athletics.

  Reprint of the 1966 ed. published by Indiana
University Press, Bloomington.
  Includes bibliographical references and indexes.
  1. Athletics--Greece. 2. Athletes--Greece.
3. Olympic games (Ancient) I. Title.
[GV21.H3 1979]   796'.0938   78-10139
ISBN 0-313-20754-2

Reprinted with the permission of Hutchinson Publishing
Group Ltd.

Reprinted in 1979 by Greenwood Press, Inc.
51 Riverside Avenue, Westport, CT 06880

Printed in the United States of America

10 9 8 7 6 5 4 3 2 1

To
My Wife

ACKNOWLEDGEMENTS

The Publishers gratefully acknowledge their indebtedness to the following:

To Messrs. Bell for permission to quote from B. B. Rogers' translation of Aristophanes.

To the Delegates of Oxford University Press and the Syndics of Cambridge University Press for permission to quote from the New English Bible, New Testament, 1961.

To the Editors of *Greece and Rome* and the Delegates of Oxford University Press for permission to reproduce three line drawings from *Greece and Rome*.

To these museums for permission to reproduce photographs of objects in their collections: the British Museum, the Ashmolean Museum, the National Museum of Wales, the American School at Athens, the Metropolitan Museum of Art, New York, the Museum of Fine Arts, Boston, the Museo Nazionale, Naples, the Staatlichen Antikensammlungen, Munich, the Staatliche Museen, Berlin, the Wagnermuseum, Wurzburg, the Musée d'Art Moderne, Paris.

Where no source is named, translations and photographs are by the author.

CONTENTS

PLATES

LINE DRAWINGS

MAPS

INTRODUCTION

By The Marquess of Exeter
Chairman of the British Olympic Association

I am very happy to have been asked to write a note at the beginning of this book and I am delighted to do so.

I commend it highly to those who are interested in sport and the Olympic Movement in particular. It must be the most comprehensive history that has been written of the ancient Olympic Games and obviously the author has done an immense amount of research. So often a book of this nature can be heavy reading, but this one I found to be most readable and one which I was loth to put down until I had finished it.

The Olympic Movement has been gaining in stature by leaps and bounds in the last 30 years and now over one hundred countries have National Olympic Committees. It will be of the greatest interest to their members to have such a comprehensive text-book of the history of the original Games. May I in particular commend to readers the last chapter headed 'Conclusions'. The author's carefully argued and logical comments on the present day situation as regards amateurism admirably put into words what so many of us who are dedicated to this movement are trying hard to achieve.

This book is an outstanding addition to sporting literature and I hope that it meets with the success that it so richly deserves.

Exeter

PREFACE

There are three groups of people who might be expected to be interested in a book on Greek athletics. There are those who know a great deal about ancient Greece but nothing about its athletics. There are those who know a great deal about modern athletics but nothing about ancient Greece. Finally there are the increasing numbers of intelligent tourists who visit Greece; they may know very little about the Greek world or its athletics, but when they find themselves in the great stadia at Olympia or Delphi they feel a natural curiosity about what went on there.

It is for the second and third of these groups that this book is primarily intended. For this reason I have kept Greek script out of the main body of the book, transliterating such technical terms as are necessary and untranslatable, and have included some history and literary comment which will be elementary to anyone with even a slight knowledge of the ancient world. At the same time I hope that scholars, judiciously skipping these parts, may find something of value to them. In my translations and in the notes I have ventured to offer some new interpretations of passages in Greek and Roman literature in which references to athletics occur, and which I believe have been imperfectly understood in the past. That some help in these matters is still needed in academic circles is obvious from the extraordinary statements about Greek athletics which continue to appear in the works of the learned. In a book published in 1962 an American archaeologist writes: 'An inscription from the Agora honors a Thasian named Theogenes who won 1300 times at Olympia.' The Greeks were less good at arithmetic than at other branches of mathematics, but any Greek could have calculated instantly that if Theogenes had entered for every athletic event at

19

every Olympiad, and won them all, the feat which he is stated to
have claimed would have required 649 years to complete.

In the spelling of Greek names the world of classical scholarship
has not yet reached a satisfactory solution. There is much to be said
for the modern practice of transliteration without Latinizing, but
some of us still cannot bring ourselves to write Aischulos or Thou-
kudides. I have pleased myself and expect to please no one else. So too
with plurals; in defiance of logic I have written stadia and gymnasia,
but palaestras and discuses.

Anyone who works in such a field as this must necessarily owe a
great debt to his predecessors. In the study of Greek athletics Dr.
E. N. Gardiner towers high above all others. Some additions to
knowledge have been made since he wrote, and some modern
developments in the world of sport enable us to see the later Greek
period with more understanding eyes; therein lies the sole justification for this book, which is in no sense intended to supersede
Gardiner's monumental works. Among later writers I owe most to
L. Moretti, who, like Gardiner, has brought to his books and
articles a combination of scholarship, knowledge of athletics and
common sense which has been all too rare in work on this subject.
The German contribution has been less happy. The Germans keep
their Greek and their athletics well apart, and show more industry in
assembling material from the sources than inspiration in interpreting
it. But any student of the subject owes much to the labours not only
of German archaeologists but of such writers as Krause and Jüthner,
particularly the latter. My debt to other writers will be evident from
the works referred to in the notes and the 'Note on Books'.

On separate points I have consulted with much profit Mr. M. N.
Tod, Professor B. R. Rees, Professor R. M. Cook, Professor G. E.
Bean, Professor E. W. Hunt, the Reverend C. R. Renowden and
Mr. D. M. Lewis. Their advice has saved me from many errors; for
those which remain I alone am responsible.

I owe a deep debt of gratitude to the Society for Hellenic Travel
and to Mrs. E. Hardie and Miss Anne Hindle of the Society's agents,
Messrs. Fairways and Swinford. The tours and cruises of the Society
have made possible visits to many of the minor sites connected with
Greek athletics, for which a busy teacher could not have found the
time by any other means.

I am indebted also to the British Broadcasting Corporation, whose televising of sporting events makes it possible for the dweller in remote parts to keep in touch with modern developments in athletic techniques even more effectively than the most favoured spectator on the spot. But for such broadcasts this book could hardly have been written.

Finally I have to thank the Pantyfedwen Trust of St. David's College for a grant making possible the provision of additional illustrations in this book.

H. A. HARRIS

St. David's College
Lampeter

I THE PROBLEM AND
THE EVIDENCE

TOWARDS the end of the first century of the Christian era, Dio
Chrysostom, writing about a dispute between two Greek cities of
very unequal importance, says:

'The situation is exactly similar to that in athletics, when a small
man is fighting one very much larger. The latter is not permitted
the slightest breach of the rules, and if he offends even accidentally,
he is flogged; the small one can do what he likes, and everyone turns
a blind eye.'[1]

In broad outline the picture is a familiar one, the sympathy of the
spectators of a sporting event with the small man and the under-dog,
and this sympathy duly reflected in the decisions of the referee or
umpire. Yet there are strange details in the picture. Why is a small
man boxing or wrestling with a big one? Why is there no division
into classes by weight? Above all, the penalty of flogging for breaking the rules in a sporting event sounds strangely in our ears. This is
but one of many hundreds of similar allusions in Greek literature to
athletics, and almost all produce the same double impression on us.
Here is a world where organized sport occupies much the same
position as it holds in the social scene today, but many of the details
puzzle the modern reader. If he tries to satisfy his curiosity about
them, and to gain a complete picture of what went on in a Greek
stadium during an athletics meeting, he soon finds that he is facing
a very difficult problem and that there are many blank spaces in his
picture.

This lack of knowledge may appear strange in view of the important place of athletics in the life of the Greek world. Today athletic sports have to compete with many other pursuits for popularity among both spectators and active participants. According to season and country the modern games player can choose from football of various codes, lawn tennis, cricket, baseball, swimming, sailing, rowing and cycling, all major sports, besides many minor but well-organized activities. In the Greek world athletics had no such rivals. The Greeks had ball games—holding about the same position as bowls or billiards with us—as well as boat races and swimming races, but none of these appear ever to have aroused much popular interest. Apart from athletics, the only well-organized activity was horse and chariot racing, an expensive pursuit in which, then as now, the majority can have participated only as spectators. There was thus a concentration of interest on athletics which has no parallel in the modern world.

Moreover, the scope of Greek athletic events seems to us strangely limited. The programme of a meeting contained only boxing, wrestling, a specialized form of wrestling called the pankration, four races* and a pentathlon made up of long jumping, throwing the discus, throwing the javelin, a foot race and wrestling. The programme was usually duplicated or further multiplied for different age-groups, but it was never extended. It was already established at Olympia before 600 B.C. and from there it spread to the many hundreds of meetings held every year all over the Greek world; so far as our evidence goes, it was still unchanged more than 1000 years later when, at the end of the fourth century A.D., a Christian Roman emperor abolished the great athletic festivals on the ground that they were pagan. With their passion for hearing new things, which St. Paul noted, the Greeks combined a degree of conservatism which to us is almost inconceivable. It is as though the Cup Final had been played every year without any important change in the rules since before the Norman Conquest.[2]

With an activity so wide-spread and enduring as this it might be

* The shortest of these races was about 200 yards in length, the distance of the Greek measurement a 'stadion'. The word came to be used of the race run over this distance and then of the track on which the race was run; in this last sense it gives us our 'stadium'. In this book 'stade' is used for the measurement and the race, 'stadium' for the sports arena.

supposed that our knowledge of it would be extensive and detailed. In fact the opposite is the truth. What is known to everyone is seldom described; authors are much more attracted by the unfamiliar. There were not even any significant changes to be recorded. As soon as the Greek boy began to play with his fellows, they initiated him into these sports, as children have always done. *Tom Brown's Schooldays* affords an excellent illustration. When Tom was learning Cotswold wrestling from Job Rudkin and Harry Winburn, the author tells us, 'all the boys knew the rules of it', and we may be sure that these village boys had not learned the rules from a book. Later, when Tom, now at Rugby, was fighting Slogger Williams, a dispute arose about whether wrestling was allowed in a school fight; it was settled instantly by the oldest boy present: 'Of course he may throw him if he catches him fairly above the waist.' This is how a sporting tradition is transmitted, whether in a school or in a nation. Even when a player takes up a game after childhood he seldom reads the rules. Such knowledge of them as he possesses he gains pragmatically. It is not surprising, then, that we have no complete set of the rules of Greek athletics. Every Greek knew them in his very bones. Furthermore, in the innumerable chance allusions in Greek literature to athletics the author could always assume in his readers a thorough acquaintance with the whole background and practice of these activities. We, who lack this familiarity, are often left groping.[3]

There is another way in which Greek literature disappoints the student of this subject. For many of us, detailed descriptions of contemporary sporting events are a regular part of our daily reading, and if this ration from the newspapers is not sufficient, modern fiction adds a lavish supply of imaginary contests and matches. The Greeks took no less delight than ourselves in such descriptions, but there is no evidence that there was ever any demand for factual accounts of contemporary events; their taste was all for the fictitious, and by a curious literary convention all these contests were set in the semi-legendary heroic age. This poses a problem which goes back to Homer himself, who set the fashion. In the *Iliad*, Homer—we are now permitted to believe in the existence of the poet—gives us an account of the sports held at the funeral of the hero Patroclus; but we do not certainly know whether this account is part of the traditional material which came down to Homer from the age which he is describing, the twelfth century B.C., or whether he is giving us a picture of the athletics of his own day, probably the eighth century, about the time when according to tradition the Olympic games were first held. All Homer's epic successors, both Greek and Roman, whose works have survived, imitate their master by including games somewhere in their poems, and the same question falls to be asked about them all. Are they simply imitating Homer, are they drawing on the athletic practice of their own day, or are they consciously trying to be 'quaint' and archaic? The same situation would arise if all modern accounts of sporting events were set in the court of King Arthur. Future generations, trying to form an impression of an international football match of 1950, might well doubt the value of a twentieth-century description of the goal-keeping feats of Sir Bedivere.

In addition to these descriptions, Greek writers from time to time wrote books on technical aspects of athletics. Diogenes Laertius tells us that even Aristotle did not disdain the task of compiling lists of Olympian and Pythian victors, and an extant inscription records the official thanks of the authorities at Delphi to him for his Pythian catalogue. These lists have not survived, but a similar list of Olympian victors, compiled in the second century A.D. by Julius Africanus, has come down to us. We hear too of a book on wrestling, now lost, written by Protagoras, the celebrated contemporary of Socrates, and of other similar works. The sole survivor from this technical literature is, however, a great disappointment. In the second and third centuries A.D. it seems to have become fashionable in intellectual circles to take a patronizing interest in the athletics of the day, which were by that time wholly professional in the upper strata, just as an interest in professional football is fashionable in similar circles today. A somewhat precious producer of *belles lettres*, Philostratus of Lemnos, during this period wrote a treatise *On Gymnastic* of which some fifty pages have survived. It is an attack on the decadent athletics of the day and an appeal for a return to earlier and sounder methods of training. But its author knows little of athletics from the inside and shows no evidence of any serious practical acquaintance with its techniques. The book is a mere literary exercise. It breaks off most tantalizingly just as the author seems about to grapple with practical details, and the surviving part contains scarcely a single hard fact which we do not already know from other sources.[4]

Much more useful is a work of about half a century earlier, the
Periegesis of Pausanias. In the second century of the Christian era,
thanks to the Roman peace, communications within the civilized
world were as safe as they have ever been before or since, and one
result of this was a great development of tourism—travel for
pleasure and to satisfy curiosity. Then, as now, Greece was one of the
first objects of travel in the Mediterranean, and to meet the needs of
these tourists Pausanias wrote his guide to the cities and monuments
of the country. The great athletic festivals had long been meeting-
points for the Greek world, and they now became tourist attractions
for the western half of the Roman empire as well. To no place does
Pausanias devote more space than to Olympia. He takes his readers
on a tour of the buildings and monuments, giving a description and
history of the most important. From the many hundreds of statues
of past victors in the games he selects those which were outstanding
as works of art or because of the interesting careers of the athletes
they commemorated. Historians complain that he was not always
sufficiently careful about the authorities on whom he drew for his
material, but without his book our knowledge of Greek athletics
would be slender indeed.

A short work by a contemporary of Pausanias deserves mention as
a source of evidence, the *Anacharsis* of Lucian. This writer, who came
from Mesopotamia and worked for a time in Gaul, was, like
Philostratus, an essayist, but a far finer literary artist. Anacharsis,
according to Herodotus, was a Scythian who visited Greece in the
sixth century B.C. and was put to death when he tried to introduce
Greek civilization among his fellow Scythians. For later Greeks he
became the embodiment of the virtues of the simple savage in
contrast to the vices of decadent civilization. Lucian's work is
an imaginary dialogue between Anarchasis, criticizing Greek
enthusiasm for athletics, and Solon, defending it. The arguments are
platitudinous, but some useful information is given incidentally. This
work, for instance, affords our sole piece of evidence that the aim of
javelin throwing in Greek athletics, as with us, was to achieve
distance, not to hit a target. Lucian was keenly interested in athletics
generally, and many casual references elsewhere in his works bring
us odd bits of knowledge.[5]

These authors, to whom we are indebted for so much of our
knowledge, belong to the time when Greece was part of the Roman

empire, and when the great athletic festivals had become entertain-
ments for the benefit of the spectators, the participants all being
professionals in the full modern sense of the term. If we seek information about the great age of Greek civilization, the sixth, fifth and
fourth centuries B.C., when most athletes belonged to the leisured
youth of the wealthier classes, the literary evidence is small, and the
bulk of what exists is exasperatingly unsatisfying. In the fifth century
it was customary for victors in the great games to commission poets
to compose odes in celebration of their achievements. Euripides and
Simonides are known to have undertaken this work, but their
victory odes survive only in fragments. Of the odes of Pindar and
Bacchylides, on the other hand, a substantial amount has come down
to us. Yet the student who searches the pages of these poets for details
of Greek athletic technique is sadly disappointed. Naturally enough,
the odes were composed for the wealthiest clients, who often sought
success in the equestrian events, where money can command victory,
rather than in the more laborious athletic programme. Even in the
odes whose hero is an athletic victor, Pindar and Bacchylides are more
concerned with the mythological origin of the victor's family and
the glories of his native city than with the details of his athletic
prowess. The descriptions of races and wrestling bouts which we
might reasonably hope to find are simply not there. Where a
technical term of athletics occurs in their pages it is almost always in
metaphor, and metaphors are unsubstantial evidence for a picture of
proceedings on a sports ground.

If the body of Greek writing devoted specifically to athletics is
small, the works of almost all Greek authors abound in sporadic
references to the subject, and it is on the patient collection and
examination of these scattered passages that we must largely rely for
our picture of Greek sporting life. Some of this work was done even
in antiquity; annotated editions of the classics are not a modern
invention, and the ancient annotators, called scholiasts, together with
the lexicographers and encyclopaedists, contribute a great deal to our
knowledge. By no means all their information is of equal value;
sometimes it goes back to early sources, but only too often the notes
are mere guess-work about a vanished age and are seriously misleading. One such source, for instance, contains the statement that
the Greek discus had a hole in the middle. No one believes this now,
but the error still lives on in the rendering 'quoit' which, even in an

age when throwing the discus is an event in every school sports, continues to disfigure modern lexicons and translations of the classics.[6]

Fortunately our evidence does not come from literature alone. The archaeologist has done much to help. His spade has brought to light many of the small objects used by athletes, their discuses, jumping weights and the strigils with which they scraped the oil and sweat from their bodies. Excavation has uncovered the stadia where the games were held, and many gymnasia and palaestras or wrestling schools in which the athletes trained. The most important discoveries are the inscriptions. Here the archaeologist and the literary student join hands. The excavator finds new inscriptions, and the epigraphist deciphers and interprets them. In many ways the Greek practice of engraving on stone or metal resembled our own. Tombstones and the panels under statues give us useful evidence of the achievements of individual athletes. But happily for us the Greek lack of cheap and abundant paper caused them to record on stone or bronze matter for which we are content with much less durable material. In this way there have survived lists of victors in some minor athletic festivals, amounts of prize-money and the cost of running the meetings. As a result of the practice of inscribing on stone the smallest details of public expenditure, we know, for instance, that the salary of the caretaker of the gymnasium at Delphi was eighty staters per annum and that the cost of laurel leaves for the sanctuary there was three obols for the same period. But bronze and dressed stone have been valuable materials in the eyes of subsequent generations, and the survival of such inscriptions, even more than that of literary works, has been subject to the hazards of time and circumstance.[7]

As with the literary evidence, the greatest number of athletic inscriptions come down to us from the Roman imperial period of Greek history. For the sixth and fifth centuries B.C. the far scantier epigraphic evidence is fortunately supplemented by a generous inheritance of vase paintings. Here, however, a warning is needed. Nothing could be sillier than the modern fashion of treating these paintings as if they were commercial photographs specially commissioned to illustrate a doctoral thesis. The Greek vase painter was an artist, faced with the task of ornamenting a panel often oddly shaped and on a curved surface. With him aesthetic considerations always came first. It would be as absurd to deduce the technique of

Greek discus throwing from the figure in Plate 1a as to use André Lhote's picture (Plate 1b) as evidence for the realities of a France v. Scotland Rugby match at the Stade Colombes. The affinities of the first picture are obviously with the ballet stage rather than the sports ground. Plate 3, an example of an oft-repeated error, is a clear warning against too ready acceptance of the evidence of the vases. The runners are depicted in an impossible attitude, with left arm and left leg advanced together. Painters so insensitive to the fundamental syntax of physical movement can hardly be regarded as sound authorities for the subtler details of athletic techniques. Convention too played its part in these paintings. Boxers and wrestlers are constantly depicted in attitudes as stereotyped as the fore-and-aft posture of galloping horses in early British sporting prints, and the Greek pictures may well be as far from reality as the British. Yet in spite of the need for this reservation, the fact remains that in athletics, as in many other activities, nothing else gives us so intimate a feeling of contact with the Greeks as these vase paintings, and no change in human fashion is more to be regretted than the one which brought an end to this style of pottery late in the fourth century B.C.[8]

Some statues of athletes survive, and no doubt athletes with their superb bodies served as models for many representations of gods. But sculptors naturally chose for the most part poses which showed the subject at rest and rarely attempted the dangerous task of depicting arrested motion; sculpture does not often help us with the details of athletic events. The most celebrated exception to this general rule, the discus thrower of Myron, which survives only in indifferent copies, has caused more controversy than enlightenment (Plate 10).[9]

A few Greek states put representations of athletes on their coins, the discus thrower of Cos and Abdera, for instance, and the wrestlers of Aspendos and Alexandria. The figures are naturally stylized, and the coins serve rather as proof of the Greek enthusiasm for athletics than as authoritative evidence of details of the activities depicted. The resemblance of the frigate on the twentieth-century British halfpenny to the twentieth-century British frigate is remote.

Such then is the problem, and such the material for solving it. Inevitably, if a writer is to preserve a proper scholarly attitude towards evidence so scanty and so unsatisfactory, the words 'probably' and 'possibly' must recur in his pages much more often than stylistic considerations would demand. The student of Greek athletics often feels himself to be in the position of a successor in A.D. 4000, trying to reconstruct the game of cricket on the evidence of the excavated foundations of the pavilion at Lord's, a few tattered pages from a *Wisden*, some cricket pictures from *Punch* and a handful of anecdotes about W. G. Grace.

II THE SPREAD OF GREEK ATHLETICS

FOR our purpose it is not necessary to enter upon the question of who the Greeks were or where they came from. We can accept their own definition of themselves as those who spoke the Greek language. According to the archaeologists Greeks first appeared in Greece at some time after 1800 B.C. and found there an incipient culture derived from the non-Greek Minoan civilization of Crete. They entered into this and from it developed a powerful and wealthy bronze-age culture of their own, generally called Mycenaean after the greatest of their cities. Its main strength lay in the Peloponnese, but by 1600 B.C. it had spread into north Greece and into many of the islands of the Aegean and Ionian seas. At a date which is still a matter of controversy, probably about 1400 B.C., the Mycenaeans appear to have been responsible for the destruction of the Minoan civilization of Crete, and some two centuries later they undertook the exploit by which they are best remembered, the siege and destruction of Troy. It was the last achievement of the age; perhaps the effort had been too great. New Greek-speaking invaders came into Greece, conveniently if not altogether accurately known as the Dorians, and the Mycenaean civilization, like the other great bronze-age cultures, crumbled away. There followed a long period of movement of peoples about which the later Greeks knew little or nothing, a dark age similar to the fifth and sixth centuries in British history. Much was destroyed, but not everything. In particular, much story and legend was preserved by oral tradition, a treasure to be drawn on freely by later Greek poets and dramatists. To the Mycenaean period belong most of the Greek stories which have excited the imagination

32

of writers, artists and sculptors ever since. From Thessaly come the
stories connected with Jason and the Argonauts, Medea and the
quest of the Golden Fleece. Thebes was the scene of another group,
to which belong the names of Cadmus, Oedipus and Antigone. Most
famous of all were the stories from Mycenae itself and the rest of the
Peloponnese, of the doom of the house of Atreus working itself out
in Agamemnon and Iphigeneia, Clytemnestra and Aegisthus, Electra
and Orestes. Agamemnon was the leader of the Greek expedition
against Troy, and this brings a further roll of famous names into the
story, Menelaus and Helen, Priam, Hector and Andromache, Achilles
and Patroclus. Oral tradition transmitted much of this in verse form,
and it is now widely accepted that about the eighth century B.C. a poet
of genius, Homer, used this material to mould his two surviving
epics, the *Iliad* and the *Odyssey*, with which Western literature begins.

It is reasonably certain that the Mycenaean Greeks enjoyed athletics.
Apart from the descriptions of the funeral games of Patroclus in the
Iliad and of the after-dinner contests of the Phaeacians in the
Odyssey, there are too many scattered references to athletics in the
epics to be explained away by any theory that Homer was ana-
chronistically introducing the sports of his own day into the
Mycenaean scene. Moreover, athletics appear in the body of
Mycenaean legend outside Homer. Hyacinthus, Acrisius and Phocus
were all killed by accidents in discus throwing. Brides were won by
the victors in foot races. The best known of these stories is that
which tells how Hippomenes won Atalanta. Others relate how
Penelope and the Danaidae were assigned in marriage to the winners
of races attended by less tragic consequences to the losers than befell
those defeated by Atalanta. Endymion, king of Elis, was said to have
decided which of his sons should be his successor by making them
run a race.[1]

Whether or not we should take the origin of athletics still further
back, to the Minoan age of Crete, is a debatable problem. There are
some concrete pieces of evidence in favour of such a theory, the most
famous being the 'Boxer' vase from Hagia Triada (Plate 2), dated by
archaeologists to about 1600 B.C. The literary tradition here and there
hints at a line of descent going back to Crete, notably the story in
Diodorus Siculus of how Androgeos, son of Minos, came from
Knossos to Athens and won popularity there by his athletic victories.
The evidence is naturally scanty and inconclusive, but there is

c

sufficient to prevent us from accepting unquestioningly Gardiner's indignant and dogmatic denial of a possible Cretan origin of Greek athletics.[2]

The Greek scene which emerges in the eighth century B.C. from the dark ages presents many changes from the Mycenaean world. The Greeks have spread over the whole Aegean and founded prosperous cities on the continental shores of Asia Minor, among them Miletus, Ephesus, Smyrna and Halicarnassus. But even this expansion was to prove inadequate to accommodate the growing population of this vigorous people, and in the eighth century a much wider movement of colonization started which in a couple of centuries was to take Greek civilization and the Greek language to most parts of the Mediterranean world. Parties of adventurers set out from their Aegean homeland and founded new cities wherever an opportunity for a more prosperous life offered itself. One important region of such colonization was the Black Sea, the Marmora and the Helles-pont. The south coast of Asia Minor, the Levant and Egypt were denied to the Greeks, but in Cyprus they disputed possession with the Phoenicians so successfully that they were able to establish several cities, with resultant problems even today. In North Africa they founded Cyrene, which exploited the fertility of Libya. The Phoenicians prevented any effective Greek settlement of the coast of Spain, but far-flung Massilia opened up the resources of the Rhône Valley and of Provence. The most important area of this expansion was Sicily and south Italy, where Hellenization was so complete that the Romans later called the region Magna Graecia. The sites of some of these colonies are now deserted, but the modern cities of Istambul, Odessa and Trebizond, of Agrigento, Syracuse, Catania and Messina, of Taranto, Reggio di Calabria, Naples and Marseilles show how excellent was the eye of the early Greeks in choosing a site.

The political organization of this extended Greek world was that of independent city states, a source at once of strength and of weakness. It was a source of strength because it gave to most Greeks a fierce local patriotism and a measure of political responsibility. If a man was fortunate enough to be a citizen of a democracy he could hardly escape playing some part in government at some time in his life; even if his city was governed by an oligarchy or a despot, at least he did not feel himself, as the citizens of great modern nations often do, the helpless victim of a distant and faceless bureaucracy. It was a source of weakness because the Greeks always found it difficult to combine against aggression from without, and they wasted much of their energy on inter-city wars and quarrels. Nevertheless, in spite of this tendency to fragmentation, there were some unifying influences in the Greek world. The most important was the Greek language; then again, the Greeks everywhere worshipped the same gods. A minor unifying factor was the wide-spread Greek love of athletics (Maps 1 and 2).

It is sometimes suggested that there was a fundamental difference between the athletic meetings of the Mycenaean age and those of later times, that the former were always held at funerals and the latter always as part of a religious festival. This is not true. Certainly the most detailed description of Mycenaean games we have is that of the funeral games for Patroclus in the *Iliad*, but the contests in the *Odyssey* have no connection with death; there is too a hint in the *Iliad* of a festival at Olympia, apart from the tradition that Heracles founded the Olympic games and won three events there in the same day. Moreover, funeral games did not end with the passing of the Mycenaean Age. Athletic sports were held at funerals at least as late as the fifth century B.C., especially at the funerals of those killed in war. They were held, too, in historic times to keep alive the memory of great statesmen and soldiers such as Brasidas of Sparta, killed in action in 422 B.C.* Undeniably, however, the most important athletic meetings of later Greece were part of religious festivals. At first sight this link is almost as odd to the modern mind as the earlier connection with funerals. Nor is it to be explained simply by the holy day becoming a holiday. With their strong anthropomorphic conception of divinity, the Greeks believed that the gods took pleasure in the same things as mortals—music, poetry, drama and dancing —and as they were held to share aesthetic pleasures, so it was believed they were delighted with displays of physical excellence. No doubt the double motive of religion and sport helped to swell the attendance at these festivals from all over the Hellenic world.[3]

By the sixth century B.C. four of the many Greek athletic meetings

---

* Even today the custom is not altogether dead. At rugby football the Mobbs memorial match is played annually in memory of a former international player who was killed in the First World War, while at Mountain Ash athletic sports are held on New Year's Eve each year to perpetuate the memory of a great Welsh runner, Guto Nyth Bran.

had become pre-eminent in importance. These were the Olympic games, held in honour of Olympian Zeus, the Pythian, which took place at Delphi at the festivals of Apollo, the Isthmian, dedicated to the god Poseidon and also commemorating the hero Archemorus, and the Nemean in honour of Zeus. The reasons for their fame were probably as accidental as those which made Canterbury or Compostella outstanding among many objects of pilgrimage in the middle ages, or those which have caused Henley and Wimbledon to tower above other regattas and tennis tournaments. Certainly convenience and ease of access can have had nothing to do with it. Olympia and Nemea in particular can never have been easy to reach.

The Olympic and Pythian games were held at four-yearly intervals; the Isthmian and Nemean were biennial, the Isthmian held in Olympic and Pythian years, the Nemean in the years between. In the period before Christ the Olympic years are those divisible by four. Thus, for example, 396 B.C. is an Olympic and Isthmian year, 395 Nemean, 394 Pythian and Isthmian, 393 Nemean and so on. In the Christian era, owing to the absence of a year 0, the Olympic years are 4n+1. Thus Olympic years were 4 B.C., A.D. 1, A.D. 5, A.D. 9 and so on.

The prizes at these games were crowns or garlands, at Olympia of wild olive, at Delphi of the laurel of Pythian Apollo, at Isthmia of pine and at Nemea of wild celery. In less famous 'crown' games elsewhere other plants were used, white poplar at Rhodes, myrtle at Thebes and Argos, barley at Eleusis. In addition a palm was put in the hand of the victor and he was wreathed in ribbons. The prizes at other festivals were more utilitarian. At Argos shields were awarded, at Megara, Sicyon and Marathon silver cups—and shields and cups are still popular sporting trophies. Sometimes the games appear to have served to advertise a local product. The prizes at Pellene in Achaea were warm leather jerkins. At Athens victors received amphorae of the olive oil for which Attica was renowned. In the fifth and fourth centuries B.C. some of these amphorae were examples of the magnificent Athenian painted pottery; the subjects of the paintings were appropriately athletic, and surviving Panathenaic amphorae are among our most valuable evidence (Plates 1a, 3, 17, 18). An inscription of the fourth century B.C. tells us that prizes for boys' and youths' events at Athens varied between thirty and sixty amphorae of oil, awards well worth having; unfortunately the statement of men's prizes is lost, but presumably they were even more valuable. We hear too of bronze cauldrons as prizes at some meetings (Plate 22b), and Herodotus mentions a festival in Caria where the prizes were bronze tripods which winners were not allowed to take away but had to dedicate in a local temple.[4]

We are sometimes called on to admire the Greek athletes of antiquity on the ground that they were content to struggle for a worthless crown, and they are held up as paragons of the purest amateurism in sport. The facts hardly support this roseate view. The winner of an event in one of the great 'crown' festivals was on a very good thing. He expected to be substantially and materially rewarded by his city for the glory which his victory had brought it. If Plutarch is to be believed, Solon, when legislating for Athens about 590 B.C., laid down maxima for these grants, 500 drachmae for an Olympic victor, 100 for an Isthmian. Even the smaller Isthmian award was almost as much as a year's earnings of a working man.[5]

For obvious reasons the majority of the competitors at the great festivals in the early centuries were drawn from the wealthier classes. They alone had the leisure to train and they alone could afford to travel to the meetings. Yet it is impossible to dogmatize on this point. The earliest recorded Olympic victor, Coroebus of Elis in 776 B.C., is said to have been a cook, but he was a local man and so would not have been put to any great expense by competing. The winner of the boxing at Olympia in 520 B.C. was a ploughman, Glaucus of Cary- stus in Euboea, about whom an interesting story was told. One day when working in the fields he hammered a ploughshare into its socket with his bare fist. During the Olympic final, when things were going badly for him, his father—or according to another account his trainer—shouted out to him a reminder of this feat, whereupon he dealt with his opponent's head as he had treated the share. Another Olympic victor, mentioned by Aristotle, was a fish-porter. Even at this early period, then, athletes were not drawn exclusively from a narrow social class. It may be that wealthy patrons sometimes helped promising athletes from the working class who could not otherwise have afforded to compete, as in the Regency period in Britain Corinthian bucks patronized boxers. Early in the third century B.C. Theocritus gives us a picture of this happening; a Sicilian land-owner, Milo, takes his cowman Aegon off to compete at Olympia, to the considerable contempt of Aegon's fellow workers. Aristotle is said to have paid the expenses of Philammon of Athens, an Olympic victor in boxing. We know too that in 472 B.C. the city of Argos won the four-horse chariot race at Olympia with a team raised and entered by the state. If the state could subsidize a chariot there seems to be no reason why it should not have helped an individual athlete. There appears, however, to be no direct evidence that any city ever did so.[6]

Though we must reject any picture of pure amateurism in Greek athletics at any period, it nevertheless remains true that Greek life from the sixth to the fourth century B.C. preserved a better balance between sport and other more important activities than did subsequent times. We do not hear of anyone, except perhaps Theogenes of Thasos, who made athletics a career. The highest achievements in sport were still open to young men with ambitions to make their mark in the world in other ways, men for whom games were only a relaxation. Many who became famous in other spheres were successful athletes in their young days; Plato competed in the Isthmian games as a wrestler. Many who won renown primarily as athletes served their cities well in peace and war, Milo and Phaÿllus of Croton, Dorieus of Rhodes and Antiochus of Lepreum. We search in vain among the later Olympic records for any such figures.[7]

At the beginning of the fifth century B.C., the Greek world was faced with the threat of being invaded and absorbed by the great Asiatic power of Persia, whose boundaries now included the whole of Asia Minor, the Levantine coast and Egypt, and stretched south and east to the Persian Gulf, Afghanistan and the Himalayas. For the first and only time since the Trojan war the Greek city states managed to achieve some degree of united action, and by heroic efforts at Marathon and Thermopylae, Salamis and Plataea, performed the almost impossible feat of throwing back the enormously superior forces of the invaders and vindicating their own freedom. This triumph inaugurated the most brilliant period of achievement of the Greek genius, a period in which the Athenians, who had fought with great distinction in the Persian wars, played a chief part. But Athens was ill guided by her leading statesman, Pericles, who lacked any Panhellenic vision and involved his city in two wars of aggression against other Greek states. He died before the second of these wars, the great Peloponnesian war of the last third of the century, had well started, but his unhappy influence survived him, and the struggle ended in the complete defeat of Athens at the hands of Sparta and her allies. Athens had still much to give the world in the cultural sphere, but the fresh bloom of her splendour was gone. It had almost all been contained within the fifth century B.C. Those who believe that success in international sport is a necessary part and a true criterion of national greatness might pause to reflect that of 158 Olympic victories in athletic events in the fifth century won by men whose names and cities are known, no more than four were Athenian.*

One of the most deplorable results of the Peloponnesian war was that it revived the Persian threat to Greece. There were far-seeing men such as Isocrates who realized the necessity of a Panhellenic union to face the danger, but they pleaded in vain, and when in the end some measure of unity was achieved it was imposed from without. Philip, King of Macedonia in north Greece, would probably have been glad to be the leader of a free alliance of Greek states, but they would have none of it and he was driven to compel them to submission by force of arms. His victory at Chaeronea in 338 over an army consisting mainly of Athenians and Thebans virtually ended the epoch of the independent city state and left him master of the Greek scene. Now he made ready to lead a combined force of reluctant allies to remove for ever the Persian menace, but just as his preparations were nearing completion he was assassinated. The task was taken up by his son, Alexander the Great. In 334, a young man only twenty-three years of age, he crossed the Hellespont into Asia at the head of his army, never to return; in the eleven years of life left to him he changed completely the course of history of the eastern Mediterranean. First he made himself master of Asia Minor and crushed the Persian army under Darius II at the battle of Issus. Then he passed through Syria, Phoenicia and Palestine and accepted the surrender of Egypt. Returning to the head of Mesopotamia, he won a second victory over Darius on the banks of the Tigris; Babylon and the immense wealth of central Persia now fell into his hands. After three years of tough guerilla fighting in Afghanistan he made his final advance into India and won the last of his great battles on the banks of the Hydaspes, a tributary of the Indus. He would

* Xenophon tells us that the younger Pericles criticized the Athenians for their inferiority to the Spartans in physical excellence, while Socrates defended them on the ground that in the games they obeyed the umpires better than anyone else. This has a very familiar ring.[8]

have pressed on further, but was thwarted by the monsoon rains. After making his way back to Babylon he was embarking on the organization of his vast conquests when he was seized with a fever and died in 323, not yet thirty-four years old.

Whether or not Alexander cherished ecumenical dreams of a whole world at peace under a single government is debatable; if that was his ambition he did not live to realize it. But what he did achieve is remarkable enough. Though his more distant conquests to the east and south east reverted almost at once to native rulers, Asia Minor, Syria, the Levant, Palestine and Egypt were thoroughly Hellenized and for many generations were ruled by Greek dynasties. The Greek language became the lingua franca of the whole region and for many of the inhabitants their only tongue. Alexander had set the example of founding new Greek cities in the countries he overran, many of them named after himself. The practice continued after his death; from these centres the Greek way of life spread to the older cities of the countries, finding expression in temples, colonnades, basilicas, theatres and works of art after the Greek pattern, many of which have survived to our own day. Among the departments of Hellenic life thus given a new and wider sphere were Greek athletic sports (Maps 3 and 4).

Alexander himself is said to have been a keen athlete, but to have avoided taking part in public games on the ground that kings should compete only against kings. The reason for this eschewal is probably revealed in an anecdote told by Plutarch; on one occasion Alexander ran a race against the leading sprinter of the day who, no doubt with the best intentions, ostentatiously eased up to allow the king to beat him, a gross affront to the dignity of a proud man.* His last recorded utterance was a play on words in a metaphor drawn from athletics, 'I foresee that there will be great funeral games for me', a grim prophecy of the fierce struggle for power which followed his death. It is not surprising, then, that the army of a king so keen on athletics took the cult with them. Two of his generals, Perdiccas and Craterus,

---

* Plutarch names the king's opponent as Crison of Himera. This must be a mistake, as Crison's three Olympic victories were in 448, 444 and 440 B.C., a century before Alexander. Plutarch's slip over the name, however, does not necessarily invalidate the anecdote; it is probably due to an unconscious recollection on his part of a remark of Socrates in Plato's *Protagoras*: 'If Crison and I ran a race, he would have to ease up; for I cannot run quickly, but he can run slowly.'

carried with them on their campaigns a huge marquee 200 yards long to enable training to be continued under all conditions of weather, perhaps the earliest example of indoor athletics. They also took baggage animals laden with powder for wrestlers. Strabo tells us that as soon as the army entered India the native craftsmen turned to the production of strigils and oil-flasks, the indispensable equipment of the Greek athlete. Alexander entrusted his Indian conquests to a native client king, and no part of the sub-continent was ever under direct Greek rule, yet we read in Philostratus of an Indian rajah of the first century A.D. who had a training ground laid out in the park of his palace where he practised throwing the discus and javelin in the Greek way. Perhaps the most astonishing evidence of the spread of enthusiasm for athletics in unexpected quarters is to be found in the complaint of the author of *Maccabees* in the second century B.C. that the young priests in Jerusalem were neglecting their temple duties in order to practise discus throwing. [9]

Very soon after the conquest, stadia were constructed all over the newly Hellenized territories, and cities vied with one another in instituting new athletic festivals after the pattern of those in older Greece. Alexandria and Antioch, Tyre and Sidon, Ascalon and Gaza, Damascus, Tarsus, Perga and Laodicea were only a few of the cities of this new Greek world in which athletic meetings were inaugurated (Map 4). Sometimes these new meetings were 'crown' games, if the promoting cities could prevail on their neighbours to grant 'isolympian' or 'isopythian' honours to the victors in them. Thus an inscription of about 280 B.C. found in the island of Amorgos records a decree of a confederacy of island cities welcoming the foundation of games at Alexandria by Ptolemy Philadelphus in honour of his father, and giving this undertaking:

'Citizens of the islands who win victories in these games shall receive the same honours as those laid down in the laws of each island city for those who win a victory at Olympia.'

Half a century later a festival of Artemis at Magnesia on the Meander in Asia Minor which had previously given money prizes was accorded 'crown' status for the first time; a series of inscriptions records decrees, granting Pythian honours to victors at these games, passed at Ithaca, at Megalopolis and eighteen other cities of

Arcadia, at Epidamnus, Calchis, Paros and seventeen other island cities.[10]

But wealth was abundant in the Greek world after Alexander's conquests, and at many of these new festivals the winners received money prizes of considerable value. The athletes themselves, as the many inscriptions recording their victories tell us, divided these meetings into 'talent' and 'half-talent' categories according to the prize-money awarded. We are fortunate in having a number of inscriptions from the not very important city of Aphrodisias in Asia Minor, enumerating the prizes in the games there early in the Christian era; the list is interesting also as showing the relative popularity of the different events. These are the prizes in the men's competitions:

Long-distance race	750 denarii.	Pentathlon	500
200 yards	1250	Wrestling	2000
400 yards	1000	Boxing	2000
Race in armour	500	Pankration	3000

The youth's prizes were roughly two-thirds and the boys' one-third of these amounts. In calculating the purchasing power of these prizes it may be remembered that at about this time a denarius was the day's wage agreed on by the labourers in the parable of the vineyard in the New Testament and that the Good Samaritan left two denarii for the maintenance of the injured man during his absence. Aphrodisias was not a particularly wealthy or important city.[11]

This pouring of money into athletics was partly a symptom and partly a cause of a change in the status of sport which probably began early in the Hellenistic period, the age which followed the death of Alexander. From being an amusement for the enjoyment of the participants in their leisure time, it became primarily an entertainment for spectators provided by full-time professional entertainers. The monetary rewards now available on a considerable scale made it well worth while for many a young man to devote the most active years of his life to this career. This did not mean that other young men and boys ceased to enjoy their athletics, but the standards of performance set by the skill of the professionals put the important meetings far out of the reach of the amateur. We have seen exactly the same thing happen in football during the last century.*

Less than two centuries after the death of Alexander, Rome, with her growing power, began to be drawn into the affairs of Greece. At first she acted simply to protect Roman interests in the eastern Mediterranean and without any intention of annexation. As time went on, partly through force of circumstances and partly through the ambitions of individual soldier-statesmen, Roman policy became more aggressive, and when, shortly before the beginning of the Christian era, the republic gave place to the empire, the whole of the Greek world had passed under Roman rule. This did not cause as much change in the life of the Hellenistic countries as might have been expected. In the west the Romans had extended their sway over countries for the most part of a culture inferior to their own, and inevitably they had imposed on their subjects their superior civilization and their own Latin tongue as a common language. In the east, on the other hand, they became rulers of subjects whose cultures they recognized as far older and in many respects finer than their own; moreover, this part of the world already possessed in Greek a common language. The Romans accepted the situation. They used Greek as an official language, and while they milked the Greek world of much of its wealth they gave it in return the Roman peace, the rule of law, and government which by the standards of the day was reasonably good and efficient. For several centuries the whole Mediterranean world was under a single central administration, yet the two halves never coalesced; they remained a Latin west and a Greek east, and when in the fourth century the imperial authorities decided in the interests of efficiency to divide the empire for administrative purposes into two parts, the division was made on this basis. After the collapse of the Latin empire in the west in the fifth century, the Greek eastern empire, with its capital at Byzantium, kept Graeco-Roman civilization alive for a further thousand years.

The contrast between the two halves of the Mediterranean world was reflected in sport and public entertainment. In the west the arena, with its brutal contests of gladiators and wild beasts, afforded the

* In 1874 the F.A. Cup was won by Oxford University, in 1879 by the Old Etonians. Both these clubs still play the game with no less enjoyment and probably with even greater skill, but it is unlikely that either of them will ever win the Cup again.

most popular amusement. In the east, enthusiasm for athletics persisted. Gladiatorial shows were not unknown there, but they never seriously challenged the supremacy of the stadium. In the same way athletics never made much headway in the west.* Athletic festivals continued into the Roman imperial era in some of the Greek cities of Sicily and south Italy, notably in Naples, but the only Latin city where athletics flourished at all was Rome itself, where for a time after the middle of the first century B.C. Greek customs were fashionable in intellectual circles. Augustus gave athletic games at Rome in a temporary wooden stadium erected near the Circus Maximus. His example was followed by Nero, who was also a keen patron of the great festivals in Greece. At the beginning of the collapse of his power Nero was in Naples when news arrived of the revolt of Gaul, and Suetonius relates how the emperor, to conceal his perturbation at the report, 'at once went to the gymnasium and with the closest attention watched the athletes at their training'. Domitian built in Rome a permanent stadium, the outlines of which can still be traced in the Piazza Navona. Here were held the Capitoline games with crowns of oak leaves as prizes, which Greek athletes in order to flatter the emperors ranked on a level with the four premier 'crown' festivals of Greece.¹²

For the athletics of the Greek world the chief result of the Roman conquest was the foundation of new festivals by emperors or the refounding of old meetings under fresh imperial titles. Games under the labels Augusteia, Antoninia, Hadrianeia, Commodeia, Trajaneia or Severeia proliferated in the eastern Mediterranean (Map 4). Many athletes prefixed Roman names, mostly derived from emperors, to their own Greek, producing such hybrids as Marcus Aurelius Demetrius, Tiberius Claudius Petrobius and Titus Domitius Prometheus.

The one new feature of the athletic scene in Roman times is the synod or xystus, the professional organization or trade union of athletes.† The first mention of this is in a papyrus recording a rescript of Mark Antony which must belong to either 41 or 33 B.C., though

* The only sport equally popular in both parts of the empire was chariot racing.
† The synod seems to have been originally the organization of all competitors at festivals, athletes, actors and musicians, while the xystus (properly a practice running track) was the athletic section of the synod. Later the two words appear to have become interchangeable.

the terms of the rescript imply that the institution had existed for some time.

'My friend the trainer Marcus Antonius Artemidorus, eponymous priest of the synod of winners in the sacred games and of crowned victors from the whole inhabited world, asked me to confirm the inviolability of the existing privileges of the synod and to make these further grants: exemption from military service, immunity from public duties and from billeting, a truce for the period of festivals and the right to wear purple.'[13]

Another papyrus records the granting in A.D. 194 of a certificate of membership of the synod to Herminus of Hermopolis in Egypt in return for a fee of 100 denarii, adding that Herminus made a payment of fifty denarii to the synod when he was acting as priest of the Asian games at Sardis. In the Roman manner the document incorporates extracts from relevant decrees of earlier times. It quotes a rescript of the emperor Claudius thanking the synod for the gift of a golden crown on his conquest of Britain in A.D. 43. It adds another expression of thanks from Claudius to the synod for organizing games performed in his honour before the kings of Commagene and Pontus in Asia Minor. Finally it quotes a rescript of Vespasian, confirming the privileges granted by Claudius.[14]

In the early stages athletes probably organized themselves in local groups. But the Roman emperors always tended to suspect any such association as a possible centre of political opposition and unrest; readers of the younger Pliny will remember how even so sensible an emperor as Trajan forbade the establishment of a much-needed fire brigade at Nicomedia on these grounds. For this reason the separate xysti were dissolved at some time in the first century and reconstituted as a single organization under the emperor. The officers of the branches, the xystarchs, thus became nominees of the emperor, and the imperial authorities retained full control over the proceedings of the synod. This professional organization of athletes is an interesting early example of the trade union as an instrument of state.[15]

A large number of inscriptions from the Christian era reveal various activities of the xystus. It organized games, gave money prizes at others, and voted statues and honours to its own members, to promoters of meetings, to benefactors and to emperors. At festivals the local xystarch had such duties as the distribution of oil among the athletes; he sometimes spent his own money. In the financial accounts of the games at Aphrodisias there is a mysterious entry, thrice repeated: 'To the xystarch for "filling up".' The amounts paid on the three occasions are 745, 647 and 250 denarii. 'Filling up' may mean simply 'repayment'. On the other hand, the xystarch may have been responsible for ensuring that the lists of entries for the events were full, and have expected some reward for his efforts.[16]

The main concern of the xystus, however, as of a modern trade union, was with the pay of its members. How far pay claims were pressed we can read in a letter sent by Pliny when he was governor of Bithynia to the emperor Trajan early in the second century. There was a category of games known as 'eiselastic' which gave the winners in them the right of a ceremonial entrance into their city on their return home and to a special money allowance from the city. Pliny reports that, whereas in the past allowances had been paid from the date of the ceremonial entry, the athletes were now claiming that they should be paid from the date of the victory; further, that in some games which Trajan had recently raised to eiselastic status, victors in previous years were now claiming that back payments of the allowance should be made. In his reply Trajan gives his decision that payment should continue to be made from the date of the entry; on the second point he shrewdly remarks that where he had demoted festivals from the eiselastic category, past winners were not required to repay allowances already received, and that the same principle should apply to games promoted to the higher level.[17]

The privileges and exemptions accorded to athletes under the Roman empire are simply an expression of the high esteem in which the leading exponents of sport were held by the people. We are apt to think of the frenzied adulation of sportsmen and entertainers as a modern phenomenon, but it was no less marked in antiquity. Oppian, looking for a simile to describe pilot-fish crowding round a ship, can find no better picture than the mob of admirers round a popular athlete:

'As an athlete crowned with fresh laurels is beset by boys, youths and men who conduct him to his house and crowd round him in troops until he crosses the threshold of his home.'

At least we in our day have not yet reached a stage at which these darlings of the people are officially granted exemption from military service and the other civic duties of the ordinary citizen.[18]

The excessive admiration of athletes did not begin in the Christian era. As early as the sixth century B.C. Xenophanes was deprecating it, and his example was followed by Euripides, Plato and Diogenes. In these early times a city would erect a statue of a victor at the scene of his victory and another in the city itself, and perhaps bestow on him the right of a daily meal at the public expense. When Exaenetus of Acragas in Sicily won his second victory in the stade at Olympia in 412 B.C. he was escorted into his native city by a procession of 300 chariots drawn by white horses. But in the imperial epoch a mere triumphal entry was not enough. City walls were broken down to make the reception more spectacular. At the beginning of the empire wise heads had realized the dangers of this favoured treatment of athletes. Maecenas urged Augustus to restrict the privileges to victors at Olympia and Delphi, but the advice was not taken. The results were what might have been expected. Philostratus tells us that in his day corruption was rife everywhere in the athletic world except at Olympia. He relates a story of a boy wrestler who sold the final of his event in the Isthmian games for 3000 drachmae, foolishly neglecting to secure payment in advance. The victor refused to pay up, and his rival had the shameless affrontery to appeal to the law, though this, of course, involved his admission of his own part in the transaction. The last official document dealing with athletics is at least as significant in what it implies as in what it states. It was a rescript of Diocletian and Maximian of about A.D. 300, laying down that exemption from civic duties was to be granted only to competitors who without corruption or bribery had won three or more crowns in sacred games, at least one of them in Rome or ancient Greece. Less than a century later the closing of the Olympic games virtually brought to an end the history of Greek athletics. Even the most passionate lover of sport could scarcely wish that it had continued longer.[19]

III ATHLETICS IN THE EPIC TRADITION

WE HAVE seen that the descriptions of games found in the epics of Greek and Roman poets are of very doubtful value as evidence for athletic practice at any period. Yet they are the only objective accounts we have and they cannot be disregarded; there is always the possibility that some detail of contemporary procedure may have been included, perhaps unconsciously, by the author.

The earliest descriptions of sports we have are those in Homer, and his works alone have any authority for the athletics of the Mycenaean age. It is clear from Homer that at that time athletics were a normal diversion for the warrior class. Competition in games is a natural sequel to a feast. Agamemnon, urging Diomedes to greater feats in battle, reminds him how his father Tydeus had once gone to Thebes and found the Thebans feasting in the palace of Eteocles:

'Then Tydeus, driver of horses, stranger as he was, did not fear, though he was alone among many Cadmeians, but he challenged them to compete with him in athletics and easily beat them all.'[1]

There is a charming picture in the *Odyssey* of such games after a feast. Odysseus, in the course of his long homeward journey, is hospitably entertained by Alcinous, king of Phaeacia. After the banquet a bard, not knowing the identity of the guest, sings of incidents in the Trojan war, which bring unhappy memories to Odysseus. To cheer him up, Alcinous proposes athletic competitions:

' "Now that we have had our fill of the rich feast of the lyre, the proper companion to a rich banquet, let us go out and enjoy contests

48

of all kinds, so that our guest, when he returns home, may tell his friends how far we surpass other men in boxing, wrestling, jumping and running."

First of all came a foot-race. The course stretched out in front of them from the starting line, and they all flew over the ground, raising a cloud of dust. Clytoneüs was far the speediest of them and beat them by a mule-team's stint of ploughing; the rest were nowhere. Then they went on to the tough sport of wrestling; at that Euryalus was supreme. Amphialus won the jump, and Elatreus was far the best with the discus, while Laodamas, the noble son of Alcinous, carried off the boxing.'

At this point Laodamas courteously suggests to his friends that they invite Odysseus to show his ability as an athlete:

' "Come, Sir, join us in ours ports if you are skilled in any of them. You look like an athlete, for nothing brings a man greater renown throughout his life than what he does with his hands and feet." '

Odysseus at first politely declines on the grounds of the hardships he has suffered, but Euryalus, the winner of the wrestling, insultingly taunts him with being a mere merchant seaman and no athlete, whereupon Odysseus, after a stinging rebuke to Euryalus, shows his prowess:

'Jumping up just as he was in his cloak, he seized a great heavy discus, far weightier than the one with which the Phaeacians competed. He swung it round and hurled it from his stout hand, and the stone hummed in its flight. Those famed seafarers, the Phaeacians of the long oars, cowered beneath the hurtling mass. Flying lightly from his hand, it pitched beyond all the marks. Athene in the likeness of a man put in the marker and addressed Odysseus: "Even a blind man fumbling with his hands could pick out your marker, for it is not with the group of the others but far in front of them. You can be sure that you have won this contest; none of the Phaeacians could equal this throw, much less beat it." '

Elated by his success, Odysseus now challenges the Phaeacian youths to match him in boxing, wrestling, or even running, refusing

D

only to box with Laodamas on the ground that he is his host. He claims to be 'not bad' at all sports, especially archery. He can throw a javelin as far as other men can shoot an arrow. Only at running is he afraid that the Phaeacians might beat him, for his legs have been stiffened by his seafaring. At this point Alcinous intervenes. He tells Odysseus that the Phaeacians do not claim for themselves exceptional merit as athletes; they are good runners but not outstanding as boxers or wrestlers; their great pride is in their seafaring, music and dancing. So the scene of the sports ends.[2]

Even more famous than the Phaeacian games of the *Odyssey* is the description in the *Iliad* of the games held in celebration of the funeral of Patroclus, with Achilles, the close friend of the dead hero, as their president. The festival opens with a chariot race, recounted in great detail by the poet; it is obvious that chariot racing is his favourite sport. The first athletic event in the programme is boxing. As soon as competitors are called for, Epeius steps forward with the confident announcement to which boxers are prone:

' "This is what I say, and this is what will happen. I will tear my opponent's flesh and smash his bones. Let all his friends stand by to carry him away when I have finished with him." '

After some hesitation Euryalus takes up the challenge. Diomedes acts as his second, putting on his trunks and 'well-cut thongs of domestic cowhide', the Greek equivalent of boxing gloves. The fight is a short one.

'As Euryalus was looking for an opening, Epeius came in and hit him on the cheek. He could not stand up any longer, for there and then his fair limbs failed beneath him. As when beneath the ripples of the North wind a fish jumps from a tangle of seaweed and then the waves cover him again, so Euryalus flew through the air at the blow.'

Epeius behaves better in victory than might have been expected from his prelude; he picks up his rival and sets him on his feet.

'Then his friends crowded round him and led him away with dragging feet and lolling head, spitting out thick blood.'

From this first event in these games we see the limitations of poetry as evidence for athletics. It is impossible to gain from Homer a coherent picture of the end of the fight; the simile does not fit the straight account. The latter tells us that Euryalus was hit on the cheek and his legs collapsed under him. When this happens the boxer sinks to the ground; the simile describes a man lifted off his feet by an uppercut, and this normally happens only if the blow lands under the jaw.

The next event in the funeral games is the wrestling, and in this again there are only two competitors, Odysseus and Ajax son of Telamon. They grapple for so long that the spectators are bored; at last Ajax makes a great effort and lifts Odysseus off his feet, but Odysseus hams him with a skilful kick behind the knee and wins the first fall. At the next grapple both fall together, and at this point Achilles stops the contest, adjudging it a draw.

Then comes the foot race, for which three competitors challenge, Odysseus, Ajax son of Oileus, and Nestor's young son Antilochus. Achilles points out the finishing post to them, a fact which seems to indicate a straight course without a turn. Ajax takes the lead from the start, closely pressed by Odysseus:

'Thus Odysseus ran close behind him and trod in his footsteps before the dust could settle in them, and on the head of Ajax fell the breath of the godlike hero running lightly and relentlessly on.'

As they come to the last few yards Odysseus prays for divine assistance. This is forthcoming from Athene, who not only inspires him to fresh efforts but causes Ajax to slip and fall in a mass of cow-dung. The event ends in a pleasant scene. Ajax receives an ox as second prize:

'He stood, holding the horns of the ox and spitting out dung, and exclaimed: "Curse it, that goddess tripped me up. She always stands by Odysseus like a mother and helps him."'

The young Antilochus, as he takes the third prize, pays a graceful tribute to the ability of the veterans who have beaten him.

The description of the race, like much else in Homer, produces in the reader two opposite sensations: at one moment he is surprised at the modernity of what he reads, at the next he feels that he is in another world. Odysseus uses tactics in the race which are commonplace today. Every runner knows how disconcerting it is to have an opponent running at his shoulder and breathing down his neck. For many a reader, on the other hand, the intervention of the goddess robs the passage of all reality and consequently of much of its appeal. Here perhaps, through not allowing for differences in literary conventions, we are not being altogether just to Homer. We all recognize the great part which luck plays in any game. The Greeks simply found it more interesting to regard this as the intervention of personal deities than as the operation of impersonal chance.

The next event in the games is a curious one, a gladiatorial duel with edged weapons between Diomedes and Ajax son of Telamon. Homer probably found the story among his traditional material but felt doubts about it because in his own day the event had long been obsolete. At any rate, in the poem as it stands the fight is ended by the spectators almost before it has started.

Then comes the discus throwing. The discus is an ingot of raw metal straight from the mould (Plate 9a), and it also serves as the prize for the contest. Homer gives no details of the throwing, but his statement that Epeius 'whirled and threw it' makes it clear that the method of throwing was fundamentally the same as that used today.

Finally, after an archery match, Achilles proclaims a contest in throwing the javelin. Two competitors come forward, Agamemnon and Meriones. There is no throwing; Achilles awards the first prize to Agamemnon on the ground of his reputation, without any protest from Meriones. The very perfunctory nature of the account suggests that Homer found nothing about javelin throwing in the tradition and included it merely because it was a familiar event in his own day.[3]

Entertaining though the descriptions are, it is evident that Homer is not deeply interested in the technique of any of the sports he recounts. By far the most vivid element in the scenes is the interplay of character which emerges in competitors and spectators alike, the dispute between Menelaus and Antilochus during the chariot race, the boasting of Epeius, and the aged Nestor giving his prosy and unwanted advice to his son about driving, and boring all with his long-winded account of his own athletic feats long ago. Perhaps the most delightful incident in the funeral games is an argument between two spectators during the chariot race. On their homeward run the chariots have passed for a time out of sight of the crowd near the finishing post. As they come into view again, still a long way off, Idomeneus the Cretan and Ajax son of Oileus start to argue about who is leading. Idomeneus says it is Diomedes; Ajax tells him that he is half blind and that the leader is Eumelus. Idomeneus asks him if he will bet on it, and they are about to come to blows when Achilles tells them to stop behaving like children and to sit and watch and they will soon know who is leading. Anyone who has ever stood in a crowd to watch a sporting event will have seen this scene re-enacted a dozen times.

There is a tradition that in his old age Homer was blind, and this adds particular poignancy to Athene's remark in the *Odyssey* that even a blind man could tell that Odysseus had won the discus throwing. Yet from one or two phrases it is difficult to believe that the poet had not been an active athlete in his youth. This is particularly true of the wrestling match with the vivid touch of the red weals on the wrestlers' bodies caused by the tight grip of the fingers, and the brilliantly swift account of the first fall. Most significant of all, perhaps, is the phrase at the beginning of the foot race in both the *Iliad* and the *Odyssey*: 'The course stretched out from the starting line.' This is not a spectator's view. It recalls perfectly what a sprinter feels in that lonely moment when he goes to his mark and the finishing post recedes into an unimaginable distance.*

So great was Homer's prestige that many subsequent poets, both Greek and Roman, who wrote of the heroic age, felt it right to imitate him by including some athletic scenes in their epics. In the third century B.C. Apollonius of Rhodes in his *Argonautica* gives us a Homeric description of a boxing match. In their travels the Argonauts come to the country of the Bebrycians, whose arrogant king Amycus compels all strangers to contend with him in boxing. His challenge is taken up on behalf of the Argonauts by Polydeuces. Apollonius's account of the fight is conventional and wooden. This was apparently the opinion of his younger contemporary Theocritus, for he has left us a description of the same encounter in a poem

* It is only fair to state that the phrase has sometimes been understood to mean 'The running was at full stretch from the start', but this seems an unnecessarily tame rendering.

clearly intended to be an improvement on his predecessor's. We think of Theocritus primarily as the idyllic pastoral poet of the peaceful countryside, but in this work he has undeniably produced one of the most spirited accounts of an athletic event which have come down to us from antiquity.

'As soon as they had put on the boxing thongs they stepped into the ring, breathing slaughter against one another. At first they manœuvred to see who should get the sun behind him. Polydeuces outwitted his opponent, and the rays fell full on Amycus' face. He rushed in, but Polydeuces stopped him with a blow to the point of the chin which infuriated him still more. Now he began to mix it and came in head down. Polydeuces, however, side-stepped this way and that, and getting home with left and right caused the other to pause in spite of his confidence. Punch-drunk he halted, spitting out red blood, while the spectators yelled with delight at the sight of the severe wounds round his mouth and jaws. His face was so swollen that his eyes were almost closed. Then Polydeuces worried him with a succession of feints with both hands, and as soon as he saw him thoroughly confused went in with a blow straight to the centre of the brow, which skinned the whole forehead to the bone and stretched him on his back. He rose to his feet, and the fight grew even fiercer. Amycus succeeded in landing blows only on his opponent's body, but Polydeuces kept hammering away at the face. At last the Bebrycian king, anxious to achieve the *coup de grâce*, seized his rival's left hand with his own to throw him off balance, and at the same time brought up his right in a furious uppercut. Had it landed, it would have knocked out Polydeuces, but he rode the blow by drawing back his head and retaliated with a right to the head which cut open Amycus' temple. He followed this with a left to the mouth and then pounded away at the face until Amycus reeled and fell to the ground, holding up both hands in admission of defeat.'[4]

The next poet to give us an account of athletics in the heroic age is Roman Virgil, who in this part of his epic leans very heavily on Homer. He includes only two athletic events in the funeral games given by Aeneas for his father Anchises, a foot race and a boxing match. In the race, as in Homer, the leader, Nisus, slips in a pool of blood and falls, leaving Salius in the lead. Here Virgil allows himself an elaboration of his original. Nisus, lying on the ground, sees that his bosom friend Euryalus is lying just behind Salius; accordingly he trips up Salius, and Euryalus gains the victory. The resultant dispute is settled by Aeneas giving prizes to everyone. The boxing match is described at considerable length, but the description is purely literary and no whiff of the ring ever comes through to us. The contest is between a veteran, Entellus, who takes a firm defensive stance, and a younger and nimbler opponent, Dares, who circles round, looking for an opening. Missing with a swing, Entellus overbalances and falls, but he recovers and abandons his immobile tactics to hunt Dares round the ring. Aeneas stops the fight to save Dares from further punishment, fortunately perhaps, as Entellus, receiving an ox as his prize, kills it with a single blow of his fist.

In his archery contest Virgil follows Homer even more slavishly than in his foot race. Only in his own addition to the games, a race between the ships of Aeneas's fleet, where Homer is not looking over his shoulder, does he achieve real liveliness.[5]

For the student of the techniques of athletics by far the most interesting of the epics is the *Thebaid* of the Roman poet Statius, written towards the end of the first century A.D. In the sixth book he gives an account of the first Nemean games, representing them as having been founded to celebrate the funeral of the young Archemorus. As a poet, Statius may not be in the first rank, yet his description of the games stands out among all such epic narratives because of the intimate knowledge he displays of what he is relating. He is also a master of the story-teller's art. The whole event of the four-horse chariot race, for instance, is made to turn on the character and disposition of a single horse, Arion, and the contrast between the expert instruction about the management of this horse given by Adrastus to Polyneices and the conventional advice on driving given by Nestor to his son in the *Iliad* is most marked. The scene in Homer is a remarkable study of human old age. Statius knows his horses.[6]

As in Virgil, the first athletic event is the foot race. For this there are several competitors, among them Idas of Pisa, a recent Olympic victor, and the Arcadian Parthenopaeus, who has inherited the speed of his mother Atalanta. The limbering up before the start is vividly described:

'*Tunc rite citatos*
explorant acuuntque gradus, variasque per artes
exstimulant docto languentia membra tumultu;
poplite nunc sidunt flexo, nunc lubrica forti
pectora conlidunt plausu, nunc ignea tollunt
crura brevemque fugam necopino fine reponunt.'

'Then they go through the ritual of tuning up and trying out their paces, and with many tricks of the game they liven their sluggish muscles with well-tried exercises. Now they do a "knees bend", now they slap their chests with loud smacks, now their fiery legs prance in "knees up" and they take short sprints and suddenly stop.'

When the race starts Parthenopaeus and Idas draw away from the others, and victory appears assured for the former. But owing to a religious vow he has never cut his hair, and as he runs it streams out in the wind behind him. The temptation is too great for Idas. Just as Parthenopaeus is about to cross the line, Idas grasps his hair, pulls him back and passes the winning post first. At once uproar breaks out. The Arcadian spectators are ready to avenge their champion's wrongs and prepare to swarm over the track. But there are others who are delighted with Idas's cunning. Parthenopaeus himself gives a performance worthy of a footballer trying to convince a sceptical referee that he has been fouled in the penalty area. He throws handfuls of earth over his head and face, bursts into sobbing, 'tears adding grace to his beauty', scratches his chest and cheeks till they bleed, and tears at the hair which has caused his defeat. It might be thought that the incident offered no very serious problem to the umpire, but the aged Adrastus dithers irresolutely, wondering what to do. In the end he orders a re-run, with the competitors on opposite sides of the track to prevent any possibility of another foul. Justice is done. Parthenopaeus wins easily, but Idas receives a second prize which he has certainly not deserved.

Even more interesting is the account of the discus throwing, and nowhere is it more tantalizingly difficult to distinguish the elements in the narrative which Statius is deriving from the epic tradition and those which come from the discus throwing of his own day. A bronze discus is brought forward for the competition of such heroic weight that its bearer can hardly carry it, but it is contemptuously tossed aside by Hippomedon, who produces one even heavier. This so dismays most of the would-be challengers that they withdraw, leaving only three. Phlegyas of Pisa is the first to throw:

'First of all he roughened the discus and his hand with sand. Then he shook off the dust and with practised skill turned the discus about to see which side best suited his fingers or lay best along his forearm.'

Before the competition proper he allows himself a practice throw straight up into the air. His success with this delights the spectators, dismays his rival Hippomedon and arouses his own hopes for an even better throw along the level (*in aequo*).* His hopes are disappointed. In his competition throw, the discus slips and falls from his hand just in front of his feet. Competitors in the games in the epics are allowed only one effort each, so Phlegyas's chances are gone. The next contestant, Menestheus, takes warning from this accident and carefully powders the discus with dust again. He makes a good throw, and the spot where the discus pitches is marked with an arrow. Then Hippomedon steps forward:

'He took up the discus which his right hand knew well, raised it aloft and gathered up the strength of his muscular flanks and vast shoulders. He swung it with a mighty whirl and followed through the throw with his body. The discus leaped forward through the air in a huge arc, and even at a distance remembered his right hand and kept a steady flight. It beat Menestheus' throw with a mark far beyond his, which left no doubt about the result.'

Nowhere does Statius's expert knowledge of athletics appear more clearly than in this passage, particularly in the line:

'*Iamque procul meminit dextrae servatque tenorem discus.*'

* The reason for sending the warming-up throw straight up into the air is to save the athlete from having to walk far to retrieve his discus. The mention of it in Statius, however, led a French critic to propose a theory that the Greeks competed in a high throw as well as a long. Gardiner shrewdly comments that measurement would have presented difficulties.

In a good throw the discus spins smoothly in the plane of flight
without any wobble, and much of the skill of the thrower consists in
his ability to impart this spin with his throwing hand and still control
the steadiness of flight. It would be difficult to imagine a way in which
this could be better expressed in verse than by the words 'Even at a
distance the discus remembered his right hand and kept a steady
flight'. They must surely have been written by a man who had often
thrown a discus himself.

The boxing match between Capaneus of Argos and the Spartan
Alcidamas follows the usual epic lines, but there are some good
individual details. At the beginning of the fight:

> 'inclinant tantum contraria iactu
> bracchia et explorant caestus hebetantque terendo.'

'They merely touched each other's fists and tested their gloves and
blunted their sharp edges by rubbing them together.'

Capaneus is the more aggressive boxer, the young Spartan the
more cautious and skilful:

'Sometimes he avoided harm by drawing back or swiftly ducking
his head; sometimes he parried with his gloves the blows aimed at
him; he feinted a forward move with his feet, but took his head back
out of reach. Often too, as his opponent came in with his superior
strength, he got inside his guard—such was his experienced ringcraft
and skill—towered over him and attacked him from above.'

Alcidamas lands a blow on Capaneus's forehead and draws blood:

'Capaneus as yet did not realize what had occurred and was
surprised at the sudden murmur which ran through the spectators
but when he happened to wipe his face with a weary hand he saw
the bloodstains on the glove.'

At once he 'sees red' and rushes recklessly at Alcidamas.

'Furiously he drove the young man all round the ring, forcing him
to give ground and throwing him back on his heels. He ground his
teeth hideously and redoubled his shower of blows; some of them

struck only air, some landed on the gloves of his opponent. With swift movement and nimble footwork the Spartan evaded the thousand threats of death which rained about his temples, never forgetting his boxing skill, and even while giving ground he sometimes stopped his enemy with a blow.'

The pace is too hot, and both fall back for a breather. Then Capaneus repeats his rush, Alcidamas skilfully eludes him and Capaneus stumbles and falls. As he rises, the Spartan floors him again. Capaneus is now mad with fury, and Adrastus, to avoid manslaughter, stops the contest and awards the prize to Alcidamas.

The wrestling match is between the short and wiry Tydeus and the much taller and more loosely knit Agylleus. At first Tydeus tries unsuccessfully to turn his short stature to advantage by forcing his opponent to stoop in order to grapple with him. The contest settles down into the usual protracted struggle. First one then the other with a grunt grasps flank or forehead, shoulders, neck, chest or legs that slip from the clutch. Sometimes they remain balanced for a long time, supported by each other's arms; then with a fierce movement they break from the grapple. At last Tydeus's superior fitness begins to tell and he takes the initiative. Feinting at his opponent's neck, he grasps at his legs, but cannot secure the hold because his arms are not long enough. The wrestlers fall to the ground with Agylleus uppermost, but he is unable to drive home his advantage. Tydeus slips from under him, gets behind him and gains a grip round his flanks and waist, while holding his legs helpless between his own thighs. Agylleus tries desperately with his right hand to tear the hold away, but in vain. Tydeus picks him up, throws him sideways to the ground, jumps on him and secures the fall and with it the match.

The poet gives us one very graphic detail during this fight. Agylleus, out of condition, is gasping and panting, and rivulets of sweat wash the caked dust from his body:

'*Ac furtim rapta sustentat pectora terra.*'

'He strengthened his chest with sand swiftly snatched up.'

Greek wrestlers seem to have found powder very refreshing, and Agylleus is seeking to replace what the sweat has washed off him. The word *'furtim'* admirably conveys the stolen movement with which he scoops up a handful of sand during a momentary break.

Now Statius follows Homer in hastening to the end of his games. The armed contest is stopped before it has started, while archery does not produce a match and is at once abandoned. Clearly the poet is interested only in the events which he knows himself.

In his expert knowledge of what he is describing, Statius offers a strong contrast to the next surviving poet who has left us an account of heroic funeral games. At the end of the fourth century A.D. Quintus of Smyrna wrote in Greek an epic in imitation of Homer, carrying on the story from the end of the *Iliad* to the fall of Troy. True to tradition, he includes funeral games in his poem. In Homer the games had been celebrated by Achilles at the funeral of his friend Patroclus; in Quintus the games are for the funeral of Achilles himself. The poet obviously derives his material from literary sources rather than from personal experience of athletics, but there are some interesting details in his account.[7]

The president of the games is Achilles' mother Thetis, and because of the presence of the sea-goddess and her Nereids the competitors wear shorts.* Except for the order of events, the games follow the usual course. For the foot race there are only two competitors, Locrian Ajax and Teucer; there is the traditional accident caused by divine intervention, but at least Quintus invents one of his own. Teucer trips over the root of a myrtle tree and sprains his ankle, leaving Ajax to finish alone.

For the wrestling also there are only two challengers, Diomedes and the other Ajax, the son of Telamon. The first fall is well described:

'Diomedes, using all his skill and strength, lifted up the mighty son of Telamon by dropping his flank, pushing his shoulder under Ajax' great muscular frame, and thrusting forward his leg behind his opponent's thigh. He hurled the gigantic hero to the ground and swooped down astride him.'

* Bronislaw Bilinski in his *L'agonistica sportiva nella Grecia Antica* considers these shorts a sign of fourth-century degeneracy in contrast to the noble nakedness of the classical Greek athlete. This is surely sociology run mad. Quintus is merely following Homer, whose competitors wore shorts.

Before the second round Ajax powders his body again and then calls on Diomedes to resume the struggle. He wins the second fall, and at this point Nestor intervenes to persuade them to leave the match a draw.

'With their hands they wiped the streaming sweat from their brows, then kissed one another and laid aside their rivalry in friendship.'

The boxing attracts only one competitor, the veteran Idomeneus, who is duly awarded the first prize. This dismays the aged Nestor, and he reproaches the younger heroes with lack of ambition, adding some details of his own youthful prowess. As a result, two young boxers come forward. The spectators make quite clear what they want: 'They urge the brave young men to mingle their stubborn hands in blood.' Before the start, both contestants do some shadow boxing, 'Testing their arms to see if they are supple as before, not stiffened by warfare.' This fight too is stopped before a decision is reached, and the boxers wipe the blood and sweat from their faces with 'many-holed sponges'. Almost a thousand years before Quintus, vase painters had often depicted sponges among the equipment of the gymnasium, but now for the first time in literature we read of them being used by athletes.[8]

The other contests are very cursorily dealt with. Alone among epic poets Quintus includes the long jump in his games, but unhappily he gives us no description of it or of the javelin throwing. Telamonian Ajax throws out a challenge to the heroes to face him in 'the contest of hands and feet together'—obviously the pankration—but such is his reputation and bodily strength that no one will accept it.

A feature of these games which Quintus probably took from the athletic meetings of his own day is the first-aid service for casualties, directed by Podaleirius. Teucer's sprained ankle is bled and then given a dressing of lint smeared with ointment; two charioteers after a crash have their wounds similarly treated. The patching up of the boxers is described in greater detail:

'First Podaleirius sucked the wounds clean. Then with his own hands he stitched them skilfully and applied medicines which his father had given him; with these even wounds from deadly strife which seem incurable are healed in one day.'

It was a century after Quintus that the last of the epics to concern us was written. Rome had fallen to the barbarian, but the Greek-speaking eastern half of the empire endured, and about A.D. 500 in Egypt Nonnus wrote a vast epic in forty-eight books in the language and metre of Homer, dealing with the career of the god Dionysus. More than a hundred years had passed since the last Olympic games had been celebrated, and while chariot racing was still a popular sport in the Byzantine empire, athletics were dying or dead. Yet Nonnus remained true to the epic tradition and included in his thirty-seventh book an account of the games held by Dionysus at the funeral of Opheltes. For the most part he follows Homer slavishly. Aristaeus gives his son Actaeon precisely the same platitudinous advice about driving that Nestor gave Antilochus in the *Iliad*, and the lapse of twelve centuries between the poems has not made it any more thrilling. The gods intervene in the events in Nonnus as in Homer. Boxing and wrestling follow the well-worn lines, and the leader in the race slips and falls in the same old patch of dung. Not surprisingly, Nonnus writes much more vividly about chariots than about athletes. His chariot race is the only one in the epics on which the spectators bet. The charioteers exchange taunts and abuse during the race, and fouls abound. The drivers snatch at one another's reins, and at last one of them deliberately crashes his own chariot into a rival's. The description leaves us with the impression that the Hippodrome at Alexandria in the fifth century A.D. must have witnessed some very spirited scenes.[9]

In the discus event the first two competitors throw with moderate success. Then Halimedes takes his turn:

'The discus, falling from the sky, bounded along the earth in long jumps, still feeling the urge of the skilled hand of the thrower and carrying its own impetus, until it had run past all the marks. All the spectators crowded round and applauded, astonished at the unchecked run of the bounding discus.'

For a moment we are tempted to wonder if Nonnus has here preserved a feature of the discus throwing of historic times, and whether the throw was really measured to the point where the discus came to rest and not to the point where it landed. But when we read on for a few lines and find that the two competitors in the javelin throw their spears at one another—the poet has run together Homer's javelin throwing and his armed contest—we realize that Nonnus is not to be regarded as an authority for anything athletic.

So commanding was the pattern set by the great Greek and Roman epics that John Milton felt compelled to conform by including some games in his *Paradise Lost*. The technical problem was formidable. There are only two human figures in the poem, one of them a woman; Death appears as a character in the narrative, but there are no funerals. The poet solved the problem by assigning his sports to the fallen angels:

> 'Part on the Plain, or in the Air sublime
> Upon the wing, or in swift race contend,
> As at th'Olympian Games or Pythian fields;
> Part curb thir fierie Steeds, or shun the Goal
> With rapid wheels, or fronted Brigads form.'

Thus Milton makes his bow to tradition, and so we take our final leave of epic athletics in Hell.[10]

IV THE EVENTS OF GREEK
ATHLETICS

(A) RUNNING

A MODERN athlete entering a Greek stadium for the first time is at once struck by the difference between what he sees and the sports grounds to which he is accustomed. We are all familiar with the modern arena with its roughly oval track, two straights joined by semicircular curves at each end, with an area of dead ground in the middle about the size of a football pitch. The Greek stadium was a strip of land about 230 yards long and 30 yards wide, with no dead ground in the middle. In races longer than a stade the runners did a full turn of 180 degrees round a post at each end of the track. The surface was dressed with sand, possibly rolled, and was probably rather softer than ours. Lucian writes of athletes running in deep, soft sand, but they appear to be not competing but following a method of training like that sometimes used by long-distance runners today.[1]

The second obvious difference to the eye between Greek sports and our own was that Greek athletes were completely naked. This had not always been the practice. In Homer, as we have seen, Euryalus wears boxing trunks, and in early historic times, according to Thucydides—and his statement is born out by the earliest vase paintings—athletes wore shorts. Two stories were told to account for the change. One of them relates that in 720 B.C. the winner of the stade at Olympia, Orrhippus or Orsippus of Megara, lost his shorts in the middle of the race and so set a new fashion. Another version, less well attested but easier to believe, ascribes the innovation to Athens, where a runner leading the field tripped and fell when his shorts came adrift, and the archon Hippomenes by edict enforced nakedness for the future to prevent any recurrence of the accident. The Greeks always regarded their own readiness to appear naked before their fellows as one of the traits which marked them out from the barbarians. On one occasion Agesilaus of Sparta when at war with the Persians exhibited naked prisoners of war to his troops so that they might be encouraged by the contrast between the flabby whiteness of the Persians and their own bronzed bodies.[2]

The Olympic programme included four races, the stade, 200 yards, the diaulos, 'double pipe', 400 yards, the race in armour, also two stades in length, and a long-distance race called the dolichos. This appears to have varied at different meetings between seven and twenty-four stades, the most likely distance for Olympia being twenty. At some games, but not at Olympia, there was another race of 800 yards called the Hippios (Horsey). It is attested at Isthmia, Nemea, Athens, Epidaurus, Argos, Plataea and elsewhere. There may have been among equestrian events a race of four lengths from which this took its name; more probably the word is a piece of athlete's jargon for this exhausting middle distance—'fit only for horses'. Pausanias tells us that Hermogenes of Xanthus, a runner who won eight crowns at Olympia between A.D. 81 and 89, was nick-named Hippos (Horse), by his fellows.[3]

The Greeks were well aware of the different actions required of runners over different distances. Philostratus describes in detail the economy of effort in the carriage of the arms in the dolichos, con-trasting it with the powerful arm action of sprinters 'moving their legs with their arms to achieve speed, as if winged by their hands'. Aristotle is deeply interested in this arm action and analyses its physiological aspects.[4]

Generally, in ancient times as in modern, it was the shortest race, the stade, which carried the highest prestige. From the time when Olympiads began to be used for dating purposes, an Olympiad was known by its number and by the winner of the stade, just as today many men date a year by the winner of the Derby. Diodorus Siculus, for instance, after naming the Athenian archon and the Roman consuls, always uses the formula 'The 93rd Olympiad was celebrated, in which Eubatus of Cyrene won the stade'. The reason for this pre-eminence of the shortest race is probably the eternal attraction of sheer speed. While the longer races have more to offer the spectator, it is the sprint which establishes 'the fastest man on earth'.

E

To a modern sprinter the stade appears rather long for the shortest race in the programme. The reason is probably connected with a fundamental Greek view of the aim of athletics, that it was to gain the satisfaction of victory and a sense of physical well-being in return for hardship, exhaustion and discomfort, 'ponos' as they called it; the resemblance to our word 'pain' is not accidental, and our 'agony' is derived from 'agōn', the Greek word for athletic contest. Here, as elsewhere in life, the price must be paid.* They would probably have felt that there was insufficient of this element in a race shorter than their stade.⁵

Most Greek stadia accommodated either twenty or sixteen runners at the start. At Olympia it was twenty. If preliminary heats were necessary it appears from an unfortunately corrupt passage in Pausanias that the first four in each heat went on to the final. In early days the signal for the start was given by trumpet. It is true that in two plays of Aristophanes where there is a parody of the start of a race, word of mouth is used, but this can hardly have been done at the big meetings. It is often necessary to recall the runners after a breakaway in a false start; in modern athletics the starter's second gun is unmistakable, but in a stadium packed with thousands of yelling spectators, to try to recall the field by shouting after them would have been a hopeless task. This probably explains the use of the trumpet, not otherwise an ideal instrument for starting a race. The chief evidence for it is that the chariot race at the Pythian games described by Sophocles in the *Electra* was started by trumpet. Even after a better way of handling the start had been devised, trumpeters, who also announced the results, remained important figures at the festivals. In Roman times there was a competition for them at many meetings, even at Olympia, and some celebrated performers are known. Athenaeus mentions one who was such a virtuoso of the instrument that he could play on two trumpets at the same time.⁶

There is no evidence that Greek sprinters ever used the modern start off the hands; indeed, without spikes it would hardly have been practicable.† Short- as well as long-distance runners used the natural standing position. The earliest Greek starting line was a simple

* Pindar is particularly insistent on the importance of 'ponos' in athletics.

† Spiked shoes were not unknown in antiquity. Strabo tells us that they were used in the Caucasus for moving over ice and snow, but there is no evidence that athletes ever wore them.

scratch (grammē) in the sand—hence our word 'scratch' in handi-caps. The first move to help the runners at the start was to provide permanent starting holes for the athletes' toes, like those which we used to dig in the track before the invention of starting blocks. The best surviving example of these is at Corinth (Plate 28b). Here is a starting line for sixteen runners. Each man has a pair of holes cut in a stone slab, left foot in front of right, twenty-five inches apart—uncomfortably far for a runner less than six feet tall. The holes are beautifully shaped, with a vertical back wall and the front edge chamfered to avoid catching the runner's toes as the foot moves forward in the first stride. A single hole of the same kind is still to be seen in the stadium at Rhodes. The stone in which it is cut has been relaid at some time so that the hole now points the wrong way, but its purpose is unmistakable.[7]

The eternal difficulty with the start of a sprint is the tendency of runners at high tension to break away before the signal is given. That this was still happening at the beginning of the fifth century B.C. we learn from a story in Herodotus, and from the same story we learn how the stewards dealt with those who 'beat the gun'. In the discussions of strategy before the battle of Salamis, the Athenian Themistocles, who was advocating an aggressive policy, was rebuked by Adeimantus the Corinthian with the words: 'In the games, those who start before the signal are flogged', to which Themistocles retorted: 'True, but those who are left at the start win no prizes.' Even this summary treatment of offenders failed to eradicate the practice, and before the end of the century a mechanical starting device had been introduced called a 'husplex', the nature of which was long disputed among modern scholars. The few references to it in Greek literature inform us that it operated by falling and that it made a loud noise. Many years ago it was conjectured that the device might be a rope stretched across the track in front of the runners and dropped for the start; incredible as it may appear, this continues to be repeated in print as if it were ascertained fact. The one certainty about it is that if it had ever been used all the runners would have tripped over it at the first stride and gone sprawling on their faces. A better explanation was needed.[8]

Several stadia, notably Olympia, Delphi and Epidaurus, have starting lines with grooves for runners' toes, separated at intervals of about three and a half feet by sockets for posts. It was often supposed

—rightly as we now know—that these sockets might be connected with the husplex, but Gardiner, usually so shrewd in his judgement of these practical points, strangely fell into the error of supposing that each runner in the longer races turned round a separate post, and that this was the purpose of the sockets. But this would inevitably have caused the runner, if he was leading his left-hand neighbour, to collide head-on with him as he rounded the post. Gardiner also granted that the sockets might have served for some form of starting gate, and in 1956 Oscar Broneer showed by his discoveries at Isthmia that this was indeed the form of the husplex and revealed the way it worked.[9]

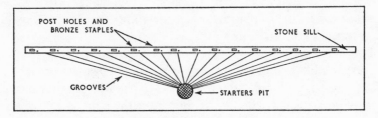

Fig. I. Husplex. Starting line and grooves (plan). (Not to scale.)

At Isthmia, the site of one of the 'crown' games, Broneer found two starting lines, both of which had been abandoned and covered over soon after their construction because of changes in the site of the stadium; this accounts for their excellent preservation. One of them is particularly significant. It is a stone sill without grooves, having at intervals sockets for posts (Plates 26a & b). A few inches from each socket is a bronze staple let into the stone, and from each staple a shallow groove runs to a starter's pit three yards behind the centre of the line (Fig. I). Each groove, near where it enters the pit, is crossed by another staple, to keep the cord in position at this end. The purpose of all this is unmistakable. Each runner had a starting gate like a railway signal. The moving arm was worked by a cord which ran from the short end of the arm through the staple and along the groove to the pit. All the cords were held by the starter standing in the pit, and when he released them, all the arms fell at the same time, thus ensuring a fair start (Fig. II).

The grooves for the runners' toes at Olympia, Delphi and Epidaurus are double, the distance between the grooves varying between four and a half and seven inches (Plates 24b, 28a & 30a). It is just possible, but unlikely, that the purpose of having two grooves was to allow the runner alternative positions for his front foot, according to whether he liked to be right up to the bar of the husplex or a little back from it. It is far more probable that the grooves were for the two feet of the athlete. To us this appears an uncomfortable stance for a start. Why has the change taken place from the natural straddle of the holes at Corinth? Almost certainly the invention of the husplex

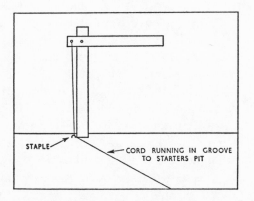

Fig. II. Husplex. Post and Arm. (Not to scale.)

was responsible. It is tempting to believe that the runner leaned as far forward as possible over the bar and so drew up his back foot until it was only just behind the front one. But in the *Phaedrus* Plato likens a charioteer reining in his horses to a runner rearing back from the husplex. This strongly suggests that runners were not allowed to lean over the bar, or that the bar was so high as to make this impossible, and that consequently it was to the athlete's advantage to keep back from it in order not to hinder its drop. This would explain the close position of the feet (Plates 5a & b).[10]

There is one conclusive piece of evidence that the post-holes did indeed serve for a starting gate. If such a gate was used we should expect sprinters to need practice with it, just as a horse today must be trained to the gate. In most places a runner practising starts would do so in the stadium and use the gates there. But at Delphi the stadium is inconveniently high up the mountainside, and a practice ground was provided for athletes lower down, just below the Castalian spring where there was an abundant supply of water for their baths. In this practice ground is a long sill of marble, and in the middle of it a single socket with a single groove beside it (Plate 29a). This could have no conceivable purpose except to allow a runner to practise starts with the gate under the eye of his trainer.

The stadia of the Greek world were not uniform in their provision of equipment at the starting line. No starter's pit has yet been found anywhere except at Isthmia. At Delos there are sockets for posts in the starting sills but no grooves. The single hole for the runner's toes at Rhodes already mentioned has a square post-socket beside it, suggesting that the long groove was not a necessary feature of the start with the husplex. The bronze staples at Isthmia have so far not been paralleled elsewhere, though at Delphi there are some holes in the sills near the sockets which may have held staples. But neither the pit nor the staple in the sill is essential to the working of the husplex; a staple fixed to the post near ground level would have served as well, and in some ways would have been more convenient. All races finished at the same end of the stadium; this meant that the stade race started at one end, while the diaulos, the armed race and almost certainly the dolichos started at the other. It was essential, therefore, that the gates should be able to be quickly taken down and set up again for the different races, and this must have been more difficult when the cords had to be threaded each time through staples in the ground.

Two inscriptions of the third century B.C. from Delos record expenditure on spare parts for the husplex there. These pose some problems: 'posts' and 'arms' are obvious; 'side-pieces' and 'eagles' or 'pediments' are less clear. An interesting part is a 'syrinx' or pipe. This probably served the same purpose as the cord-grooves at Isthmia. The cords working the gates were taken through pipes so that they should not become entangled with the feet of nervous runners as they moved to their marks.'[11]

Another inscription of the third century, from Epidaurus, is also of interest. The engineer of the husplex there, Philo of Corinth, had been fined 500 Alexandrian drachmae by the president and stewards of the games, presumably for breach of contract or inefficiency at his job. He appealed to the senate of Epidaurus, who confirmed the fine, deducted from it his pay of 200 drachmae and added 50 per cent to the remainder because the fine had not been paid before the time limit, leaving the unfortunate Philo with 450 drachmae still to pay.[12]

The problems of the stade race are all connected with the start. In the diaulos, and to some extent in the dolichos, there is the added problem of the turn round the post (*kamptēr*). These posts were set in the middle of the starting sills. At Olympia, in the west sill where the kampter was used only for the dolichos, the centre husplex socket is larger than the others, four and a half inches square against three inches, obviously to accommodate this post; at the east end there is a separate socket for the post, used in the diaulos and the dolichos, slightly north of centre (Plate 28*a*). All turns were made left-handed. The technical problems of this turn were formidable. Short-distance runners today often complain about the tight bends on some modern tracks, but the difficulties of the sharpest and most inconvenient bend are negligible compared with the task of rounding a post at full speed—and the times of modern races show that 400 yards can be run at practically full speed throughout. The side pressure, the risk of slipping with bare feet on a loose surface of sand and the possibility of collisions between runners subject to these strains seem to present difficulties almost insurmountable. It is one of the many mysteries of Greek athletics that in the whole of Greek literature there does not appear to be any reference whatever to this problem, and the vase painters were equally uninterested. This is in strong contrast to the attention paid by ancient writers from Homer onward to the same problem in chariot racing; the collisions and crashes in foot races were no doubt less spectacular than those with chariots, but they can hardly have been less numerous. Occasionally the poets use the kampter as a metaphor for the prime of life, the turning-point after which a man, in our phrase, is going downhill; even so, the metaphor is as likely to be from the hippodrome as the stadium.

The first impulse of a runner having to turn a post at full speed is to grasp it with the left hand and swing round it. Had this been the practice of the Greeks we should surely know of it through literary metaphor or vase paintings. It is probable that in order to prevent it the foot of the post was surrounded by a base sufficiently large and high to make it impossible. The vases give some hint of this (Plates 12*a*, 20).[13]

Even though a first leg of 200 yards would string out the field to some extent, to be one of twenty runners converging on point X at the post (Fig. III) must have been an alarming experience. The difficulty of the turn would appear greatest to the runners at the extreme left of the line, point A on the plan. It was probably in order to accommodate these unfortunates as far as possible that the post at Olympia was placed slightly left of centre. In any case, runners starting at the outside of the line at either end had a little longer to run on the first leg than those in the centre. It is true that the extra distance amounted to only about fifteen inches, but it no doubt appeared much more to highly strung athletes awaiting the start. Runners at the extreme right, point C, had at least the consolation that the turn was easiest for them owing to their angle of approach.

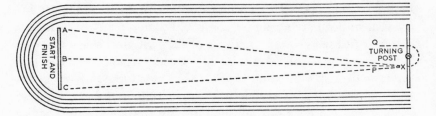

Fig. III. Plan of stadium.

It was probably because of the difficulties of runners in the left half of the starting line that at Delphi this part, A—B on the plan, was abandoned and only the right half, B—C, used. At some time the left half of the sill was taken up and relaid very roughly a foot higher than the right half, without any attempt to keep the grooves on the top surface.* Some evidence of the date of this change is afforded by an inscription of 271 B.C. from Delphi, recording the gift by Eudoxus of Argos of ten shields for use in the armed race at the Pythian games. The fact that the number is ten, not twenty, suggests that before this date half of the starting line had been abandoned for this race, which, like the diaulos, was two stades in length.[14]

A further problem of the turn round the post must have been the opportunity which it afforded for sharp practice. A runner who had failed during the first leg to secure a good position for the turn must have been under a strong temptation to take a short cut from P to Q in the plan and hope to hide himself among the body of runners who had rounded the post. The detection of offenders cannot have been

* This sill presents a problem; in its present state it cannot have been used either as a starting or as a finishing line.

an easy task for the umpires at this point (Plate 4*b*); naked Greek athletes carried no numbers. It is perhaps from this manœuvre that Aeschylus draws a metaphor in the Agamemnon; the Chorus, anxious not to be guilty of excess or deficiency in the warmth of their welcome to the king, ask how they can avoid 'cutting in before the turning-post of politeness or taking too wide a sweep beyond it'.[15]

As the Greeks were fortunate enough not to possess stop-watches, we have no means of comparing their running with ours, but it is highly probable that their best diaulos runners were fully equal to our best performers in the quarter-mile or 400 metres. It must have been of the utmost importance for a diaulos runner to be clear of the field when he came to the turn, and this must have ensured a very fast first leg in the race. It is within living memory that quarter-milers have dispensed with an 'easing up' in the middle section of their race. The Greeks must very early have learned how to do without it.

Of the dolichos we know little. Different authorities give as its length 7, 8, 10, 12, 20 and 24 stades—from just under one mile to about three. We need not believe that the distance was the same everywhere. Moreover at some games there were dolichos races for boys and youths, and it is reasonable to suppose that the distance was shorter for the younger runners.* Tactics were obviously much as today. The encyclopaedists give us Greek terms for running at another man's shoulder and for letting a tearaway runner have his head in the early stages. Moralists, anxious to extol the virtue of perseverance, point out that it is the position at the end of the race that matters. Aristotle, dealing with the problems of motion, gives us in characteristically crabbed language what is surely a description of a runner's changes of speed in the course of a long-distance race.

'If motion is change from one place to another, there are different forms of this too, flying, human movement on foot, jumping and so on. Not only so, but there are differences in human movement on foot itself; for the change from one place to another is not the same in a race in the stadium as in part of it, or the same in one part of it as

---

* Lucian makes a neat use of this fact in his essay on *How to write History*. The author of a work which claimed to cover the history of a large part of Asia over a long period of time in fewer than 500 short lines had announced himself in the title, 'almost longer than the book itself', as 'Antiochianus, victor at a sacred festival'. Lucian comments 'I suppose he won the boys' dolichos'.

in another part; crossing the line and turning the post is not the same at one end as at the other. For the runner does not merely cross a line, but a line in a specific place, and the line at one end of the stadium is not the same as the line at the other end.'[16]

Far more vivid is the description of a race in a simile of Oppian in his poem on fish. He is describing the rush of male parrot-wrasses towards the female decoy:

'As runners on the track, leaping forward from the start and urging their swift limbs ever on and on, raise clouds of dust in their eagerness to reach the distant post; each of them longs to win through to the finish to receive the sweet reward of success, to force his way first to the line and place on his brow the victor's wreath.'[17]

Even more entertaining are the writers of satirical epigrams. The Greeks worshipped success. They appear to have had little to say in praise of the good loser; Pindar twice speaks of defeated competitors slinking home in shame from the great festivals. It is not surprising, then, that the wits of the Hellenistic and imperial epochs directed their shafts at unsuccessful performers. Lucilius tells of a runner, Eutychides, slow on the track but a flier to his meals, and of another, Erasistratus, whom not even an earthquake could inspire to show a turn of speed. Nicharchus has an epigram about Charmus, a dolichos runner who finished seventh in a field of six. A friend ran alongside him shouting, 'Keep going, Charmus,' and, although fully dressed, beat him; 'And if he had had five friends he would have finished twelfth.' Best of all is Lucilius's story of Marcus, a long-distance runner who was moving so slowly that the groundsmen mistook him for a statue and closed the stadium for the night. When they opened it next morning Marcus had still not finished the race.*[18]

The race in armour or Hoplite race, even though it came late into the Olympic programme, was a survival of the time when all athletic competition was part of training for war. In historic times the armour had been reduced to a symbolic helmet and shield, later to a shield alone; the distance was two stades. All the evidence suggests that the race was less and less esteemed as time went on, and that it came to be

* I have adopted the more charitable rendering 'next morning'; the phrase more often means 'next year'.

regarded by athletes much as an egg-and-spoon race would be today if it had survived in any serious sports meeting. Fewer and fewer runners trouble to mention it in the inscriptions recording their victories; sometimes a dolichos winner will add that he also won the diaulos and hoplite race on the same day, but that is all. There is some reason for believing that runners came to look on it as a consolation race.[19]

Among the Greeks, as today, there was a constantly increasing degree of specialization among athletes; the inscriptions make this quite clear. A stade runner could generally make the diaulos as well, or he might take on the pentathlon; sometimes a dolichos runner had enough speed for success in the diaulos; but this versatility became increasingly rarer. Occasionally, even in Hellenistic and Roman times, an outstanding performer could command success in several events, even in the best company. Leonidas of Rhodes won the stade, diaulos and armed race in four successive Olympiads between 164 and 152 B.C., and as late as A.D. 69, Polites of Caria won the stade, diaulos and dolichos at Olympia on the same day. But these were exceptions. Much more characteristic of the imperial epoch is an inscription of about A.D. 90, in which Titus Flavius Metrobius announces himself as a dolichos runner, gives details of twenty victories and adds that he won 120 others in important festivals, leaving the reader to infer that they were all in the dolichos.[20]

There are a few recorded instances of long-distance races run outside the stadium. The most famous of these was the Eleutheria at Plataea, a race in armour founded to commemorate the great victory there over the Persians in 479 B.C. The starting-point was the trophy set up on the battlefield. Apparently no one was allowed to win this race twice. The legend was that if a past winner entered and failed to repeat his victory, he was put to death; this sounds like a story told by old hands in athletic dressing-rooms to gullible youngsters.[21]

Another running event which took place outside the stadium was the torch race, the Greek form of relay race. It was no part of an ordinary athletic meeting, and was connected with quite different religious festivals from those to which the usual games were dedicated. In origin it no doubt went back to a time when men knew the use of fire but did not know how to kindle it, and so the ability to carry it from place to place without extinguishing it was of great importance. In the torch race a lighted torch took the place of our baton, and in order to win, a team had to get the first man home with his torch still alight. We know from Aristophanes that such a race took place through the streets of Athens. The most famous torch races were held on the island of Delos, but we hear of them also in many parts of the Greek world. In the opening pages of the *Republic* Plato mentions an experiment in holding a torch race on horseback at a festival of Bendis in the Peiraeus.

Of the inscriptions from which we derive most of our knowledge of torch races, so large a proportion deal with boys' races that it is a reasonable assumption that the event was considered particularly suitable for younger athletes. The same source also tells us that the number of runners in a team was often eight or ten. It must have been an exciting and spectacular event. Strangely enough, it seems to have appealed more to the imagination of the Romans than the Greeks. Certainly it afforded the poet Lucretius one of his most memorable lines. Describing the mystery by which life is transmitted by succeeding generations, he writes of them:

'Quasi cursores vitai lampada tradunt.'

'Like runners they hand on the torch of life.'

Less happily, the torch, which in antiquity had no connection with Olympia, has been dragged into the Hollywood tushery with which it is considered necessary to open the modern Olympic Games.[22]

There is one modern event which bears a Greek name, but which had no place in the Greek athletics of antiquity, the marathon. When the Persians landed at Marathon in 490 B.C. to attack Athens, the Athenians sent off a runner, Pheidippides, to summon help from the Spartans under their treaty obligations. Herodotus tells us that he arrived in Sparta on the second day; that is, he had covered the 160 miles between the two cities along a route which passed through the mountainous country of Arcadia, in less than forty-eight hours. Another and much later story told by Plutarch is that an Athenian named Eucles returned to Athens from abroad after the army had marched out to Marathon. He ran out to take his place in the ranks, arrived just in time to fight in the battle, and then ran back to announce the victory in Athens, dying as he did so.[23]

When the first modern Olympic games were held at Athens in

1896 it was felt that these feats of pedestrianism at Athens' finest hour should be mirrored in the proceedings. Accordingly a race was arranged from Marathon to Athens, a distance of twenty-four miles, 1500 yards; appropriately it was won by a Greek. Since then the race has formed part of every Olympiad, and it is often included in the programme of other meetings. In early Olympiads the distance varied to suit local conditions, but since 1924 it has been standardized at twenty-six miles, 385 yards, the length of the marathon at the London Olympics of 1908. The Greeks never raced over such a distance. As we have seen, they recognized the value of 'ponos' or toughness in athletics, but in all departments of life they followed their excellent principle, 'Nothing in excess'.

(B) THE PENTATHLON

The pentathlon was a grouped event of five sections: long jump, discus, javelin, a foot race, almost certainly a stade in length, and wrestling. Of these, the first three belonged solely to the pentathlon, while running and wrestling were also separate events in their own right. Not the least of the many problems of the pentathlon is its origin. Homer knows nothing of it; in his funeral games the jump, the discus and the javelin are separate events like the rest, with their own prizes. We can only conjecture why those who introduced the pentathlon into the Olympic games in 708 B.C., when the event is heard of for the first time, found it necessary to put them together. Later Greeks held two incompatible views about the event. For Plato it was the opportunity for the second-rate performer. In the eyes of others it was the supreme test of the all-rounder. Today field events are often less highly esteemed than those on the track, and a similar attitude among the Greeks may have been partly responsible for the grouping. If it is strange that the pentathlon should have been invented, it is even more remarkable that it should have lasted so long. We find it difficult to understand athletes tolerating for a thousand years a situation in which a man might be the finest long jumper in the world, yet if he could not throw and wrestle he had no chance of ever winning a prize at any meeting.

In the second century A.D. Philostratus produced a legend set in the heroic age to explain the origin of the pentathlon. According to this, Peleus was second best among the Argonauts in every event except wrestling, in which he surpassed them all. So Jason, when he arranged games in Lemnos, grouped the events together to accommodate Peleus. As an aetiological myth this is poor; it is certainly not a convincing or even a plausible explanation. Yet it has bedevilled all modern consideration of the pentathlon, particularly the attempts to solve the second great problem of the event, how the winner was decided. Misled by Peleus's second places, and perhaps unconsciously influenced by modern practice, all authorities have tried to impose on the Greeks a system of scoring by points awarded for places. There is no evidence for this, and it runs counter to the whole Greek outlook on victory. It is true that in minor meetings second prizes were sometimes awarded, but in the great 'crown' festivals the principle was 'Win or nothing'. To be convincing, any suggestion about victory in the pentathlon must be based on wins in the separate events.

Another point which must be borne in mind is the time available. At Olympia and the other great festivals all the athletic events were crowded into two days, and less important meetings no doubt occupied only one. It is hardly conceivable that all competitors can have taken part in the wrestling of the pentathlon, still more inconceivable that the wrestling should have been continued long enough to decide places after the first. The imagination boggles at the thought of *repêchage* bouts in the stadium for all those defeated by the ultimate winner.[24]

At the present state of our knowledge, certainty is impossible, but the following procedure, based on first places only, appears reasonably practicable and accords with the little evidence we have.* The statement of a scholiast on Aristides that only three wins were needed for victory, and the phrase, frequently occurring in inscriptions, 'winner in the first triad', make it probable that the pentathlon was conducted like a five-set tennis match, that as soon as one competitor had won three events, the others were abandoned as unnecessary. The first three events held were those peculiar to the pentathlon, the two throws and the jump. If no competitor won all three, a stade race was held. If there was still no competitor with three wins, the situation must have been one of these: two men with two

* How haphazard this evidence is may be seen from the fact that one of the most important items is a chance phrase in Plutarch's essay on 'Why A is the first letter of the alphabet'.

wins each; one with two wins and two with one each; or four with one win each. In the first case the two men wrestled, and the winner then had the necessary three victories. In the second the two men with one win each wrestled a semi-final, and the winner of that, now with two wins, wrestled a final with the third man. In the third case two semi-finals and a final in wrestling decided the victor.[25]

This view of the machinery of the pentathlon is supported by what Herodotus tells us about a Spartan named Tisamenus, who later fought in the battle of Plataea. 'He failed by a single wrestling throw to win the pentathlon at Olympia, encountering there Hieronymus of Andros.' Pausanias adds the information that Tisamenus won the jump and the race; Hieronymus must therefore have won the discus and javelin and then defeated Tisamenus in the wrestling by two falls to one. Further evidence comes in the eighth ode of Bacchylides, in which he celebrates the victory of Automedes of Phlius in the pentathlon at Nemea. Automedes won the discus and javelin, and the last event, the wrestling.

'He shone among the other pentathletes as the bright moon in the middle of the month dims the radiance of the stars; even thus he showed his lovely body to the great ring of watching Greeks, as he threw the round discus and hurled the shaft of black-leaved elder from his grasp to the steep heights of heaven, and roused the cheers of the spectators by his lithe movements in the wrestling at the end.'

The same combination of events brought success in the pentathlon to an Ephesian athlete of the second century A.D. whose name is lost. The surviving part of his inscription records twenty-seven victories, and at the end he claims that he was never beaten in discus, javelin or wrestling. Clearly, like Automedes, he was no runner or jumper.[26]

The shifts to which the organisers of festivals were driven by shortage of time are illustrated by an incident related by Xenophon. In 364 B.C. the Arcadians and Pisatans had contrived to seize control of the Olympic games, and the people of Elis, in whose territory Olympia lay and who had always been responsible for the games, took the opportunity of the festival to attempt to regain control by an armed coup. Their army attacked at the moment when the horse race and the 'running events' of the pentathlon were finished, and 'when those who had gone forward to the wrestling were competing, not in the stadium but between the stadium and the altar'. This means that the wrestling of the pentathlon was being held in the Altis or sacred enclosure, near the great temple of Zeus, and this can have been only because the stadium was occupied by other events.[27]

There is one technical question which every modern athlete will ask about the field events of the pentathlon—how many attempts each competitor was allowed in the jump and the throws. In Homer and his epic successors it is only one each, but this may be due merely to poetic convenience. It is difficult enough to make the story of a throwing competition exciting even with the utmost speed of narration; the risk of tedium increases enormously with the multiplication of efforts. Recently an inscription has been discovered near the stadium at Rhodes which may throw some light on the question. Unfortunately it is in a very fragmentary condition, but enough survives to show that it contained regulations for the pentathlon. The word 'five times' occurs in a place which suggests that it may well refer to the number of throws allowed each competitor in the discus. Even if this is by no means certain, it is at least reasonable, and it is the nearest to direct evidence that we have. The only other possible indication is Pausanias's statement that three discuses, provided by the authorities and stored in the treasury of the Sicyonians, were used at Olympia. This may imply that each competitor was allowed three throws, one with each discus.[28]

(C) THE JUMP

So far as we know, the Greeks practised only one jump, the long. The Greek countryside is furrowed by so many ravines that the ability to long jump is valuable for moving across it rapidly in war, while there are few natural obstacles which demand high-jumping skill.* The long jump appears a straightforward enough event, yet there is no department of Greek athletics which bristles with so many unanswered questions.

One way in which Greek jumping differed from ours is that the Greeks used weights (halteres). Several of these have been found, and

* Vase paintings show that Greek cavalrymen, lacking stirrups, sometimes used their lances to help them to vault on to their horses, but this form of pole-jumping appears never to have been made the basis of a competition in the games.

they are often depicted in vase paintings; some of them resemble flat-irons, others telephone hand-pieces, while one recently discovered at Isthmia is a stone cylinder with grooves to fit the fingers. They generally weigh from four to eight pounds. Even now the purpose of these weights is not perfectly certain. Weights can help the effort of a jumper, long or high, if he throws them backwards in mid-air, but there is no evidence that Greek jumpers did this. Indeed, vase paintings show jumpers on the point of landing with the weights still in their hands (Plates 6, 7), and Philostratus says that the use of weights is to bring the jumper firmly to his landing. Lucian clearly looks on the halteres as a handicap to make the exercise more difficult: 'We train them to jump over a ditch if necessary, or any other obstacle, even carrying in their hands lead weights as large as they can hold.' But Aristotle says that athletes jump further with weights than without, and it is unlikely that he would have made such a categorical statement without accurate knowledge derived from experience.[29]

This by no means exhausts the perplexities of the subject. Two jumps are known from antiquity. An epigram records of Phaÿllus of Croton, who commanded a ship at the battle of Salamis: 'He jumped five over fifty feet, but threw the discus five short of a hundred.' Ancient commentators on this epigram inform us that the pit was normally dug to accommodate a leap of fifty feet, but that Phaÿllus jumped well beyond it and broke his leg when he landed on the hard ground. The second recorded jump is one of fifty-two feet by Chionis of Sparta, winner of the stade and diaulos in three Olympiads between 664 and 656 B.C. It may be noted that in spite of this great leap, presumably the best on record until it was beaten by Phaÿllus, even so fine a runner as Chionis was unable to win the pentathlon; clearly he was no thrower or wrestler.[30]

Another odd point about Greek jumping is that Philostratus tells us that because it was the most difficult of all athletic events, the authorities allowed it to be accompanied by a flute player (Plate 7). Most of us would consider the two throws far more difficult, and it is not easy to think of any human activity less likely to be helped by a flute obbligato than our long jumping.[31]

The inescapable conclusion from all this would seem to be that the Greek long jump was a triple or more probably a double jump. It was this interpretation which caused the introduction into modern

F

athletics of the triple jump, which we used to call the hop, step and jump. At the moment of writing the world's record at this event is 55 ft. 10½ in. If Greek jumpers gained some help from their weights, this makes Phaÿllus's fifty-five feet and Chionis's fifty-two feet plausible as exceptional feats by outstanding performers at a double jump.

The conclusion that the Greek jump was not a single one appears to be inevitable if we accept a statement by Themistius in his commentary on Aristotle's *Physics*, where he cites the jump of the pentathlon as an example of motion which is not continuous. It is not easy to think of any human movement which is more continuous than a single jump from the moment of take-off to the moment of landing. On the other hand, a double or triple jump is necessarily broken into parts and therefore discontinuous.

There is some supporting evidence for the theory of the double as against the triple jump. The Greek word for the take-off board was batēr; this is defined by one encyclopaedist of the first century A.D. as 'the edge from which they make the first jump', and by another as 'the middle from which, having jumped, they jump again'. The words 'first' and 'again' in these definitions seem to prove decisively that the jump was not a single one like ours. A curious pointer in favour of the double rather than the triple leap comes in Plato's *Laws*. He is arguing against the belief that we are naturally right or left handed; he attributes the general prevalence of right-handedness to the folly of nurses and mothers, 'making us, as it were, lame in our hands'. As part of his proof he states categorically: 'It is obvious that there is no difference at all between the feet and legs in active exertion' (the Greek word is 'ponos').* Now Plato was himself a fine athlete and must have spent a great deal of time in the gymnasium and palaestra. Had the Greek jump been a single one, he could not have failed to notice that some jumpers invariably take off from the right foot and others equally invariably from the left. Had the jump been triple, he must have noticed a similar preference among athletes for one foot or the other for two of the three parts of the effort. But if the jump was a double one, every first-class jumper must have had to be equally powerful with either foot, and to secure this equality he would naturally practise using either foot for the first half of his leap. Plato's misconception is then readily understandable.[32]

* Incidentally, this makes it quite certain that the Greeks of Plato's time did not play football.

Although vase paintings sometimes depict an athlete possibly about to make a standing jump, the vastly greater number showing a jumper running with his weights suggests that the Greek jump, like ours, was done with a run; the standing jump was no doubt part of the training routine. The take-off for the jump was probably the starting sill of the runners. In vase paintings showing a jumper there is often a pillar which appears to be the runners' turning post in the centre of the line. This belief is supported by a statement of the encyclopaedist Pollux, who gives 'batēr' as a synonym for 'finishing line'. If the Greek jumper did in fact take off from this line, he had to be content with a much shorter run than his modern counterpart. At Olympia the distance between the edge of the stadium and the starting sill is not more than twenty yards, and few stadia allow more than this. The technique demanded by the use of the weights may well have made a long run inadvisable.*³³

Pollux adds a Greek proverb drawn from the jump. It may be rendered, 'He has made the batēr resound' or, 'He has hit the take-off with a bang', a lively equivalent of our, 'He has hit the nail on the head'. It conjures up a vivid impression of the loud slap of the jumper's bare foot on the take-off, heard clearly in the moment of silence while he is in mid-air.

Philostratus tells us that the rules did not allow the jump to be measured unless the impression left by the jumper on the surface of the pit was clear. In the fragment of inscription from Rhodes already mentioned, the phrase 'of two feet' occurs in connection with the jump and its pit. Moretti thinks that it is part of a regulation that the pit must be two feet wide; Bean, with more probability, that the pit must be dug to a depth of two feet. As the word 'measuring rods' appears in the next line of the inscription, it is possible that the phrase was part of the rule mentioned by Philostratus, that there must be an impression of the two feet of the jumper.³⁴

Lucian in the *Anacharsis* describes athletes performing an exercise consisting of jumping up and kicking the air. It is tempting to see in this a method of training for the kick in the middle of the long jump which is part of the modern technique. But it must be emphasized that there is no further evidence for this, and it would be unwise to state dogmatically that the Greeks had discovered the trick of the

* Ebert argues interestingly that the Greek jump was a quintuple standing leap. I remain unconvinced.

kick in mid-air; nor is it certain how this kick would combine with
the use of the weights, which must have made the Greek technique
different from ours.³⁵

The employment of the halteres probably explains the function of
the flute player in Greek jumping. Fundamentally, success in the long
jump depends on speed and spring at the take-off, with correct
elevation, the kick, and the swing of the arms playing their part.
With the use of the weights, the arms must have been even more
important than in our jump. The difference between a good and
an outstanding leap came from an exact correlation between
movements of arms and legs, with the two rhythms coinciding
precisely at the moment of take-off. Staccato music from a flute,
particularly the Greek double flute which is often seen in the vase
paintings (Plate 7), may well have helped with this rhythmic
problem.

In order to perfect this synchronization of arms and legs, jumpers
used to practise swinging the arms while carrying the weights. This
was found to be beneficial to physical development generally, and
Greek medical writers advocate these exercises for others besides
specialists in the long jump. The weights were thus the ancestors of
the dumb-bells which used to be employed in children's physical
training half a century ago. A pair of lead halteres in the British
Museum, weighing about two and a quarter pounds each, were
probably made specially for this purpose; they are scarcely heavy
enough to be an effective help in jumping.³⁶

A pleasant picture of Greek athletes practising the jump is evoked
by a famous passage in the *Clouds* of Aristophanes. A disciple of
Socrates is describing to an old countryman the wonderful scientific
achievements of his master:

'DISC. A short time ago Socrates was asking Chaerophon how
    many times its own feet a flea could jump. For one had just
    bitten Chaerophon on the eyebrow and jumped off on to
    Socrates' head.
STR. How in the world did he measure that?
DISC. Very cleverly. He melted some wax and then took the flea
    and dipped its feet into it. Then, when the wax cooled
    Persian slippers had grown on the flea's feet. He took them
    off and measured the distance.'

Every member of the audience must often have seen athletes practising the jump, and one of them picking up a sandal with which to make a rough measurement of a leap. So in Aristophanes' wild logic, wild as the White Knight's, if a flea's jump is to be measured one must have a flea's shoe.[37]

(D) THROWING THE DISCUS

The first question to ask about this event is why a missile of this particular and not very convenient shape should have been chosen. The ability to throw stones is sometimes useful in warfare. In one of the duels in the *Iliad*, Ajax and Hector, having discharged their spears at one another, pick up stones with which to continue the engagement. For this purpose a flat discus-shaped stone is the least suitable. It is difficult to throw at all and still more difficult to throw accurately at a target. The most effective missile of this kind with which to injure an enemy is a roughly spherical stone rather larger than a tennis ball, weighing about three or four pounds; this is heavy enough to disable a man, and light enough to command an effective range. It is noteworthy that Lucian makes the Scythian Anacharsis criticize discus throwing on the ground that it is useless for war, and suggest that the Greeks would do better to train their young men in throwing 'stones that fill the hand'.[38]

Late writers tell us that the discuses used in competition in early historic times were of stone, unlike those of their own day which were of bronze. It is therefore tempting to assume that the athletic event rose out of attempts to throw the flat water-washed stones of the sea-shore or river bed. Almost certainly this was not so. In the *Iliad*, as we have seen, the prize in the weight-throwing competition was an ingot of raw metal which went to the man who could throw it farthest. Modern authorities distinguish this weight, the 'solos', from the discus, but they are not justified in doing so. In ancient smelting the molten ore was poured into a circular mould hollowed in the sand; this produced a round ingot with a curved under surface derived from the bottom of the mould and a flat upper face. There are excellent examples, dating from the Roman occupation of Britain, in the National Museum of Wales (Plate 9a). This button-shaped ingot was the 'solos' of Homer and the first discus; it is obvious why

Greek writers compare the shape of the discus to the lentil or the moon. Homer's solos was no doubt much heavier than the discus of later competition—the ingots at Cardiff vary from twenty-nine to forty-nine pounds—but the most effective way of throwing it was the swinging motion using centrifugal force which is the foundation of all subsequent discus throwing.[39]

In post-Homeric times the discus undoubtedly became smaller and lighter, but it must be admitted that beyond that we know very little about the Greek discus. Several examples have been found, varying in diameter between six and a half and thirteen and a half inches, and in weight between three and fifteen pounds. There is no need to assume exact uniformity throughout the Greek world or at all periods of Greek athletic history. We have seen that at Olympia the authorities supplied the discuses for competition, and this was probably done everywhere to ensure perfect fairness. Pausanias tells us that when some gigantic bones, thought to be those of Ajax, were discovered on Salamis, the knee-cap was 'as big as a boys' discus'. This shows that, as with us, the missile used by boys was smaller than the men's. Vase paintings of the fifth century B.C. mostly show the discus extending well up the forearm of the thrower, and therefore two to four inches greater in diameter than ours, but this is precisely the kind of detail for which we cannot depend on the vases. On the whole, the most reliable pieces of evidence, the surviving ancient examples, suggest that the Greek discus of the historic period did not differ much from the modern one, eight inches in diameter and four and a half pounds in weight, which indeed was based on those examples.[40]

When we come to the method of throwing we have once again very little direct evidence. The word used from Homer onward of the throw, 'whirling round', makes it clear that with the Greeks as with us, propulsion depended on centrifugal force rather than on the action of the joints at elbow and wrist as in a true throw. The vases give us very little help. Painters generally preferred to depict a moment of rest during action rather than movement itself. Before the throw proper an athlete always swings the discus backwards and forwards a few times to loosen and warm his muscles. At the top of the backward swing he prevents the discus from slipping from his grasp by an outward turn of the wrist. At the top of the forward swing he brings up his left hand to steady the discus and to avoid tightening the muscles of his throwing arm by having to grip the discus firmly with his fingers at this point. It is these two points of rest as the movement is reversed that appear most often on the vases, especially the latter (Plate 11*b*), but these pictures tell us little or nothing about the throw itself. The top of the backward swing was chosen by the sculptor Myron as the pose for the most celebrated work of art depicting an athlete of which we know (Plate 10). The original has disappeared, and we have only copies variously restored. Myron was renowned in antiquity for his realism; one of his works was a bronze cow so lifelike that, according to the epigrammatists, real calves used to try to suck from its udders. But it is possible that in the Discobolos his realism has failed him, and that the statue is not quite so perfect a representation of a thrower in action as has generally been supposed. Myron wanted his statue to stand on its own feet. But, as anyone who has ever thrown a discus knows, the top of the backward swing is not a true moment of balance. In order to prevent the vigorous swing from toppling him over on his back, the thrower starts the forward movement of his body just before the arm reaches its most backward point. The athlete who stood as model for Myron was faced with an impossible task and had to adopt a compromise. To achieve a balanced pose by keeping his centre of gravity directly above his feet, as it never is during an actual throw, he bent both knee and hip joints much more than a thrower would ever do in practice. Even so, the balance of the statue was so delicate that the carver of the best-known copy, that in the Vatican, found it necessary to support his version with the conventional tree-trunk.[41]

It is unfortunate that the only literary account we have of discus throwing is simply a description of Myron's statue. Philostratus is describing a picture of the accident in which Apollo killed Hyacinthus with a discus. These are his words:

'A throwing-point is marked off on all sides except the rear, small but large enough for a man standing. In the picture it is supporting the thrower's right leg. The top part of his body is leaning forward and taking the weight off his other leg, which he has to bring forward to follow through with his right hand. The attitude of the thrower is this; he must turn his head to the right and bend it forward far enough to look along his flank; he makes the throw by heaving up. as it were, and following through with the whole of his right side,

That, no doubt, is how Apollo threw the discus, for there was no
other way in which he could do it.'

The concluding words suggest that Philostratus was not altogether
happy about the accuracy of his description. In his account of the
'balbis' or throwing-point he seems to be thinking as much of the
small base on which a statue stands as of a sports stadium. The one
detail which does appear to come from real throwing is that the
throwing 'box' was not restricted at the rear. It seems to have been
marked out thus:

Direction of throw ————→

If, as seems probable, the line behind which the throw had to be made
was the runner's starting sill, the purpose of the side lines has to be
explained. They were probably a practical safety measure, ensuring
that the throwing was done from a point near the central axis of the
stadium. Had the throwers been allowed to throw from anywhere
they pleased behind the line, a discus thrown from a spot near the
side of the stadium, swerving only a little towards that side, would
have landed in the spectators' seats. A central balbis reduced this risk
considerably.[42]

Unhappily a corruption in one manuscript of Philostratus produced in the description of the balbis in this passage the reading
'heaped up' instead of 'marked out'. When discus throwing was
revived by modern athletes at the end of the nineteenth century, this
rendering of Philostratus, together with some very bad reconstruc-
tions of Myron's statue, gave birth to a style of throwing believed to
represent the method of the Greeks of antiquity. This so-called 'Greek
style' was executed from a small raised platform and demanded that
the right foot be kept in front of the left throughout the throw.
Fortunately the northern peoples, especially the Finns, refused to be
restricted by these academically inspired contortions, and they
developed the modern method which adds grace to our sports
meetings today. There is little reason to doubt that the Greeks, with
their centuries of experience, arrived at much the same conclusion.
The 'Greek style' lingered on in the modern Olympic games until

the London Olympiad of 1908, after which it vanished from the athletic scene, one hopes for ever.

A successful throw of the discus depends primarily on the speed at which the missile leaves the hand. This speed is achieved by a combination of three bodily movements. The first is the reversal of the position of the feet which turns the whole body round; the second is the swing of the trunk from the hips; the third and most important is the swing of the arm from the shoulder across the body. The thrower must also impart the correct elevation to the flight of the discus. Equally essential to a good throw is the maintenance of the plane of the discus in the plane of flight without flap or wobble until the moment of landing. This depends on accuracy of release and especially on the spin imparted to the discus by the fingers of the throwing hand, particularly the outside of the little finger. This is well brought out in Statius's memorable line about the discus in flight 'remembering the thrower's right hand'.[43]

The Greek method possibly differed in some details from our own. There is no evidence that they threw from a circle; on the contrary, Philostratus's account implies that they were allowed an unlimited run up to the throwing line if they wished to use it. It is, however, extremely unlikely that they did so; the basis of discus throwing is a circular motion, which would be hindered rather than helped by a run. (The shape of the balbis is probably accounted for by its being used for the javelin as well as the discus; for javelin throwing a run is essential.) The evidence of the few vases which depict a discus thrower in action (e.g. Plate 1a) is that the Greek method included a reversal of the feet, and this is implied also in Myron's statue and Philostratus's description; whether this reversal produced a turn of the body through a full circle or only a half-circle we do not know.

It is possible that the greatest difference between the Greek method and ours lay in the way in which elevation was achieved. For the best results, the discus must be dispatched at the optimum angle of 45 degrees to the horizontal. In the epic stage of the event, when the missile was a ponderous ingot weighing perhaps thirty pounds, the only way of imparting this elevation was to swing the discus close to the ground with the body bent and to help the lift by an upward thrust from the feet, straightening knees and hips together. In modern throwing with the lighter discus, the swing is done with the body erect and the throwing arm almost parallel with the ground, so that the discus is only slightly below the level of the shoulder. The necessary elevation is given by an upward sweep of the throwing arm from the shoulder in the last part of the swing. But the same result can be achieved if the plane of the circular sweep of the arm is tilted by bending the trunk from the hips; elevation is then produced by releasing the discus at the point midway between the lowest and highest points of this plane. Myron's statue and Philostratus's description suggest that this method may have been used at least by some throwers. On the other hand, the majority of the few vases which attempt to show the action of the throw depict an upright stance. By far the most convincing representation of a discus thrower that has come down to us from antiquity is a fragment of a red-figured vase now in Würzburg (Plate 9b). The lower half of the thrower's body is lost, but even the small piece remaining gives a vivid impression of the tremendous concentration of the athlete's effort. The artist has perhaps shown the discus too full-faced; the oblique view of a shield or discus presented a problem which few Greek sculptors or painters mastered. Yet the picture is unmistakably of a thrower using a method fundamentally the same as that of today.

Little can be said about the standard of Greek discus throwing. Only one throw has been recorded, that already quoted in the epigram about Phaÿllus: 'He jumped five over fifty feet, but threw the discus five short of a hundred.'

There is a strange disparity between the endless discussion in modern times of Phaÿllus's jump and the almost complete silence about his throw. Partly no doubt this is due to the feeling that in our uncertainty about the weight of Phaÿlus's discus there is little point in examining the statement. It may be too that the throw has seemed less remarkable to modern writers because of the strange coincidence that at the first modern Olympics of 1896, the winner of the discus, R. S. Garrett of U.S.A., threw 95 ft. 7¾ in. But there is a noteworthy difference between the ancient and modern performances. Garrett went to Athens in 1896 to take part in another event. Three weeks before the Olympic games he had never even seen a discus in his life. Today the world's record stands at over 200 feet; such is the improvement that sixty years of a developing technique can achieve. Phaÿllus was an outstanding pentathlete at a time when discus throwing had been practised for centuries and when every possibility of technical improvement in method must have been explored. How then are we to explain the epigram?

Gardiner, who believed that the Greek jump was a single one, assumed that both statements in the epigram were wild exaggerations. This would be possible only if the discus of Phaÿllus's time, about 480 B.C., was very much heavier than ours. But discuses of approximately the modern weight have been found which archaeologists date to the previous century. Moreover, an epigram based on mere exaggeration of figures would be a very feeble one. Hyperbole is a legitimate weapon of the epigrammatist, but to be effective it must be expressed in figurative language, not in statistics. When the poet writes of Jessop:

> 'He wrecked the roofs of distant towns
> When set in his assault',

he carries the reader along with him in the superb sweep of his exaggeration; had he written that the batsman hit the ball one mile 832 yards the effect would have been simply silly. It gives more point to the epigram if we assume that Phaÿllus's discus was much like ours, and that Phaÿllus, an outstanding runner and jumper, was a very poor thrower.* The epigrammatist, in fact, is consoling ordinary humanity by pointing out that even the finest performers have their weak spots.

For the student of Greek athletics in keen pursuit of solid fact, one of the most tantalizing passages in ancient literature is found in the *Heroicus* of Philostratus. In this delicate fantasy the author is describing a vineyard near the tip of the peninsula of Gallipoli, haunted by the ghost of Protesilaus, the first Greek to be killed in the Trojan war. This amiable revenant, ten cubits tall, when he is not helping the farmer, spends his time in athletic pursuits, and Philostratus tells us that he can throw a discus 100 cubits, even though it is twice the weight of the Olympic one. There is a certain interest in the author's use of the phrase 'the Olympic discus,' rather than 'the discus of today'; it may imply that the authorities at Olympia, always conservative, had retained an old-fashioned heavy discus long after a lighter model had become customary everywhere else. But our chief

---

* He must have owed his victories in the pentathlon to his running, jumping and wrestling.

feeling is one of annoyance that Philostratus, when he might easily have revealed a single normal human throw which would have told us so much that we want to know, has instead described this 150-foot cast of an overweight discus by a fifteen-foot ghost.[44]

(E) THROWING THE JAVELIN

Of all athletic events javelin throwing was the one which remained longest and most closely linked with war. In both Greek and Roman armies the thrown javelin was for many centuries the secondary armament of the infantryman, whose primary equipment was sword and shield. Missile weapons enabled him to strike the enemy before coming close enough to use his sword. For this purpose javelins had an advantage over arrows; once they were thrown, the soldier was not hampered by surplus equipment as the archer was by his bow and quiver. In warfare two qualities are required of a good thrower: accuracy and long range. The necessity of the first is obvious; long range enables the soldier to hit the enemy before the enemy can hit him. It is perfectly possible to devise competitions which will test both these qualities in a throw, as contests in archery and rifle shooting at varying ranges show. But the method of scoring for victory is inevitably complicated, and, as we have seen, in athletic games the Greeks liked a simple and clear-cut issue. It is true that both in military training and in the gymnasium they practised throwing at a mark for accuracy, but in their athletics the javelin throwing of the pentathlon was like ours, a contest simply in achieving distance.[45]

The Greek athletic javelin was reduced to the utmost simplicity, a shaft of wood which in the vase paintings is sometimes rather shorter than the height of the thrower and sometimes rather longer. We learn from a chance reference in Bacchylides that it was of elder wood; the shaft of the military javelin was made of the much harder and heavier cornel wood. For practice purposes—and the vases often represent scenes in the gymnasium rather than the stadium—it was often blunt. In competition it must have been pointed, and the vases confirm this. In order to be valid a throw must have pitched on the point, as with us, and measurement is much easier if the javelin sticks in the ground. It is not certain whether athletic javelins had metal points; practical considerations both of penetrative power and of wear and tear would suggest that they had. Pindar twice, in metaphor but in an athletic context, calls a javelin 'bronze cheeked', an epithet which Homer appropriately uses of helmets, but which is not well suited to the metal tip of the javelin, which on the evidence of the vases simply continued the taper of the wooden shaft. Two bronze ferrules found at Olympia may well be such tips, though they may equally well have served as the butt-end ferrules of military javelins.[46]

The Greek method of throwing the javelin differed from our own in one important detail. Whether in war or on the sports field the Greeks threw with the help of a thong looped over the first finger or the first two fingers of the throwing hand. The characteristic grip which this involves is constantly portrayed in vase paintings and sculpture (Plates 11b, 12a). Even the great bronze statue in Athens of Zeus hurling the thunderbolt has the right forefinger cocked in this unmistakable way. There are two quite distinct functions which the thong can perform. It can give additional leverage and thus add force and distance to the throw, serving the same purpose as the cord of a sling. In its other use the thong has the same function as the cord of a peg-top; it causes the javelin to spin round its own axis and so secures a steadier flight, as do the spiral grooves of a rifle barrel by causing the bullet to spin in the same way. It has generally been assumed that both these ends can be attained at the same time. This is open to doubt.

A javelin can be thrown with a thong in several different ways. The thong can be firmly fixed to the shaft and the throw can then be made with the thong either straight or twisted round the shaft. Otherwise the thong can be twisted round the shaft without being attached to it, the cord being held in place by a half-hitch; in this case the thong can be retained in the throwing hand as when spinning a peg-top, or it can be allowed to slip from the fingers as in throwing with a fixed thong. Gardiner records, by hearsay, experiments in throwing with a thong which produced phenomenal improvement in performance, as much as 300 per cent. Some experiments recently carried out by the author suggest that these figures should be regarded with considerable suspicion. An account of them may be of interest.[47]

The javelin used was a standard modern all-metal eight-foot weapon. To reduce the number of variables, all throws were done without a run, using as far as possible the same effort. A number of throws were performed in the normal way without a thong, in order to establish and maintain a 'control' standard, and these were repeated at intervals between the other experiments. Of twenty-four throws done in this way, only eight pitched on the point, but the distances were reassuringly constant, varying only 4 per cent above and below the mean standard S. The first experiment was with a fixed thong eighteen inches long, not twisted round the shaft. Of fourteen throws done thus, thirteen pitched on the point; the average distance was S+4 per cent, the throws varying between S+20 per cent and S—16 per cent. It was surprising to find that when the thong was lengthened to three feet, distance fell off. Of five throws, four pitched on the point; the mean distance was S—6 per cent, the throws varying between S+4 per cent and S—10 per cent.

The next series of throws was done with the eighteen-inch fixed thong twisted round the shaft to produce spin as well as leverage. All twelve throws pitched on the point, but the mean distance was S—2 per cent, the throws varying between S+16 per cent and S—20 per cent.

In the first experiments with the free thong, a very few throws were sufficient to show that no technique was practicable in which the thong was retained in the hand after throwing, as in spinning a peg-top. Even with only two turns of the cord round the shaft, the minimum necessary to keep the half-hitch taut, the drag caused loss of distance. Moreover in five throws out of six the javelin failed to pitch on the point. It was evident that with a free thong as with a fixed, the loop must be allowed to slip off the fingers on delivery. In all the best throws the thong dropped off the javelin in mid-flight. Of twenty-five throws done with the free thong, twenty-three landed on the point; the mean distance was S+1 per cent, the throws varying between S+10 per cent and S—10 per cent. The optimum number of twists round the shaft appeared to be three; with five twists, distance fell off badly.

These experiments certainly established the superiority of thonged over thongless throwing. Although the gain in distance was never spectacular, the improvement in steadiness of flight and security of pitching on the point was most marked. The results gave no decisive answer to the question whether the Greeks threw the athletic javelin with a fixed or a free thong. The evidence from antiquity on this point is equally inconclusive. Many vases show javelins without thongs; a few depict an athlete holding a thongless javelin in one hand and a loose thong in the other. One (Plate 12c) shows a thrower tightening the loop by holding it under his foot. On the other hand, javelins are often depicted, especially in pairs, with thongs looped on them. This does not necessarily prove permanent attachment; naked Greek athletes had no pockets, and this would be a natural way of carrying a loose thong or of tying two or three javelins together. The experiments produced two pieces of evidence which weigh slightly in favour of the belief that the Greeks used the free thong. The chief difficulty of throwing with the free thong is to keep it taut right up to the moment of delivery and so prevent the half-hitch from slipping. The easiest way to do this is to press the shaft back with the left hand against the pull of the loop in the right. Many vases (Plate 11b) show a thrower doing just this. The necessity does not arise with the fixed loop, since the weight of the javelin tautens the thong as the hand is taken back for the throw. Again, when throwing with the free thong there is a strong temptation to look back at the loop at the moment of throwing to make sure that it is taut, instead of following the natural impulse to look forward to the point of aim. Here too the vases show that this was frequently done by Greek throwers (Plates 11b & 12a).

Apart from these details consequent upon the use of the thong, Greek javelin throwing appears to have been identical with our own. The thrower ran up to the mark carrying the javelin on a level with his ear (Plate 12b), took it back for the throw, at the same time extending his left arm to help his balance, and threw without over-stepping the line. A vase from Spina (Fig. IV) shows an interesting variation. The thrower as he runs up to the mark is carrying the javelin as a pole jumper carries his pole. There is no doubt about the object being a javelin; the artist has clearly represented the thong on the right hand. This painting does not imply any radical difference in the method of throwing. The arm can be taken back to the throwing position as easily from this underarm carriage as from the more usual overarm.

Of Greek standards of performance with the javelin we know even less than of their achievements in the jump and discus throwing. We have nothing here comparable even with the cryptic epigram about Phaÿllus. In the whole of ancient literature there appears to be only one passage which throws any light at all on the subject, and it is a very oblique light. Statius, describing in the Thebaid the course for the chariot race, says that in length it was three times a bow shot and four times a javelin throw:

> 'finem iacet inter utrumque
> quale quater iaculo spatium, ter harundine vincas.'

We know that a few great hippodromes of the ancient world, Olympia, Byzantium and the Circus Maximus at Rome for example, were about 600 yards long, while others, that at Lepcis Magna for instance, were about 400 yards. This must have been the minimum length; crashes were frequent enough in ancient chariot racing, but without a first leg of the course long enough to enable the field to spread out before the first turn round the post, racing would have been impossible. We know something of the achievements of Greek archery. An inscription from Olbia of the late fourth century B.C.

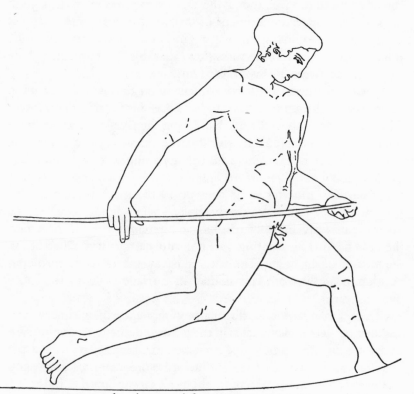

Fig. IV. Javelin thrower (after a vase in Spina Museum)

records that a man named Anaxagoras shot an arrow 282 fathoms, well over 500 yards, and Strabo mentions a bow-shot by Mithridates from the temple of Artemis at Ephesus of rather more than a stade, 200 yards. It is clear then that Statius's hippodrome could have been 600 yards long and still well within three bow-shots; this would give a javelin throw of 450 feet. If we take the shorter hippodrome of 400 yards, this gives 300 feet for the javelin. This is slightly longer than the modern world record at the moment of writing. But we have to remember that an elder-wood shaft eight feet long is four to eight ounces lighter than the modern athletic javelin; this must have made far greater distances possible, especially when the javelin was thrown down wind. Moreover, the use of the thong improved performances considerably. We are probably justified in assuming that the best Greek throwers could achieve well over 300 feet.[48]

(F) BOXING

The Greeks called boxing, wrestling and the pankration 'the heavy events'. They had no classes for different weights, but only for different age-groups, and it is to these contests, where sheer muscular strength counts so much, that the old adage best applies: 'The good big 'un will always beat the good little 'un.' So, while no doubt small men wrestled and boxed with one another in palaestra and gymnasium, in open competition only the biggest had any chance of success.

While none of these events presents a problem as fundamental or as clear-cut as that of the single or double jump or the weight of the discus, our knowledge of the details of them is often vague. It is very difficult to discover precisely what was allowed and what was illegal in each of these closely allied fighting contests. Even more than in other departments of athletics, tradition governs the rules in such events; what is permitted in one age and country is looked on as the dirtiest of fouls in another. There is some evidence from literature, for instance, that kicking was allowed in Greek boxing; the only argument against the assumption is that in the descriptions of boxing matches in the epics, kicking is never mentioned. Many who regard everything Greek through rosy spectacles would recoil with horror at the thought of Greek boxers kicking one another, yet in Thai

G

boxing today, a very civilized sport, kicking is perfectly legitimate.
Whether or not kicking was allowed, we know from Plutarch that
boxers were not permitted to grapple. Amid these complexities of
distinction between the three heavyweight events, there is one
redeeming simplicity; owing to the prestige of Olympia the rules
were in all probability uniform throughout the Greek world.
Philostratus tells us that the Olympic rules for boxing were drawn
up by Onomastus of Smyrna, who in 688 B.C. was the first winner of
the event at Olympia; he adds that the rules were accepted 'although
they came from effeminate Ionia'. We learn from Diogenes Laertius
that exactly a century later, Pythagoras of Samos, Olympic victor in
588 B.C., was the first man ever to box scientifically. He must have
been an outstanding performer; Diogenes says that he tried to enter
for the boys' boxing but was not accepted, presumably because he
could not give proof of his age, and that he thereupon entered in the
men's class and won. It is an intriguing thought that he may well
have been an uncle of the celebrated mathematician and philosopher
of the same name.[49]

Greek boxing differed from ours in one important particular. A
bout was not divided into rounds; it continued uninterrupted until
one of the competitors was knocked out or held up his hand in
acknowledgement of defeat (Plate 16). This must have made their
matches short compared with ours. Instead of gloves, Greek boxers
wore leather straps or thongs (himantes) round their hands; the purpose of these was probably to protect the fingers of the striker rather
than to soften the blow to the recipient; they corresponded, in fact,
to the bandages worn under our gloves rather than to the gloves
themselves. In the colloquial jargon of athletes they were called 'ants'
(murmekes) because they stung. The binding of these thongs was
carried up the forearm, where in later times it held in position a band
of sheepskin with which the wearer could wipe the sweat from his
forehead to prevent it from trickling into his eyes, a device which
tennis players have recently begun to copy. For training, boxers
wore something much more softly padded, which they called
'spheres' or' balls'. Modern writers continue to repeat the extraordinary statement, for which there is no evidence whatever, that
these spheres were iron balls which boxers held in their hands; one
German pundit even suggested that this was the purpose of an eight-
pound stone jumping-weight. The only result of such a device, of

course, would be to smash the fingers of the unfortunate holder the first time he landed a blow. Plato's advocacy of the use of spheres in training makes their purpose unmistakable. 'If we were boxers in training', he writes, 'we should come as near to the real thing as possible, and put on spheres instead of himantes, in order to have the best possible practice in delivering and parrying blows.' At first sight, putting on soft gloves instead of those used in competition does not look like 'coming as near to the real thing as possible', but Plato knew perfectly well that sparring partners do not throw themselves whole-heartedly into their task unless they are sure that there is little risk of getting hurt if they do so. Boxers in training, like their modern counterparts, also wore ear-guards. We owe our knowledge of this fact to the accident that Plutarch remarks that they would be more suitably worn by children to prevent them from hearing bad language. Apparently they were not worn in competition; at any rate, cauliflower ears are frequently mentioned in Greek literature as the trade-mark of the boxer. For training purposes boxers used the punch-ball and practised shadow-boxing.[50]

It is sometimes stated that in Roman imperial times Greek boxing deteriorated and became more bloodthirsty, with the boxers wearing a fearsome caestus loaded with lead and fitted with projecting spikes. This mistake is made by those who fail to detect the differing traditions of the Latin western and the Greek eastern parts of the empire. In the west boxing was incorporated into the gladiatorial games and developed as we should expect in order to satisfy the blood-lust of the spectators in the amphitheatre. There is no indication that the boxing of the Greek stadium followed the same course. Rather there is evidence of a very different development. Dio Chrysostom relates of Melancomas of Caria, an Olympic victor of the first century A.D., that although he was a boxer, his face was as unmarked as if he had been a runner. Moreover, not only did he avoid being hit himself, but he won his victories without finding it necessary to hit his opponents. The exchange of blows he considered to be the refuge of those who had no lasting power and wanted to finish the bout as soon as possible. The true excellence of a boxer in his view was endurance without being overcome by the weight of the hands, by shortage of breath or by the heat. So he skipped round his opponents in the ring until they held up their hands in acceptance of defeat, either through sheer exhaustion or perhaps because they disliked being made to look foolish. Dio tells us that Melancomas could keep this up for two days. Even allowing for the exaggeration of the moralist, we must recognize that Dio could not have told the story if in his day Greek boxing had declined into mere brutal slugging. It is worth noting that the only two fatal boxing accidents of which we know any details both occurred in the so-called 'golden age' of Greek athletics. In 496 or 492 B.C. Cleomedes of Astypalaea killed Iccus of Epidaurus at Olympia by a foul. About 400 B.C. an extraordinary scene was enacted at Nemea. The finalists, Damoxenus of Syracuse and Creugas of Epidamnus, were still boxing as night drew on. They agreed before witnesses that to decide the result, each should deal an unopposed blow at the other. Creugas hit Damoxenus on the head, but without knocking him out. Damoxenus then struck his opponent below the ribs with his hand straight out; he was wearing the soft thongs of the time, which left the fingers uncovered. His nails were so sharp that his hand pierced Creugas's stomach, caught his entrails and tore them out. Creugas died on the spot, but was awarded the crown posthumously. Whatever happened to Greek boxing in Roman times could hardly have been a degeneration from this conduct.[51]

We have one piece of evidence for Greek boxing tactics from an unexpected source. Cicero, discussing in a letter to his friend Atticus the question of a suitable term for a philosopher's suspension of judgement, approves the suggestion of Carneades of Cyrene that the Greek word 'probolē' would fill the gap. This word, which literally means 'thrusting forward', is a technical term of boxing, where it is used for the boxer's stance. When we take into account the purpose for which Cicero proposed to adopt it, it is a fair assumption that the Greek boxer employed the classic stance of the right-hander, with the left shoulder forward to protect the chin and the left hand 'thrusting forward', and that this prodding left was primarily a weapon of defence; a philosopher suspending judgement is not in an aggressive mood.[52]

But for our mental picture of Greek boxing we have to rely, apart from the epics, chiefly on the vases. Many of the paintings, especially those which depict the combatants squaring up to one another, remind us of Harry East's picture of Tom Crib in a posture of defence 'which did no credit to the science of that hero, if truly represented'. But some of the more animated ones are wonderfully

vivid (Plates 15, 16, 19). It is not always possible to be certain whether
the contest depicted is boxing or the pankration, in which hitting
was permitted. We are generally told that if the fighters are wearing
thongs, they are boxers, if not, the event is the pankration, but this is
surely to attribute too much significance to the presence or absence
of a few lines on the vase. If the evidence of the paintings is to be
trusted, Greek boxers often delivered a blow with the heel of the hand
with the fist unclenched, and also with the side of the hand, using the
fist as if it were a hammer. The latter manœuvre may explain why
in some of the boxing matches described in the epics the final
decisive blow is a downward one, unusual in modern boxing.[53]

As we might expect, the satiric epigrammatists found rich material
in boxers, particularly in their battered appearance. Lucilius warns
one of them, Olympicus, an old fighter much the worse for wear,
never to look at his own reflection in a pool, or he will die like
Narcissus, but for very different reasons. The same poet has a delightful inscription for a statue erected in honour of the boxer Apis by his
grateful opponents: 'For he never hurt one of them.' A third epigram
of Lucilius tells of a boxer, Cleombrotus, who retired from the ring
and got married; 'and now he endures at home all the blows of
Isthmia and Nemea. His wife is an old battleaxe, hitting harder than
an Olympic victor, and he dreads seeing the inside of his own house
more than he ever dreaded the stadium'. This is an unexpected
glimpse of Greek married life.[54]

We have seen that accounts of athletic events are almost unknown
in Greek literature outside the epics. A very brief description of the
end of a boxing match comes in a simile in Oppian's poem on hunting. He is describing the last stages of a lion hunt, when the quarry,
beset by its enemies, is facing death:

'Like a man who has been crowned with many an olive wreath for
victories in boxing but now is overcome by blow after blow as he
faces a stronger opponent. At first he keeps his feet, though bathed in
streams of blood and with lolling head, like a drunken man; at
last his legs give way under him and he lies stretched out on the
ground.'

It is the sad but all too familiar story of the veteran who has gone
on for just one fight too many.[55]

(G) WRESTLING

Whatever spectators may have thought, there is little doubt that among Greek athletes themselves wrestling was by far the most popular sport. This is readily understandable. It is less painful than boxing or the pankration and requires less space than running or the field events. Palaestras or wrestling schools abounded in Greek cities from the sixth century B.C. to the end of the Roman imperial epoch. By a curious convention which we learn from Plutarch, these were used only for wrestling and the pankration, not for boxing, training for which was done in the gymnasium. A young Greek joined one of the palaestras in his city, as today he would join a club, and spent much of his spare time there; his friends knew where to find him. Plato in the Symposium gives us a charming picture of the middle-aged Socrates and the young Alcibiades at one of these palaestras often engaging in wrestling bouts with one another as naturally as today they would have a round of golf or play a set of tennis together. The popularity of the sport is attested also by the frequency with which metaphors drawn from it occur in literature, especially poetry.[56]

Unlike boxing, in which a bout continued without a break until victory was conceded, a wrestling match was broken into sections by the falls, but there appears to have been no interval after a throw; the combatants re-engaged at once. A match was for the best of three falls. We have no clear statement of what constituted a fall, and there is no point over which the wrestling rules of different countries and ages are more at variance. A passage in Aristophanes, describing a wrestler who has been thrown, hastily wiping the sand from his shoulders, presumably to remove the evidence of what had happened before the referee could see it, suggests that a fair throw was established by the shoulders touching the ground. The boast of a wrestler in an epigram of Philippus that he never marked the sand with his back points the same way, and there is some other supporting evidence for this belief.[57]

Like all other Greek athletes, wrestlers rubbed olive oil all over themselves before training or competition. This was a hygienic measure, designed to keep sand and dust out of the pores. After exercise, the athlete took a bath and then scraped the oil off with a curved bronze instrument called a strigil or stlengis. It is sometimes suggested that a wrestler's motive in using oil was primarily to make it difficult for his opponent to secure a hold, but this would have reduced a fine sport to the level of hunting the greasy pig. In fact, after putting on the oil, wrestlers dusted themselves with fine powder, and, if a somewhat confused passage in Lucian's *Anacharsis* is to be believed, powdered one another. Presumably a wrestler was allowed to ensure that his opponent's body was adequately covered. Yet a passage in Aristophanes hints that after this dusting an unscrupulous athlete sometimes gave a surreptitious wipe with an oily hand to a part of his body which his opponent was likely to grasp; in Aristophanes it is the neck.[58]

We know a considerable number of technical terms of Greek wrestling, but unhappily we do not know their exact application, and a very slight acquaintance with the vocabulary of any modern game will suggest that it is unwise to deduce the meaning of a term of athletic jargon from the literal significance of the word. We have only to think of the various meanings of the very ordinary word 'leg' in the mouth of a cricketer. But we do know enough to be able to state that there were two tactical approaches to wrestling. In the first, the wrestler attempted to seize the hands, wrists or arms of his opponent and to throw him by a sudden twist (Plate 13*a*); this was called akrocheirismos. In the second he came to close quarters and tried to secure a h ld on the body (Plate 13*b*). An unpleasant variation of the first method was introduced by Leontiscus of Messana, who won two victories at Olympia, in 456 and 452 B.C. He seized his opponent's hand immediately upon engagement and broke his fingers by bending them backwards. We do not hear of this again, so presumably it was made illegal.[59]

A fragment of papyrus of the second century A.D. gives us a graphic scene of a trainer instructing two boys in the tricks of wrestling. He throws a command at each in turn, telling one how to perform a manœuvre and immediately instructing the other in the proper riposte to it. The terms are all common Greek words, but what their exact significance may have been for a wrestler we can only conjecture.

'Put your hip alongside his and grasp his head with your right.— You, throw both arms around him.—You, get under his grip.—You, push your foot between his and close with him.—You, get your right under him.—You, grip the hand he is getting under you and thrust your left down on his flank.—You, push him back with your left.— You, reverse your feet and close with him.—You, counter his reverse.—You, grasp both his arms.—You, push forward your foot. —You, grasp him between the legs.—You, push forward and bend him back.—You, step forward and throw your head back.'

At this point the papyrus unfortunately becomes so fragmentary as to be unintelligible.[60]

The competitions in boxing, wrestling and the pankration took place in a part of the stadium called the skamma. This word, which literally means 'dug up part', was also used for the jumpers' pit, but the two places cannot have been the same. A jumping pit must be soft to prevent injury to the athlete on landing; boxing and wrestling demand a firm foothold. No doubt a rather thicker layer of sand was spread over the part used for these contests than over the rest of the stadium, to lessen the shock to the wrestler when thrown. Most Greek athletic meetings were held in the summer when the stadium was dry and dusty, but from time to time in a Greek summer a heavy thunderstorm occurs which produces a sea of mud everywhere for a few hours. Because wrestlers might for this reason find themselves competing on such a surface, they used to practise wrestling under these conditions, and every palaestra had two rings, a wet and a dry. In the *Gymnastic* Philostratus discusses how training time may best be apportioned between the two rings. For the wet one he uses the word 'mud'. Athletes colloquially called the sticky mess 'beeswax', keroma; this Greek word, oddly enough, is found more often in Latin literature than in Greek. The two rings gave rise to a proverbial expression, 'Out of the sand into the mud',—our 'Out of the frying pan into the fire'. Seneca in one of his letters uses very neatly a literal application of this proverb. Travelling from Naples to Baiae he passed from the mud of the road to the dust of the Naples tunnel:

'*Totum athletarum fatum mihi illo die perpetiendum fuit; a ceromate nos haphe excepit in crypta Neopolitana.*'

'On that day I had to endure all the lot of a wrestler; the mud-ring was followed by the sand of the tunnel to Naples.'

Martial has a brief poem which he sends to a friend with a gift of a leather wrestling cap:

'*Ne lutet immundum nitidos ceroma capillos,*
  hac poteris madidas condere pelle comas.'

'You will be able to cover your brilliantined locks with this cap, so that the dirty mud of the ring may not soil your sleek coiffure.'

A wrestler's hair was always a problem; if worn long it might afford a hold to his opponents. We know from a chance remark in the *Bacchae* of Euripides that for this reason Greek wrestlers kept their hair short:

'Long curls withal! That shows thou ne'er hast been
A wrestler.'
                                            (Tr. Murray)[61]

Though wrestling is a less dangerous sport than boxing, it too had its tragedy in antiquity. In the fifth century B.C. a member of a famous athletic family, Telemachus of Pharsalia, killed his opponent when winning the wrestling at Olympia. The inscription in which he records his regret at the accident, as well as the statue of his celebrated brother Hagias, can still be seen at Delphi.[62]

(H) THE PANKRATION

We are sometimes told that we must not try to conceive the past in terms of the present; a foolish prohibition, for there are no other terms in which we can conceive it; the unknown can only be approached through, and expressed in terms of, the known. Yet there is a real danger against which this dictum attempts to warn us, and no better example of it could be found than the definition sometimes given of the pankration as all-in wrestling. That entertainment has become all too familiar to many people of recent years. Before we accept it as a true equivalent of the pankration in its heyday, we should do well to remember that no fewer than eight of Pindar's odes celebrate victories in this event. It is not easy to believe that

members of the aristocratic families which alone could afford to
employ the poet ever devoted themselves to a sport which bore any
strong resemblance to knockabout clowning. Nor would Marcus
Aurelius in his *Meditations* have grouped the pankration with song
and dance if it had been merely brutal fighting. Even so, in later
times, when the games became professional entertainment for the
spectators, the pankration, as we shall see, did develop into something like this. A second definition is that it was a mixture of boxing
and wrestling; perhaps it would be better to call it a specialized form
of wrestling in which hitting with the fist was allowed. Another way
of describing it would be to say that it was unarmed combat
converted into a scientific sport.[63]

The chief difference between the pankration and ordinary or 'upright' wrestling, as the Greeks called it, was that, whereas in the latter
the aim was to throw the opponent, in the pankration the object was
to bring him to a point where he was compelled to admit defeat, as
in boxing. This could be done by treating the bout as if it were a
boxing match; a better and more scientific way was to secure a hold
on the opponent such that if he did not surrender he would be
throttled or have a limb broken or a joint dislocated; the parallel
with modern judo is obvious. The use of the fists was almost certainly
subordinate to this main aim. No boxing thongs were worn, because
they would have interfered with the wrestling holds. A pankratiast
probably fell back on fisticuffs only to try to compel his opponent to
relax a hold; an arm which is being used for hitting cannot be
employed for the more effective purpose of securing a stranglehold.
There was no point in avoiding being thrown, so much of the action
of the pankration took place with the combatants rolling on the
ground (Plate 21). This meant that superior size and weight were not
so decisive as in boxing or wrestling. Philostratus tells us of a Cilician
pankratiast, nicknamed 'Jumping-weight' because of his small
stature, who, acting on the advice of an oracle, achieved a great
reputation and an unbeaten record by working out a technique of
falling to the ground with his opponent on top of him and developing the struggle from this firm base.[64]

Of the rules and conventions governing this event we know only
that while kicking and hitting were allowed, biting and gouging
were illegal; the rules were enforced by umpires standing ready with
rods to flog any athlete who broke them (Plates 13*a*, 14*a*, 15, 16, 18,

19c, 20). In spite of this deterrent the rules were often broken, especially in later times. Lucian, satirizing the contemporary fashion of bestowing hyperbolic terms of praise on popular athletic stars, makes one of his characters remark that pankratiasts were well called 'Lions' because of the amount of biting they did (Plate 17). In the first century A.D. Epictetus, describing the hardships of a pankratiast's career, enumerates the rigours of training and the plain and restricted diet, and goes on:

'Then in the contest itself he must face being gouged, sometimes dislocating a wrist or twisting an ankle, swallowing lots of sand, being flogged, and with all this very often being defeated.'

The gouging to which Epictetus refers, and which was forbidden by the rules, was thrusting a finger or thumb into an opponent's eye or other soft spot (Plate 20). The Greek term for it is the ordinary word for 'to dig'. But Epictetus, like most other late writers, here uses not the simple verb but a compound of it, which means 'to gouge alongside the other man'. Here we see how unchanging is human nature. It is notorious that no player of any game ever starts dirty play. When guilty of the most blatant foul he always claims that he acted in retaliation. So no Greek pankratiast ever gouged; he only 'gouged back' or gave 'dig for dig', and the compound verb ousted the simple as the normal term of athletes' colloquial speech.*[65]

The early moves in a pankration contest must have been very similar to those in a wrestling match, with both combatants looking for a good opening hold. This probably explains why the finger-breaking trick, which Pausanias tells us was used in wrestling by Leontiscus in 456 B.C., was according to the same authority imitated 100 years later in the pankration by Sostratus of Sicyon, three times victor at Olympia. We might be tempted to think that we had here two versions of the same story, but Pausanias's account is very circumstantial; he tells us that the victor statues of the two athletes stood close to one another at Olympia. Moreover, there is nothing impossible about his story. A century was quite long enough for the

* The term caused some difficulty to the first English translator of *Epictetus*, Mrs. Elizabeth Carter, whose version was published in 1758. Unversed in the niceties of the pankration, she rendered the opening words 'Then in combat, you may be thrown into a ditch.'

scandal about Leontiscus to have faded from men's minds, and Sostratus may well have noticed that while the trick may have been forbidden in wrestling, there was still nothing in the rules of the pankration to make it illegal, and have taken advantage of this.[66]

The most famous of all pankratiasts was an athlete of the sixth century B.C., Arrichion of Phigaleia, whose last fight is described by both Pausanias and Philostratus. The latter, who claims to be describing a picture of the incident, gives a much fuller account, to which we owe much of our knowledge of the pankration. In 564, after victories in the two previous Olympiads, Arrichion faced a rival whose name we do not know. This man secured a winning hold on Arrichion. He had leaped on his back and with one arm was pressing on his throat, slowly throttling him. At the same time he had clasped Arrichion's waist between his own legs and hooked a foot behind each of his knees from inside his legs. The match appeared to be over. At this point Arrichion's trainer, Eryxias, shouted out to him in desperation: 'What a noble epitaph, "He was never defeated at Olympia."' It happened that at this moment the opponent slightly relaxed the grip of his legs. Arrichion was fast losing consciousness, but he had sufficient strength for a final effort. He threw all his weight on to his left leg and closed his legs together, thus trapping his opponent's legs between his own. Then, as he toppled over on to his left side, he kicked his right foot backwards towards his buttock. His rival's right foot was locked behind the knee of this leg, and the result of the kick was to dislocate the ankle joint. In the agony of the moment the man threw up a hand—the token of defeat. But it was too late. The combination of the stranglehold and the effort of his last move had been fatal to Arrichion. The umpires awarded him the victory and placed the crown on his dead body. An archaic statue found near Phigaleia, which used to be in the caretaker's house at Bassae and is now in the museum at Olympia, may well be the victor statue of Arrichion mentioned by Pausanias.[67]

The pankration was always a favourite event among the Greeks, especially the spectators; for them it was the supreme test of strength and skill in combination. In the *Wasps* of Aristophanes, the young Bdelucleon, trying to train his rough diamond of a father Philocleon in the ways of polite society, suggests to him that the pankration would be a suitable subject of conversation in such circles.

'BDEL. Still you must tell how splendidly, for instance,
Ephudion fought the pankratiastic fight
With young Ascondas; how the game old man,
Though grey, had ample sides, strong hands, firm flanks,
An iron chest.
PHIL. What humbug! Could a man
Fight the pankration with an iron chest?
BDEL. This is the way our clever fellows talk.'

(Tr. Rogers.)

Later in the play, Philocleon, now quarrelling with his son and threatening physical violence, neatly uses the suggested topic as a warning:

'PHIL. Now look ye here;
Once, a spectator at the Olympian games
I saw how splendidly Ephudion fought
With young Ascondas; saw the game old man
Up with his fist and knock the youngster down.
So mind your eye, or you'll be pummelled too.
BDEL. Troth, you have learned Olympia to some purpose.'

(Tr. Rogers.)

In Roman imperial times, as the prize-money at Aphrodisias shows, the pankration far excelled all other events in spectator appeal. This may imply that skill was still highly esteemed by the onlookers. But if Melancomas' boxing technique as described by Dio was at all typical of the boxers of the time it looks as if it was boxing that had developed along lines of pure skill, while the crowds, now clamouring more and more for mere violent action, turned increasingly for satisfaction to the pankration.[68]

Lacking further information from literature, we have to look for evidence about the pankration, as about the other heavyweight events, to the vase paintings, with all the problems of interpretation which that involves (Plates 17, 18, 19b, 20, 21). Until a papyrus containing a training manual turns up, or an inscription is found with a complete set of the rules, any attempt to give more than a broad outline of these events is bound to be a waste of time.

V SOME GREEK ATHLETES

IT USED to be an article of faith with our grandfathers that games train character. Many who have played games all their lives will be sceptical about this, but there can be no doubt that few human activities are more generous in revealing character. Perhaps this is less true of athletics than of team games, yet in antiquity, as in modern times, some athletes impressed themselves on their contemporaries and on posterity through qualities and quirks of character which bore no relationship to their sporting achievements. Leonidas of Rhodes, who won twelve victories in four Olympiads between 164 and 152 B.C., is no more than a name to us. Phaÿllus of Croton, without a single Olympic victory to his credit, is still a figure of flesh and blood. Admittedly much of our knowledge is accidental. Greek literature had no Bernard Darwin or Neville Cardus, or, if it had, their works have not come down to us. But then, as now, one of the signs of a man's being a 'character' was that anecdotes gathered round his name. It is from these anecdotes and the scanty factual records that we must try to build up our picture of these remarkable men.

The first Greek athlete to answer this description is Milo of Croton in south Italy. Even before his day this city had acquired a considerable reputation for its athletes. The inadequate records include the names of seven Crotoniates, six of them sprinters, who won at Olympia before Milo's first appearance there. At one Olympiad, probably that of 576 B.C., the first seven to finish in the stade were all men of Croton, a performance which not even the U.S.A. or U.S.S.R. has equalled in our day. This preoccupation of Croton with physical excellence may have been partly due to the proximity of the much larger and wealthier city of Sybaris. The Sybarites achieved one Olympic victory, that of Philytas in the boys' boxing in 616 B.C., the first occasion on which the event was held. Thereafter they affected to despise athletics and devoted themselves so successfully to the acquiring of wealth that they became and have remained ever since a byword for luxurious living. On their side the Crotoniates' passion for athletics reflected their contempt for Sybaritic softness.* Their reputation in sport was consolidated by the truly remarkable achievements of Milo as a wrestler. His Olympic career opened with a victory in the boys' event in 540 B.C. Then in five successive Olympiads, from 536 to 520, he won the men's wrestling. To these victories he added a victory in the boys' and six in the men's event at the Pythian games at Delphi, ten in the Isthmian and nine in the Nemean. Five times he was Periodonikēs or winner of the quadruple crown, a title bestowed on a man who won at all four of these 'crown' festivals in the same cycle. Even these triumphs did not satisfy him. He entered the men's event at Olympia for the seventh time, but was defeated by a younger Crotoniate, Timasitheus, who avoided coming to close quarters with the old warrior and won by using the 'akrocheirismos' technique.[1]

It is not surprising that stories of legendary feats were told of such a man. He was reported to have carried a four-year-old bull round the stadium at Olympia and then eaten it in one day. His normal daily diet, we hear, was twenty pounds of meat, the same weight of bread and eighteen pints of wine. Victors at Olympia were allowed to put up statues of themselves there. Milo unaided carried his own statue to the place where it was to be erected. Another group of anecdotes describes his exhibitions of his strength. He used to stand on a greased discus and defy all comers to push him off it. He would hold a pomegranate in his hand and challenge men to uncurl his fingers from it, resisting all their efforts without ever crushing the pomegranate. He used to bind a ribbon round his forehead and break it by swelling his veins, a feat which recalls the stories of Italian tenors shattering wineglasses with their top notes. This last group of

* The enmity of Croton and Sybaris at this time resulted in a sad incident, related by Herodotus. One of Croton's Olympic victors, Philippus, fell in love with a Sybarite girl and became engaged to her. But this Hellenic Romeo and Juliet were not destined to bring about a reconciliation of their warring cities. The Crotoniates, furious at this flirtation with the old foe, banished Philippus. The girl jilted him, and he went off to the wars and was killed in Sicily.

stories probably arose from the misinterpretation of a statue of Milo holding in his hand an apple, the prize for the Pythian games in early times, and garlanded with the ribbons which victors wore in addition to their crowns. Statues were normally carved or cast with the feet on a round or oblong disc which fitted into a recess cut for the purpose in the base; this no doubt accounts for the discus legend.

Milo was not merely a great athlete. He held high command in the Crotoniate army which in 510 ended the long quarrel with Sybaris by a victory which resulted in the complete destruction of that city. Diodorus tells us that to encourage his men he went into action wearing his Olympic crowns and with the lion-skin and club of Heracles, an eccentricity of uniform in a Commanding Officer not without parallel in more recent times. A group of stories too numerous to disregard links him with the circle which gathered at Croton round Pythagoras, whose contributions to mathematics and musical theory and speculations about the transmigration of souls made him one of the most influential thinkers of the Greek world. Pythagoras is said to have been accidentally killed in a fire which burnt down Milo's house when he was a guest there. Another story is that Milo married Pythagoras's daughter Muia. This match appears as eugenically admirable as the proposed alliance between Isadora Duncan and Bernard Shaw. If it really took place and was productive, the results would seem to have justified Shaw's fears. The athletic supremacy of Croton vanished in the century after Milo, and we hear of no compensatory intellectual achievements of Crotoniates at that time. If Muia did marry Milo, it is almost certain that she was not his only wife. Herodotus tells us of a daughter of Milo who married a doctor named Democedes, and it is hardly conceivable that, had she been a grand-daughter of Pythagoras, Herodotus would not have mentioned the fact.[2]

This Democedes had a most romantic career. A native of Croton, which was almost as famous for its medical school as for its athletes, he is the earliest known practitioner in a national health service; he was employed by the state in Aegina as public doctor and then was lured away by a higher salary to a similar post in Athens. Later, tempted by still more pay, he entered the service of Polycrates, the tyrant of Samos, and when that ruler was defeated by the Persians, Democedes was taken as a slave to the Persian capital Susa. There he won favour with King Darius by curing his dislocated ankle after the native doctors had failed; no doubt he had had plenty of experience of such accidents when working among Greek athletes. Later, by performing a similar service for the queen, he obtained permission to pay a visit to his native south Italy. It was at this time that he wooed and won Milo's daughter, paying her father a large sum of money for the privilege; this was contrary to the usual custom of Greek men, who generally expected a considerable dowry with their brides. Herodotus tells us that Democedes sent a special message about his marriage to Darius whom he knew to be a great admirer of his prospective father-in-law. The Persian king can have learned about Milo only from Democedes himself, and we can conjure up a delightful picture of the Greek doctor applying his dressings to the royal ankle and at the same time expounding the athletic triumphs of his fellow Crotoniate.

The story of Milo's death is well known. It is said that in a lonely forest he saw a tree-trunk which had had wedges inserted in it to split it. In an ostentatious attempt to demonstrate his strength he opened the split with his fingers, but the trunk closed on them, and, unable to free himself, Milo was killed and eaten by a pack of wolves. The sceptic will ask why, if eyewitnesses were present, they did not intervene to save him, or, if there were no eyewitnesses, how the manner of his death was known. It seems more probable that when travelling alone he was attacked by wolves and just failed to escape from them by climbing a tree, near which his remains were found later. Moralists then improved the occasion as moralists will.

We do not know the date of Milo's death, but if he lived the normal human span he must often in his old age, as he walked the streets of Croton, have been gazed on with admiration by a boy who was destined to bring still more glory to the city. This was Phaÿllus, whose jumping and discus throwing we have already examined. Compared with Milo's, his list of victories was meagre. We know of only three, two in the pentathlon and one in the stade, all at Delphi. He never won at Olympia, but the motive which led him to forego his best chance of an Olympic crown brought him more honour than any athletic achievement could possibly have done.

As we have seen, he must have been an outstanding jumper, a very fine sprinter and no mean wrestler, but a poor thrower. Apparently at one Pythian festival he was beaten in the stade, but if his conqueror entered for the pentathlon, Phaÿllus must have turned the tables on

H

him in that event. In all probability Phaÿllus won one or two of his
Pythian victories in the games of 482 B.C. With high hopes of an
Olympic crown, he set out for Greece in the spring of 480, in order
to put in the months of training at Elis demanded of competitors
before the games in August. He must have been a man of considerable wealth, for he sailed in command of his own ship. But when he
reached mainland Greece there were more important things than
athletics to think of. The invading army and navy of Persia were
approaching, threatening to deprive the Greek world for ever of its
liberties. Phaÿllus added his ship to the combined Greek navy, in
which he was the sole representative of the western Greeks. Soon
after his departure from Croton, the Phoenicians of Carthage and
west Sicily, acting in concert with their kinsmen from Tyre who
furnished a large part of Xerxes' fleet in the Aegean, mounted an
attack on the Greek cities of south Italy and Sicily; the Greeks of the
west were now far too busy with their own defence to be able to send
help to the country of their origin. Phaÿllus stayed with the Greek
fleet in the Aegean during the strategic moves of July and August,
and in September fought in the crowning victory of Salamis; on the
same day, according to tradition, a victory at Himera in north Sicily
freed the western Greeks from the Carthaginian threat. But by the
time Salamis was fought the Olympic festival was over. Phaÿllus had
seen where his duty lay and had done it. His Olympic hopes were
still in the future.

It was probably at Delphi in 478 that he completed his trio of
Pythian victories, and his record jump may well have been performed
at this meeting. In accomplishing the feat, according to Suidas, he
injured his leg. Perhaps this accident put an end to his athletic career;
perhaps when the Olympiad of 476 came round, he was past his best.
We do not know. But certainly the Olympic crown, the ambition
of every athlete, had eluded him. Yet Greece did not forget him. Half
a century later, Aristophanes, wishing to name a great runner of the
past, uses none of the Olympic winners he could have recalled, but
Phaÿllus. His old Acharnian charcoal burner, out of breath after
his pursuit of Dicaeopolis, pants out a lament for the loss of his
youth:

'O were I   Now as spry   As in youthful days gone by,
When I stuck   Like a man   To Phaÿllus as he ran,

And achieved   Second place   In the race,
Not so light   From my sight   Had this treaty-bearer fled.'

(Tr. Rogers.)

A century later still, Alexander the Great, after the battle of Issus, sent a share of the spoils to two cities of Greece in recognition of their heroic deeds in the past; to Plataea because of the part her citizens had played at Marathon; to Croton because of Phaÿllus's action at the time of Salamis.[3]

Not all Greek athletes were as unselfish as Phaÿllus in the hour of their country's danger. In that hot August, when the Persian armies were bearing down on the cities of the mainland, and Leonidas and his three hundred Spartans were preparing to die at Thermopylae, the Olympic games went on as usual. Among the winners at the festival was one of the greatest of all Greek athletes, a man whose life is better known to us than that of any other figure in the sport of antiquity. This was the boxer and pankratiast Theogenes. He was born in Thasos, the chief city of the island of the same name in the north Aegean. Some centuries earlier the gold mines of this island had been worked by Phoenicians; they had long since departed, but they had left behind the cult of a god whom the Greeks identified with their own Heracles and whose worship they continued, although there was a difference between the two. The Phoenician deity was a full god, and so entitled to a temple, while the Greek Heracles was only a demigod, the son of Zeus and a mortal woman, Alcmene. Theogenes' father was priest of this temple, the remains of which can still be seen in Thasos; the distinction between god and demigod was to have a curious effect on the later years of the athlete's life. The young Theogenes must obviously have been impressed by the story of Milo carrying his own statue to Olympia, for the first notice we have of him is that one day, when only eight years old, he arrived home carrying a statue which he had lifted off its base in the agora. The escapade might have had serious consequences for him, as the statue was one of a god, but the peccadillo was forgiven on condition that he carried the statue back to where he had found it, and he was spared to become the leading boxer of the day. An inscription found at Delphi records his career. He had two victories at Olympia, one in boxing and one in the pankration. He won the boxing three times at the Pythian games; at

the Isthmian, the boxing nine times and the pankration once, at the
same festival as one of the boxing victories; he won the boxing nine
times at Nemea, and the long-distance race at Argos. The inscription
adds that he won 1300 victories in other meetings, and was unbeaten
at boxing for twenty-two years. The victory in the dolichos at
Argos is remarkable for a heavyweight. Theogenes was clearly very
proud of it, for it is the only victory outside the 'crown' games which
he is careful to mention on the base of his statue at Delphi. Pausanias
gives us the clue to this pride. He says that Theogenes went to Phthia
in Thessaly and won the dolichos there, being anxious to equal
Homer's 'fleet-footed Achilles' in his own sport on his home ground.
He states that the total of Theogenes' victories was 1400, while
Plutarch says it was 1200, sourly commenting that most of them did
not amount to much.[4]

An interesting conclusion to be drawn from these figures is that
one Olympic victor at least did not think it beneath his dignity to
appear at humble sports meetings. This did not involve so much
strenuous competition as might be supposed. In the painful heavyweight events there was a reluctance to face a man who was thought
to be certain to win. Greek champions did not feel it incumbent on
them to deal gently with inexperienced opponents, and such an
expert was often given a walk-over, in Greek athletic jargon a
victory 'without dust' (akoniti). Even in the great Pythian games,
second in importance only to Olympia, Theogenes on his third
appearance found no one willing to oppose him and won a victory of
this kind. So we may assume that at most of the smaller meetings he
had to do nothing but appear and take his prize.

His experiences in the Olympic games throw a strange light on the
administration of that festival. When he first went there, in 480, the
year of the Persian invasion, he entered for the boxing and pankration
and reached the final in both. In boxing he faced the winner of the
event at the previous Olympiad, Euthymus of Epizephyrian Locri in
south Italy, and defeated him, but he was so exhausted by his efforts
that he was unable to appear in the pankration, and his opponent,
Dromeus of Mantinea, was awarded the victory akoniti; it was the
first time this had ever happened at Olympia. For scratching from
the pankration final Theogenes was summoned before the stewards,
who came to a remarkable decision. The games being in honour of
Olympian Zeus, they condemned him to pay a fine of one talent 'to

the god', a neat euphemism for 'to themselves', and one talent to
Euthymus for the injury done to him, 'because it seemed to them
that it was only to spite him that Theogenes had entered for the
boxing'. Strange as this edict was, its outcome was even more
extraordinary. Theogenes paid the fine to the authorities—he had no
alternative if he wished to compete at Olympia again—but he
came to a private arrangement with Euthymus that his part of the
fine should be remitted on condition that Theogenes did not enter
for the boxing at the next Olympiad, an agreement which seems to
us the most disreputable feature of the whole affair. Its result was all
that Euthymus could have wished. With Theogenes out of the way,
he was able to win the boxing in 476 and 472, while Theogenes,
debarred by his undertaking from the boxing, which was obviously
his best event, was content with a victory in the pankration in 476.

   In recognition of his prowess, statues of him were erected at
Olympia, in Delphi and in the city of Thasos. But success and a
consciousness of his own strength went to his head, as has happened
to many another boxer. Relying no doubt on his name—Theogenes
means 'god-born'—he claimed that he was the son not of the priest
of the temple but of the god himself, and so was entitled to the
honours due to a demigod. It is here that the status of the Thasian
Heracles is important. A son of the Greek demigod Heracles would
not be a demigod and would be entitled to no special honours such
as the son of a god could claim. Plutarch records a scene of hooligan-
ism at a ritual feast at which Theogenes thought he was not being
accorded proper treatment. It is probable too that he dabbled in
Thasian political life, which in the middle of the fifth century was in
a state of ferment. Thasos was a member of the Delian League, for all
practical purposes a subject state of Athens, and as in all such states at
that time there was a pro-Athenian and an anti-Athenian faction. The
latter so far prevailed that in 465 Thasos revolted from Athens and
was brought back to subjection only after a siege. At such a time any
prominent citizen will inevitably have many enemies, and Theogenes
was obviously the kind of man to arouse more than ordinary hatred.
During his lifetime his enemies were powerless to harm him, but
after his death one of them tried to express what he had felt about
him by stealing out at night and flogging his statue in the agora.
Unfortunately it fell on the man and killed him. Under the law of
the time even an inanimate object which had caused a death had to

be punished, so the statue was taken out to sea in a ship and thrown overboard. Soon afterwards Thasos began to suffer from failure of crops which brought severe famine. The oracle at Delphi was asked for advice and sent orders that the Thasians should recall their political exiles. They complied, but the famine continued. A further appeal to Delphi elicited the reminder that they had forgotten Theogenes. As he had now been dead for some time, his restoration appeared to present an insoluble problem. But shortly afterwards some fishermen found their nets fouled by an object on the sea bed and they dragged up the statue of the old boxer. As soon as it had been replaced on its base the famine ended. The base, which can still be seen in Thasos, has metal rings set into the stonework. It looks as if the Thasians were determined not to risk losing the statue again and chained it down.

This was not the end of Theogenes. It was believed by the Greeks that the statues of great athletes had the power to cure illness, presumably on the ground that a man who had enjoyed such super-abundant strength and vitality during his life would have some to spare for less fortunate mortals after his death. Lucian tells us that the statue of Theogenes in Thasos was renowned for these cures, and Pausanias says that he knows of other statues of him which had been erected in the Greek world and even in barbarian countries for this special purpose. The cult was long-lived. An inscription found at Thasos, containing regulations for the financial side of the procedure, is assigned by epigraphists to a date four centuries after Theogenes' death:

'Those sacrificing to Theogenes must make a preliminary offering to the treasury of not less than one obol; if anyone does not make this prescribed offering, it will lie on his conscience. The money thus contributed shall be given each year to the magistrate in charge of religious affairs; he shall keep it until 1,000 drachmas have accumulated. When the prescribed sum has accumulated, the Council and People shall decide on what offering or piece of equipment in honour of Theogenes it shall be spent.'

The whole routine was clearly very well organized; to continue so long it must have produced some results. We need not be too superior about this. It is true that, while the memory of Dr. W. G. Grace is still held in great honour, we do not expect him to exercise after death that office of healing which he so sadly neglected during his life in order to play his favourite game. Yet the curative cult of the dead Greek athlete was merely a form of faith healing, probably as well founded as much of modern psychiatry and doing little more harm.

An interesting postscript to the story of Theogenes turned up in another inscription found in Thasos, containing a list of magistrates of about 400 B.C. Among them appears a Disolympius, 'Twice Olympian', a name unparalleled elsewhere in Greek nomenclature. It can hardly be doubted that it is connected with Theogenes' two Olympic victories, and that its bearer was a son or grandson of the great athlete. Whether it was a true name, bestowed by a proud father in commemoration of his successes, or a nickname, which afterwards achieved respectability and remained in the family, first applied to Theogenes himself by contemporaries who were tired of hearing him talking about his own prowess, we do not know.

By a curious coincidence, while the healing rites of Theogenes were being established in Thasos, in faraway Locri in Italy a similar cult was growing up round the figure of his old opponent Euthymus. The story of the later days of this boxer affords an excellent example of the way in which legends more suited to the heroic age were attached to the names of these great athletes of history. Strabo and Pausanias tell us that in Euthymus's time the territory of Temesa, a city on the west coast of the toe of Italy, was ravaged by the ghost of one of Odysseus's companions, Polites, who had been killed by the inhabitants when Odysseus's ships were in those waters. This ghost used to demand the annual tribute of a maiden. On one occasion Euthymus arrived at Temesa just as the offering was about to be made. He saw the girl, fell in love with her, defeated the ghost in combat, freed Temesa for ever from the menace and married the lady. He did not die the ordinary death of mortals but was taken from human sight by the river god Caecinus, said to be his father, for Euthymus, like Theogenes, claimed divine origin. We are back in the fairyland of the *Odyssey*.

A similar ending to life is recorded of an older contemporary of Euthymus, Cleomedes of Astypalaea, who, as we have already seen, accidentally killed his opponent Iccus in the final of the boxing at Olympia. Disqualified by the umpires, he returned home an embittered man, perhaps suffering from the complaint which we now call punch-drunkenness. At any rate he lost his reason, and in a fit of madness pulled down the roof of a school in which there were sixty children. For this act he was set upon by the citizens and fled for refuge to the temple of Athene. There, like the heroine of *The Mistletoe Bough*, he jumped into a chest and pulled the lid down on himself. When after a long struggle the Astypalaeans opened the chest it was empty. They sent to Delphi to ask what had happened to him, and the oracle, which seems to have had a soft spot for boxers, replied that he was now a demigod and must be honoured as one; so a cult of this undeserving hero was established, which was still maintained in Astypalaea in Pausanias's time.[5]

This cropping up of the supernatural is always disconcerting to a student of the Greek world of antiquity. The athletes we are considering were historical figures with sporting feats to their credit as well attested as those of Paavo Nurmi or Jesse Owens. Yet interwoven with the narrative is this thread of supernatural incidents, completely incredible to us, related by such writers as Strabo and Pausanias, who are obviously trying to be factual. It serves as a healthy reminder that, while in many respects the Greek experience of life was very similar to our own, there are some points in which it was utterly different, and that at times in our attempt to gain a coherent conception of ancient Greece we are moving in a very strange world.

Another athlete whose statue was thought to have curative properties was Polydamas of Scotussa in Thessaly. He won only once at Olympia, in the pankration in 408 B.C., but his fame outstripped that of many men with far more victories, perhaps because he was, according to Pausanias, the tallest man on record. Many feats of strength are told of him. He killed a lion with his bare hands on mount Olympus. He held a bull by its hind foot until it tore itself free, leaving its hoof in his hand. He stopped a chariot going at full speed by seizing the back of it with one hand. Invited by the king of Persia to give an exhibition of his skill at Susa, he repaid the kindness of his host rather oddly by killing in unarmed combat three of the royal bodyguard, the Immortals. On his return to Greece he went to Olympia in 404 to defend his title in the pankration. His opponent in the final was Promachus of Pellene, who was not unnaturally somewhat apprehensive about the result in view of the great reputation of Polydamas. Philostratus tells us the stratagem by which his trainer overcame these terrors. Learning that his protégé was in love, he brought him a message purporting to come from the lady: 'She would not think you an unworthy lover, if you should win an Olympic victory.' This considerable meiosis might appear to be rather frigid encouragement, but the trainer clearly knew his man, for Promachus was so inspired by it that he succeeded in defeating his formidable antagonist.[6]

The manner of the death of Polydamas was as famous as that of Milo. One hot summer's day he went into a cave with some friends to seek shade. The roof of the cave started to collapse, and the old pankratiast held it up long enough for his companions to escape and then was crushed to death.

The people of Pellene were naturally proud of Promachus after his victory over the mighty Polydamas, and they erected a statue of him in their city as well as one at Olympia; they were less proud of another citizen with an even better record half a century later, Chaeron, who won the wrestling at Olympia four times between 356 and 344. When Alexander the Great reduced Greece to subjection he appointed Chaeron ruler of Pellene, no doubt hoping that his outstanding athletic achievements would recommend him to his fellow citizens. But Alexander had misjudged them; they regarded Chaeron as a quisling, and, Pausanias tells us, never again spoke of him with pride. Athenaeus informs us that he had been a pupil of Plato, and, after recounting his harsh rule, comments: 'That was all the benefit he derived from the noble *Republic* and the lawless *Laws*.'[7]

In 408, the year in which Polydamas won the pankration at Olympia, the victor in the stade was Eubatus, a sprinter from Cyrene. This runner had been promised success by an oracle, and he had so much confidence in this assurance that he had his victor statue made before the games and took it with him to Olympia when he went to compete. While he was in Greece for the festival he was seen by the famous courtesan Lais, who conceived a great passion for him and tried to seduce him. Eubatas resisted her advances, but she succeeded in persuading him that he had promised to take her back to North Africa with him after the games. He found a way to escape from her clutches and at the same time to satisfy his own scruples of conscience over breaking a promise by taking home a portrait of her, and as a reward for this conjugal fidelity his wife erected another statue of him, in Cyrene. In moral rectitude he was even surpassed by another athlete, Cleitomachus of Thebes, winner of three Olympic crowns for wrestling and the pankration two centuries after Eubatas; it is related of him that if any improper story was told in his presence he rose and left the company.[8]

By no means all Greek athletes were of this blameless character. In 336 B.C. the Olympic crown for the pankration went to Dioxippus of Athens. What his other victories may have been we do not know, but they must have been numerous and decisive, for at Olympia no opponents appeared to face him and he won by a walk-over, akoniti. On his return to his native city he was given the civic reception always accorded to Olympic victors, and while he was riding in a chariot in the procession through the streets of Athens he caused unfavourable comment by ostentatiously ogling a pretty girl among the crowd. This gave Diogenes the Cynic the opportunity for a characteristically dry remark: 'Look at your great wrestler now; that young minx has got him by the short hairs already.' Dioxippus's family was involved in a far more serious scandal than this. His sister was accused by her husband of adultery; the co-respondent, Lyco-phron, was said to have attempted to seduce her actually at the marriage ceremony. Some fragments of the speech written for the defence by the orator Hyperides have survived, and in one of them Lycophron is made to argue very reasonably that he was hardly likely to have behaved in this way at the wedding, seeing that Dioxippus and his sparring partner Euphraeus, 'generally admitted to be the strongest men in Greece', were both present.[9]

The end of Dioxippus was a sad one. By astute flattery he became a favourite of Alexander the Great, and accompanied him on his expedition against Persia. During the course of this he quarrelled with a Macedonian named Coragus and challenged him to a duel. Diodorus vividly describes the scene. Coragus appeared in full armour, with javelin, lance and sword as his weapons. Dioxippus, as befitted an athlete, was completedly naked, gleaming with olive oil and armed only with a club. First Coragus threw his javelin, which Dioxippus easily dodged. Next he charged with the lance, but Dioxippus shattered its shaft with a blow of his club. Then, as he tried to draw his sword, Dioxippus grasped his sword-arm with his own left hand, and with his right threw Coragus off his balance; at the same moment, with the skill of a trained pankratiast, he swept his feet from under him. He crashed to the ground, and as he lay prostrate Dioxippus marked the completeness of his triumph by setting his foot on his enemy's neck. The victory was popular among the other Greeks of Alexander's army, but not with the Macedonians and not with the Macedonian king. Dioxippus was never in favour again. His enemies seized their opportunity; they stole a gold cup, planted it in his quarters and accused him of the theft. Amid the scandal caused when the cup was found in its compromising position Dioxippus committed suicide.

Heredity has always been important in the athletic world. In Greece, as today, there were sons who repeated or surpassed their fathers' feats. Towards the end of the seventh century B.C. Hipposthenes of Sparta won the wrestling at Olympia six times, and at the beginning of the next century his son Hetoemocles won five Olympic victories in the same event. But these were the times when the competitors at Olympia were still drawn from a small number of cities in the Peloponnese (Map 1). Far more impressive is the tally of Olympic victories of a Rhodian family at the end of the fifth century, when athletes came to Olympia from all over the Greek world. The story starts with Diagoras, who won the boxing in 464 B.C., and whose victory was celebrated by Pindar in his seventh Olympian Ode.* His eldest son Damagetus won the pankration in 452. At the next Olympiad Damagetus won the pankration again, and his brother Acusilaus won the boxing. Pausanias has a pleasant story of this year 448. After their victories Damagetus and Acusilaus carried their father, sixteen years after his own triumph, through the crowd of spectators, who pelted him with flowers and congratulated him on having two such sons. There were further successes to come. In 432 a third son, Dorieus, won the pankration, and he repeated his victory in 428 and again in 424. Twenty years later two grandsons revived the memories of the family greatness. In 404 Eucles, a son of Diagoras's daughter Callipateira, won the boxing, while Pisorrhodus, son of another daughter Pherenice, was the victor in the boys' boxing. Here is a remarkable case of a male quality being transmitted through the female line, for we do not hear that any of Diagoras's victor sons himself fathered a winner.[10]

One of these mothers of victors made history at Olympia.

* According to the Scholiast on Pindar, this ode was inscribed in golden letter on the walls of the temple of Athene in Lindos.

According to one version of the story, she disguised herself as a man, so keen was she to see her son compete, and went into the trainers' enclosure. When her son was victorious she was so excited that she jumped over the wall of the enclosure as she rushed forward to congratulate him, and in doing so she betrayed her sex. Because of her family connections she was forgiven for having broken the strict rule of the time that no woman except the priestess of Demeter was admitted to the games, but, to prevent any recurrence of the scandal, trainers thereafter were compelled to attend the games as naked as the athletes. Another version is that the daughter of Diagoras—the names in these stories vary from author to author—applied to the authorities at Olympia for a special dispensation to be allowed to see the games, on the ground that she was the daughter, sister, aunt and mother of Olympic champions, and won her point.

The most distinguished member of this remarkable family, both in sport and in other fields, was Dorieus. Pausanias gives the number of his victories as three at Olympia, eight Isthmian and seven Nemean, and adds, without giving the total of his Pythian victories, that he won at Delphi akoniti. If, as appears probable, an inscription from Delphi refers to him, he had four Pythian victories; in addition, according to the inscription, he had four at the Panathenaea at Athens, four at the Asclepieia at Epidaurus, three at the Hecatomboea at Argos and three at the Lycaea in Arcadia. He was thus, like his father, a periodonikes certainly once, probably more than once. He was also a military commander of some eminence. When he was about to embark on his athletic career the Peloponnesian war broke out between Athens and Sparta. Rhodes was an ally or subject of Athens, but there was in the city a strong anti-Athenian party to which Dorieus belonged. As a result of this strife of faction, he was exiled to Thurii in Italy, and while in exile he commanded a fleet against Athens in 410. He was captured and condemned to death as a rebel, but the Athenians, remembering his great athletic feats, relented and set him free. Later, after Rhodes had actively entered the war on the side of Athens, Dorieus happened to be in the Peloponnese and was captured by the Spartans. Although he was taking no part in the war, he was put to death.

Another family of outstanding athletes was that of the Oligaethidae of Corinth. Even before the time of their most famous champion they had, Pindar tells us, won sixty victories at Isthmia and Nemea. A member of this clan, Thessalus, with victories to his credit in the stade and diaulos at Delphi and the stade, diaulos and armed race at Athens, won an Olympic crown in 504 B.C., probably in the diaulos. His son Xenophon—not to be confused with the Athenian author of the same name—was even more successful. Before he went to compete at Olympia in 464 he made a vow to the goddess Aphrodite that if victorious he would dedicate 100 slave girls to the service of her temple on Acrocorinth. At the games he won the stade and the pentathlon; later Pindar composed his thirteenth Olympian ode to celebrate the achievement. Then Xenophon made good his vow, and at the ceremony, during which the girls were consecrated to the goddess, they sang a song, also written by Pindar, of which some fragments survive.'[11]

There are some athletes who are remembered only for a single anecdote told about them. Such was Amesinas of Barce in North Africa, who won the wrestling at Olympia in 460 B.C. He used to practise wrestling with a bull, and when he went to Olympia to compete he took this unconventional sparring partner with him. There was a boxer or pankratiast, Echeclous of Samos, long stricken with dumbness, who suddenly recovered his speech through sheer fury at being unfairly treated at a sports meeting. Aulus Gellius says that the athlete detected that the draw was being rigged against him; Valerius Maximus, that he won his fight but was robbed of his victory by the decision of the umpire. The best of all these stories relates to a boxer from Cyrene named Eurydamas, who after receiving a blow in the face found himself with a mouthful of his own teeth. Reflecting that if he spat them out the sight could not fail to bring comfort and encouragement to his opponent, he swallowed them.[12]

Most of these 'characters' belong to the period when Greece was still free. When we come to the athletes of Roman imperial times we often know more of their feats in the stadium, for while earlier champions were content to record in stone only their victories in the more important games, their successors frequently enumerated their achievements in very minor meetings; but we know less of them as persons. These long inscriptions are, of course, valuable to the student, enabling him to expand his list of festivals and giving evidence of the growth in the number of fixtures from which athletes could make their choice. Sometimes they give us interesting technical details. One such inscription from Anazarbus in Asia Minor, listing the victories in the third century A.D. of Demetrius of Salamis, a pentathlete, tells us that in Naples he defeated eighty-seven competitors. This at once raises the question of how long it took to put eighty-seven men through the discus, javelin and jump. The same inscription reveals that at the joint Asian games, Demetrius dead-heated four times in the stade with another competitor, Optatus, and beat him only at the fifth attempt.[13]

Very occasionally some trait of character does peep through the cold enumerations of the stones. These athletes were as keen as their modern counterparts on 'records'. They were happily free from the tyranny of the stop-watch, and so could not break records in running, and, as we have seen, they were curiously careless about statistical achievement in the events which they could measure, the throws and the jump. Their records consisted in being the first to achieve some victory or combination of victories, just as today we remember the first man to beat six feet in the high jump or four minutes in the mile long after those feats have become commonplace. Most Greek athletes were content to announce when they were 'first of all men' to do something; but there is an inscription of the first century A.D. about a runner from Miletus, whose name is lost, which shows an amusing anxiety to establish some category of priority for all his successes:

'I won the diaulos at the 190th. Olympic Games; in the Pythian, the men's stade, diaulos and armed race on the same day; at Nemea I was first of all men to win stade, diaulos and armed race in succession in the same year; at the Eleutheria at Plataea I was the first of the men of Asia to win the stade and the armed race from the trophy and to be proclaimed "The best man of Greece"; at the Great Caesarea at Actium I was first of all men to win the men's stade, diaulos and armed race on the same day; at Nemea I again won the diaulos and armed race; at the Sebasta Romaea given by the Community of Asia I was first of the Ionians to win the armed race, at Isthmia the first Milesian to win the armed race, and at the Pythian games the first of the Ionians to win the stade and the armed race for the second time; at the games given by the crowned winners of the whole world I was the first of all men to win the stade, diaulos and armed race; at the Heraea of Argos I won the stade (the first Milesian to do this) and the armed race; at Nemea once again, I was the first of the Ionians to win the stade, diaulos and armed race; at the Halieia in Rhodes I won the stade and the armed race; at the Eleutheria in Plataea again I won the stade, diaulos and armed race, and I was the first and only man to win the armed race from the trophy for the second time* and to be proclaimed "The best man of Greece", and for this I was honoured by the Community of the Greeks with a gold crown of triumph; at Isthmia I won the armed race for the second time; at the Great Eleusinia given by the people of Athens I won the diaulos and armed race, and was honoured by the people of Athens with the grant of citizenship, a statue and a crown of leaves for my excellence.'[14]

The most elaborate of all these inscriptions is one from Rome, containing the exploits of a pankratiast who won an Olympic crown in A.D. 181. It includes a number of technical terms of athletics, not all of them yet explained with certainty, but it is of even greater interest for the character of the man, at which it hints at least as much by what it leaves unsaid as by what it states:

'I, Marcus Aurelius Asclepiades, also called Hermodorus, was the son of Marcus Aurelius Demetrius, high priest of the world-wide Xystus of athletes, xystarch for life, keeper of the Imperial Baths, citizen of Alexandria and Hermopolis, periodonikes in the pankra-tion and wrestler extraordinary. I was senior temple guardian of the great Serapis, high priest of the world-wide Xystus of athletes, xystarch for life, keeper of the Imperial Baths, citizen of Alexandria, Hermopolis, Puteoli and Naples, senator of Elis and Athens, and citizen and senator of many other cities. I was a periodonikes, un-defeated in the pankration. I was never dismissed from the ring in a "no contest" and never disqualified, but won every event for which I entered. I never appealed for a foul, nor did anyone ever dare to appeal against me for a foul. I never drew a fight nor made a protest nor scratched nor withdrew, nor did I ever undertake a contest to win royal favour. I never won after a fresh fight had been ordered, but was always crowned in the ring in every event for which I

---

* This shows that the rule mentioned above (p. 75), which laid it down that this event must not be won twice by the same man had by this time become a dead letter.

entered, and I was always approved in the preliminary investigations before these events. I competed in three countries, Italy, Greece and Asia, and won victories in the following games, all in the pankration: the 240th celebration of the Olympic Games in Pisa; the Pythian in Delphi; at Isthmia twice; at Nemea twice, on the second occasion causing my opponents to withdraw; at the Shield of Hera in Argos; at the Capitolia in Rome twice, on the second occasion causing my opponents to withdraw after the first round; at the Eusebeia in Puteoli twice, on the second occasion causing my opponents to withdraw after the second round; at the Sebasta in Naples twice, on the second occasion causing my opponents to withdraw after the second round; at the Actia in Nicopolis twice, on the second occasion causing my opponents to withdraw; in Athens five times, at the Panathenaea, the Olympia, the Panhellenia and twice at the Hadriana; in Smyrna five times, twice at the Joint Asian, on the second occasion causing my opponents to withdraw, and—also in Smyrna—at the Olympia and twice at the Hadriana Olympia; in Pergamum at the Augustea three times, on the second occasion causing my opponents to withdraw before the start, and on the third causing them to withdraw after the first round; in Ephesus three times, at the Hadriana, the Olympia and the Barbillea, causing my opponents to withdraw after the first round; in Epidaurus at the Asclepeia; in Rhodes at the Haleia; in Sardis at the Chrysanthina; and at even more festivals with money prizes, among them the Eurycleia in Sparta, the Mantinia and others. After competing for six years in all, I retired from athletics at the age of twenty-five, because of the risks and the jealousies which I encountered. A long time after my retirement, I yielded to compulsion and won the pankration at the sixth Olympiad of the Olympic games in my native Alexandria.'

Surely the athlete doth protest too much. There would have been no need for all these asseverations of blameless innocence if there had not been something to conceal. We cannot help suspecting that after these six years without an appeal against him for a foul, such an appeal was made and upheld, and that he was suspended or else retired through pique; the word 'jealousies' is significant. Of all this Asclepiades naturally makes no mention. What may have been the nature of the compulsion which caused his return to the ring we cannot say. But he must have been almost forty years of age when he

1A Discus thrower. Panathenaic amphora

(By courtesy of the
Museo Nazionale, Naples)

1B Rugby football. A. Lhote.
1917

(By courtesy of the Conservateur
des Musées Nationaux, Paris)

2 Cretan bo[x]
Minoan va[se]
from Hag[ia]
Triada

(*By courtesy* [of the]
Ashmolean Mu[seum,]
Oxford)

3 Runners. Panathenaic
amphora
(By courtesy of the
British Museum)

4A Runners
(*By courtesy of the Wagnermuseum, Würzburg*)

4B Umpire at the turning post.
From the same vase

5A Runner awaiting the start. Small bronze

(By courtesy of the Metropolitan Museum of Art, Rogers Fund, 1908)

5B Runner practising start under instruction

(By courtesy of the Ashmolean Museum, Oxford)

6 Jumper landing (*By courtesy of the British Museum*)

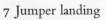

7 Jumper landing

(*By courtesy of the Metropolitan Museum of Art, Rogers Fund, 1908*)

8 Jumper in mid-air (*By courtesy of the Museum of Fine Arts, Boston*)

I INCH

9A Ingot of bronze from North Wales
(*By courtesy of the National Museum of Wales, Cardiff*)

9B Discus thrower. Fragment of a vase
(*By courtesy of the Wagnermuseum, Würzburg*)

10 Discus thrower. Small bronze copy of Myron's statue
(*By courtesy of the Staatlichen Antikensammlungen, Munich*)

11A Discus thrower putting in a peg to mark his throw
(*By courtesy of the Wagnermuseum, Würzburg*)

11B Discus thrower and javelin thrower
(*By courtesy of the Staatlichen Antikensammlungen, Munich*

12A Javelin thrower (*By courtesy of the Staatliche Museen, Berlin 2*)

12B Discus thrower and javelin thrower (*By courtesy of the Staatliche Museen, Berlin 1*)

12C Javelin thrower tightening thong under his foot
(*By courtesy of the Wagnermuseum, Würzburg*)

13A Wrestlers. Athlete with pickaxe. Boxer with 'himas'
(By courtesy of the Ashmolean Museum, Oxford)

13B Two pairs of wrestlers
(By courtesy of the Staatliche Museen, Berlin 1)

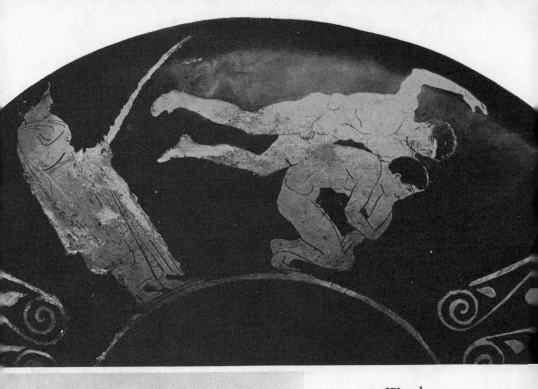

14A Wrestlers
(*By courtesy of the British Museum*)

14B Wrestlers. Small bronze
(*By courtesy of the
Staatlichen Antikensammlungen, Munich*)

15 Boxers
(By courtesy of the Staatliche
Antikensammlungen, Munich)

16 Boxers
(By courtesy of the British Museum)

17 Pankratiast biting his opponent. Panathenaic amphora
(*By courtesy of the British Museum*)

18 Pankratiasts

(By courtesy of the
Metropolitan Museum
of Art, Rogers
Fund, 1916)

19A Boxers
*(By courtesy of the
Staatliche Museen, Berlin 1)*

19B Boxers or
pankratiasts
*(By courtesy of the
Staatliche Museen, Berlin 2)*

19C Boxers
*(By courtesy of the
British Museum)*

20 Pankratiasts gouging. Boxers
(By courtesy of the British Museum)

21 Pankratiasts rolling on the ground

(By courtesy of the Metropolitan
Museum of Art, Rogers Fund, 1905)

22A Oil-flask in the shape of a kneeling boy athlete binding his head with a ribbon

(By courtesy of the American School of Classical Studies, Athens)

22B Bronze cauldron given as a prize

(By courtesy of the British Museum)

22C Base of victor statue with reliefs of trophies

(By courtesy of the Metropolitan Museum of Art, Rogers Fund, 1959)

23A Olympia. The stadium

23B Olympia. Foundation of the east wall of early stadium

23C Olympia. Foundation of grandstand

24A Delphi. Stadium from the east

24B Delphi. Starting grooves at east end of stadium

25A Perga. Stadium. Interior

25B Perga. Stadium. Exterior of spectators' banking

26A Isthmia. Starting line with post sockets, cord grooves and starter's pit of 'husplex'

26B Isthmia. Starter's pit and grooves for cords of 'husplex'

27A Ephesus. Statue bases of façade of stadium

27B Ephesus. Vault under spectators' banking in stadium

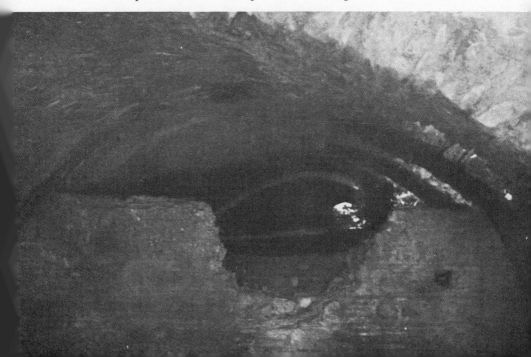

28A Olympia. Starting grooves at east end of stadium

28B Corinth. Starting holes for runners

29A Delphi. Groove and socket
for practice starting gate

29B Olympia. Foundation
of covered practice track
in gymnasium

30A Epidaurus. Stadium

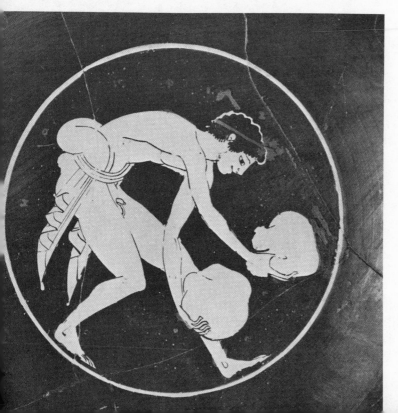

30B Athlete clearing
stadium

(By courtesy of the
Wagnermuseum, Würzbu

31A Delphi. Circular bath and washing facilities near gymnasium

31B Olympia. Small baths for athletes near gymnasium

32 Two sides of the same vase.
Victor with wreath and palm

(*By courtesy of the
Wagnermuseum, Würzburg*)

won this last victory, and it is perhaps not the least of his achievements that he so completely rebutted the old adage: 'They never come back'.[15]

No sport or game is fully represented by its star performers alone. Almost equally important, but too often forgotten, are the great mass of very ordinary players, who take part in games for enjoyment, seeking satisfaction in competing with those of their own class, and without any ambition for higher flights. Then, too, there are the spectators, the best of them old players, who understand the finer points of the game and enjoy watching because of the memories of their active past which the young performers of the present arouse. The athletics of the Greek world, no less than the games of today, had this submerged mass of ordinary participants, spectators and enthusiastic supporters, little regarded, like their present-day counterparts, either in ancient literature or by modern writers on the subject. As Greek civilization was extended after the time of Alexander the Great, so this body of enthusiasts expanded and came to include many who were not Greek by race. Among them, it is interesting to note, we must number St. Paul.

The evidence for the belief that in his boyhood the great apostle was a lover of athletics is, of course, to be found in the way in which the language of athletics constantly springs to his pen, and in that habit of his mind by which time and time again the Christian life is visualized as an athletic contest. The effects of this are deeply marked in Christian thought and language. The soul must be trained as the athlete trains—the word 'ascetic' is the Greek for an athlete in full training—and the reward for the Christian life is the prize, the crown or the palm, the reward of the victorious athlete in the games. Most modern readers probably fail to realize the force of this last metaphor. For us the word 'crown' is associated chiefly with royalty; the Greek word had no such connotations.* Apart from his use of the word to denote the supreme reward of the Christian, Paul twice, in Philippians and Thessalonians, calls a body of converts his crown, the reward of his efforts.[16]

His most elaborate exposition of the Christian life in athletic terms comes in the first Epistle to the Corinthians:

* The New English Bible, by translating the single Greek word promiscuously as 'crown', 'wreath' or 'garland', conceals from the reader the frequency of Paul's use of the metaphor.

I

'You know (do you not?) that at the sports all the runners run the race, though only one wins the prize. Like them, run to win! But every athlete goes into strict training. They do it to win a fading wreath; we, a wreath that never fades. For my part, I run with a clear goal before me; I am like a boxer who does not beat the air; I bruise my own body and make it know its master, for fear that after preaching to others I should find myself rejected.'

(New English Bible)

The metaphor in the Greek is carried further than this translation reveals. The last sentence plays on the idea of the herald who proclaimed the victors at the games; it means, 'lest after announcing victory for others I should myself be among those who win no prize'. A similar literary use of the athletic parallel is found in Philippians:

'All I can say is this; forgetting what is behind me, and reaching out for that which lies ahead, I press towards the goal to win the prize which is God's call to the life above.'

(New English Bible)

In writing to the young Gentile Timothy, who was probably as keen a lover of athletics as he had been himself, he naturally appeals to his experience of the games;

'No athlete can win a prize unless he has kept the rules.'

And:

'Keep yourself in training for the practice of religion. The training of the body does bring limited benefit, but the benefits of religion are without limit, since it holds promise not only for this life but for the life to come.'

(New English Bible)

This last passage is significant. The conventional Greek moralists, Xenophanes, Euripides and Diogenes for instance, were apt to deny any merit to athletic training; St. Paul is far too honest and too clear-sighted for that.[17]

It might fairly be said that such references to athletics are not rare in the literature of the first century A.D. Epictetus has quite as many as the Christian writer, and Epictetus, born a slave, was certainly no practising athlete. But anyone who knows a game well can always detect, when an author refers to the game, whether the allusion is based on personal experience or not. It does not need a very perceptive reader of *Pickwick Papers* and of *Tom Brown's Schooldays* to decide that Hughes knew cricket from the inside while Dickens did not; the slips by which an author gives himself away when he ventures into the dangerous country of an unfamiliar sport are generally more subtle than that. Judged by this purely subjective test, St. Paul knew his athletics, while Epictetus did not. In Epictetus the allusions are a literary device to embellish his writing; in Paul they are part of his thought. Even if we assumed that many of his images were no more than attempts to captivate his readers by appeals to what he believed interested them, it is impossible to conceive that at the end of his life, when he was proudly summing up his dedication to his great cause, he would have stooped to a mere literary trick. The mould in which a man casts his thoughts at such a moment is surely significant:

'I have fought a good fight, I have finished my course, I have kept the faith; henceforth there is laid up for me a crown of righteousness.'
(Authorized Version)

The opening phrase of this passage presents the translator with an impossible task. 'I have fought a good fight', if it suggests an athletic metaphor at all, limits the image to boxing and wrestling. The New English Bible's 'I have run the great race' similarly restricts the picture to running. The expression could have been used by any athlete, runner, jumper, thrower or heavyweight. It means 'I have finished playing my part in the great Games'; but the English language does not provide a phrase which will combine complete accuracy with the dignity which so moving a pronouncement demands. The words 'I have kept the faith' continue the metaphor; they refer to the promise, given by an athlete before competing, to keep the rules and do his best.[18]

Even more significant than these extended metaphors are the occurrences of single words and phrases of athletes' slang in St. Paul's writing. The Greek verb in 'I am like a boxer who does not *beat the air*' means literally 'flay the hide off'; it had been boxers' slang for 'give a hiding to' for several centuries before Paul used it. Far more

expressive is the word translated 'I *bruise* my own body' in the New
English Bible. The Authorized Version renders it by the sober
metaphor 'I *keep under* my body'. The Greek word is a splendidly
vigorous metaphor from athletic jargon, meaning literally 'I *give a
black eye to* my body'; the modern equivalent would be 'I take the
mickey out of my body'. The Authorized Version does at least make
it clear that the word is a metaphor. The New English Bible's
rendering 'bruise', which suggests that Paul was a paranoiac maso-
chist, has nothing to recommend it. Paul appears to have been the
first Greek author to use the word in the metaphorical sense. It is
interesting to note that St. Luke once uses it metaphorically in his
Gospel; he may well have picked it up from his friend.[19]

Another athletic colloquialism which Paul uses twice, in Galatians
and Philippians, is the phrase for useless endeavour, 'to run in vain'
or, as we should say, 'to be an also ran'. A passage in Ephesians is a
good illustration of how much is lost if we fail to follow the apostle
in his athletic metaphors. In the Authorized Version it runs:

'We wrestle not against flesh and blood, but against principalities,
against powers, against the rulers of the darkness of this world,
against spiritual wickedness in high places.'

St. Paul is describing the fight against the powers of evil. A man
cannot go into that struggle like a naked wrestler against a naked
opponent. The powers of darkness are armed at all points; the Christian must therefore put on the whole armour of God. The New
English Bible rendering, 'Our fight is not against human foes', by
missing the metaphor of wrestling, loses all the picturesque vigour of
the original.[20]

Another vivid piece of athletic jargon occurs when Paul is warning
the Gentile Colossians not to allow anyone to turn them out of
the Church if they refuse to accept irrelevant parts of the Jewish
law:

'You are not to be disqualified by the decision of people who go in
for self-mortification and angel-worship.'

(New English Bible)

The rare Greek verb is formed from the noun 'Brabeus', an umpire in the games, and means 'to give an unjust decision in one's capacity as Brabeus'. Any cricketer who has ever believed himself to have been 'umpired out' will know exactly what was in Paul's mind. He had probably picked up the term in boyhood, as boys do, and in his moment of indignation many years later it sprang unbidden to his pen.[21]

It might be thought that there is a difficulty about believing that St. Paul was ever an athlete. He came from a devout Jewish family of the Dispersion, and the Jewish tradition was against the nakedness which was inseparable from athletics as practised by the Greeks and their imitators. Nevertheless, apart from the evidence of the discus throwing among the priests in Jerusalem at the time of the Maccabees, there is some reason for doubting whether this feeling persisted among Jews living in strongly Hellenized communities. A letter from the emperor Claudius to the people of Alexandria in Egypt, written when Paul was a young man, contains an injunction to the Jews of that city, bidding them refrain from trying to enter for the athletic games there; this would have been unnecessary if they had not been attempting to do so. In the Jewish catacombs at Rome there is a picture of Victory crowning a naked youth who holds a palm branch in his left hand. The most recent Jewish authorities on the subject declare that this is authentic Jewish work of the late first or early second century A.D. Thus it appears that nakedness would not have been an insuperable objection.[22]

It was perfectly easy for Paul to have plenty of experience of athletics in his early life. Tarsus had a stadium, and we know of at least four important athletic festivals regularly held there in Roman imperial times. It had also a young men's gymnasium on the banks of the river Cydnus.* It is unlikely that he was able to take an active part in athletics after his schooldays; while still young he went to Jerusalem to study theology. But many a man who has had no opportunity to play a game since his schooldays nevertheless preserves a passion for it all the rest of his life. Paul's enthusiasm for athletics left its mark on him in more ways than one. We have only to think of his proud boast to the Corinthians:

* Strabo, to whom we owe this information, mentions a scandal in the athletic life of Tarsus some years before St. Paul's birth. A man named Boethus, appointed acting Gymnasiarch by Mark Antony and put in control of expenditure, was detected embezzling, among other things, the olive oil.

'Five times the Jews have given me the thirty-nine strokes; three times I have been beaten with rods; once I was stoned; three times I have been shipwrecked, and for twenty-four hours I was adrift on the open sea. I have been constantly on the road; I have met dangers from rivers, dangers from robbers, dangers from my fellow-countrymen, dangers from foreigners, dangers in towns, dangers in the country, dangers at sea, dangers from false friends. I have toiled and drudged, I have often gone without sleep; hungry and thirsty, I have often gone fasting; and I have suffered from cold and exposure.'

(New English Bible)

The man who could write that was tough by any standards.[23]

Whether or not he ever indulged his enthusiasm by watching athletic sports in later life it is impossible to say. His journeys through Asia Minor and Greece must have given him many opportunities to do so, and he would have been unfortunate if his eighteen months' stay in Corinth did not cover a celebration of the biennial Isthmian festival. When most of the male inhabitants of the city made the short journey to see the games, he must have been under a strong temptation to join them, for the four senior 'crown' festivals of mainland Greece, of which the Isthmian was one, still had a considerable prestige among followers of athletics all over the Greek world.* Certainly he did not live to share the delight of his fellow citizens when in A.D. 85 for the first and so far as we know the only time an Olympic victory fell to a man from Tarsus, Apollophanes, winner of the stade.[24]

It is not difficult to deduce what his favourite event must have been. According to a very ancient Christian tradition he was a small man. He is always represented thus in early Byzantine art; and when in Lystra he and his companion were mistaken for Greek gods, it was Barnabas who was thought to be the mighty Zeus, while Paul was taken to be the less impressive Hermes. So while Paul no doubt boxed and wrestled for fun with boys of his own size—he shows some knowledge of these sports, as we have seen—he would know that success in competition would be beyond his powers, and like all boys would turn his attention to a more suitable field, in his case,

* If Paul did go to Isthmia he was following the example of another great man. The only occasion on which Socrates ever left Athens except on military service was when he went to see the Isthmian games.

running. Among the running events all the evidence points in one direction. Although it is not beyond the power of men not above average size to reach the very highest levels at the shorter distances, as W. R. Applegarth showed in this century, yet most sprinters are big men. It is over the long distances that the small man, with less weight to carry, comes into his own, and it is a reasonable assumption that it was here that Paul's heart lay. In such a race even to finish the course is something of which the runner may be justly proud, and it is noteworthy that St. Paul twice touches on this theme:

'For myself, I set no store by life; I only want to finish the race and complete the task which the Lord Jesus assigned to me.'

And again in the great summing up of his life:

'I have run the great race, I have finished the course, I have kept faith.'

(New English Bible)

Paul knew that in the greater game of which he was thinking it is not only the man who passes the post first for whom a crown of glory is laid up.[25]

None of this, of course, is capable of being proved with certainty, but there can be no harm in believing that Paul's passionate longing to convert the Gentiles to Christianity may have owed something to boyhood memories of happy days spent in running and wrestling with young pagans in the sunny sports grounds of Tarsus.

VI THE BUILDINGS FOR GREEK ATHLETICS

THE buildings needed for Greek athletics were the stadium, the practice track, the palaestra or wrestling school and the bath-house. The stadium was used for competition proper, the practice track by athletes training for running, jumping, throwing or boxing, and the palaestra by wrestlers and pankratiasts. The bath-house was a necessary appendage, for a bath was a regular part of the training routine. For obvious reasons the last three buildings were often grouped together. The word 'gymnasium', which literally means no more than a place where men exercise naked, was used especially of the practice track; sometimes it covered the complex of track, palaestra and bath, sometimes it is used of a palaestra, and very occasionally of a stadium.

The fundamental requirement of a stadium for Greek athletics is a flat area rather more than 200 yards long and wide enough to accommodate several runners and allow them space to turn round the posts in the longer races. In early times this was found in the agora of the city or near the temple of the god in whose honour the games were held. The starting sills at Corinth and Isthmia are evidence of this. The disadvantages of this situation must soon have become apparent. The erection of new buildings interfered with the straight course; it is significant that both at Isthmia and at Corinth there are two sills at an angle to each other, showing that the axis of the stadium must have been changed to meet new circumstances. Another drawback of holding an athletics meeting in a market place is the difficulty of the accommodation and control of spectators. It was, of course, possible to erect temporary wooden stands; Suetonius tells us that when the emperor Augustus was introducing Greek athletics into Rome he had stands of this kind put up in the Campus Martius. But the erection of such stands is laborious and costly; a permanent stadium with provision for spectators is far preferable. The easiest way to secure this is to level the bottom of a small valley, the sides and upper end of which then serve as banking for the on-lookers. When this is done, the end of the stadium at the top of the valley is semicircular and the bottom end is open; if it is to be enclosed the obvious method is by a straight wall. This gives the conventional shape of the Greek stadium (Fig. III, Plates 24a, 25a). Stadia were constructed in this way at Athens, where a short valley running down to the Ilissus afforded a suitable site, at Sicyon, where the valley was so short and the ground fell away so quickly that the square end of the stadium had to be supported by a wall, at Rhodes, at Nemea and in many other places; the later stadium at Isthmia is also of this pattern.[1]

If a suitable valley was not to be found, a second method of making a stadium was to level a terrace on a hillside or to use a flat strip running along the bottom of a slope. This was done at Olympia, Delphi, Delos and Ephesus. Under these circumstances the lower edge of the terrace sometimes had to be supported by a wall, as at Delphi and Delos, especially if banking for spectators was to be placed along that side. Often, too, the ends of such terrace stadia are both square. But there was no hard and fast rule about this. At Delphi, a terrace stadium, a convenient shoulder on the hillside made the construction of a rounded end easy (Plate 24a). At Epidaurus, on the other hand, where a valley was flattened, the top end was squared (Plate 30a). When stadia came to be built in the wealthy Hellenistic cities of Asia Minor the conventional pattern of one round and one square end was generally followed, whatever the lie of the land, as at Aspendos and Perga. Aphrodisias and Laodicea appear to have been alone in providing more accommodation for spectators by having both ends round, as in a Roman circus. At Ephesus the terrace stadium, which must have existed for centuries before, was elaborately reconstructed in the time of Nero; whatever its earlier shape may have been, it now has a round end supported by a fine piece of walling.

When we look at a stadium of the conventional shape it is tempting to think of the square end as the one appropriate to the finishing line and the curved end as fitted to the turn of the runners in the diaulos. This is, in fact, the reverse of what actually happened. All races, of whatever length, finished at the round end. This is obvious from the stadia at Delphi and Sicyon. At Delphi runners in a close finish at the square end would have dashed out their brains on the massive pillars of the great ornamental arch, which are only a few feet behind the starting sill at that end (Plate 24b), while at Sicyon they would have plunged over a vertical drop of several feet. Moreover, the additional seating at the curved end was available for spectators at the point where most spectators at a sports meeting wish to be—near the winning post. For the same reason we may deduce that the discus and javelin were thrown from the rounded end. Most spectators like to be nearer the thrower in order to study his technique, and in view of the fate of Hyacinthus it is always advisable to have the crowd massed behind the thrower.

Either of the two methods of construction provided good accommodation. In the valley stadium there were the two sides and the head of the valley. In the terrace type the hillside often afforded almost unlimited space. It could be increased if necessary by artificial banking along the downhill side of the stadium. Where this was held in place by a wall, as at Delphi and Delos, the weight to be supported was enormous. Some idea of the amount of soil shifted in these operations is afforded by an inscription from Athens of 330 B.C., recording a vote of thanks to Eudemus of Plataea for giving a thousand waggons for use in making 'the Panathenaic stadium and spectators' accommodation'. Pliny reports in a letter to Trajan that at Nicaea in Bithynia a wall twenty-two feet thick was collapsing under its burden. The problem was sometimes solved by leaning another construction against the back of the bank. Pausanias tells us that at Aegina the stadium and theatre supported each other in this way. At Olympia the difficulty was not so great, because the stadium was not a terrace on the hillside but a strip at the foot of it, but here too the banking on the south side served a double purpose. It divided the stadium from the hippodrome, and spectators stood on its north slope to watch the athletes and on its south slope to see the chariots. Such a bank is constantly subsiding and losing height. This probably explains an inscription from Eleusis of about 288 B.C., directing that the soil from the excavations for a new stoa was to be dumped 'in the spectators' part of the stadium'. The order is not as feckless as it

appears at first sight; the intention no doubt was to raise the bank of
the Eleusinian stadium and so improve the onlookers' view.[2]

Arrangements for seating the spectators varied from place to place.
The smaller stadia probably provided wooden seats. The elaborate
stone seats still to be seen at Delphi, Rhodes, Perga and elsewhere
belong to the wealthier times of the Greek world; none of them is
earlier than the fourth century B.C. At Athens the stadium was reconstructed by Lycurgus just before 300 B.C., restored by Heraclitus in 277 B.C., probably after damage sustained in the Gallic
invasion of 279, and finally completely rebuilt by Herodes Atticus in
the second century A.D., an operation which according to Philostratus
took four years. It was this Herodes who put in the stone seating at
Delphi which still survives. He would no doubt have been glad to do
the same at Olympia, but the authorities there would have none of it.
Instead, they allowed him to improve the water supply by installing
the fountain in the form of an exedra, whose remains can still be
seen.[3]

On the island of Delos a small stone grandstand was erected in the
middle of one of the long sides of the stadium. The festivals at Delos
were important, yet these few stone seats bear a pathetic resemblance
to the tiny grandstands sometimes seen on village football grounds.
The stone seating at Epidaurus, unless stone-robbing has changed the
scene completely, was concentrated at the finishing end of the
stadium (Plate 30a). We have always to remember the attraction of
dressed stone for the people who have lived since the time of the
ancient world. Pausanias tells us that in his day the stadium at
Isthmia was equipped with seats of white marble; they have all
completely disappeared. Gone, too, from all the stadia are the many
statues of gods, goddesses and victorious athletes which once
embellished them.[4]

Olympia demands special attention. It is now known that the site
of the stadium there was twice changed. According to a scholiast on
Pindar, the western turning-point for the races was originally the
tomb of Pelops, which was situated in the Altis or sacred enclosure
between the temples of Hera and Zeus (Fig. V). The recent excavations discovered traces of this archaic stadium, which was used until
the fifth century B.C. Then it was moved eastward; the excavators
were able to lay down the position of this second stadium more
accurately, as they uncovered the foundations of its eastern boundary

wall (Fig. V, Plate 23*b*). The wall was slightly curved. Its foundations furnish evidence that there was no very extensive provision for spectators at this period, for a wall on so slight a base could not possibly support heavy banking. In the fourth century B.C. the stadium was moved still further east to the position which it now occupies and assumed the appearance which the excavations have revealed (Plate 23*a*). This eastward shift had two results. It allowed the east side of the Altis to be defined and enclosed by the Echo Stoa, and it permitted the construction of a bank at the west end of the stadium abutting on the stoa and giving increased

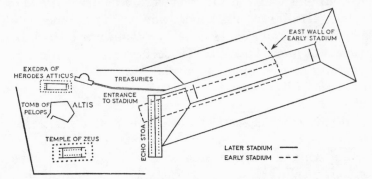

Fig. V. Olympia. Plan showing relation of existing and early stadia.

accommodation for spectators. To allow access for athletes and officials to the stadium from the Altis, a vaulted tunnel was driven through this bank; a single arch of the vault still remains (Frontispiece). A similar tunnel under the banking can be seen at Epidaurus. The arrangement was like that on many modern football grounds, where the players enter the arena through a tunnel under the stands.[5]

No provision for seating the spectators was ever made at Olympia. On the south side of the stadium there was a small stand of wooden seats on stone supports for the officials—the Hellanodikai—and very important visitors; the stone supports were discovered in the recent excavations (Plate 23*c*). Other spectators stood or sat on the ground. There can be no doubt that, had the authorities wished, many wealthy benefactors would have been glad enough to equip Olympia as lavishly as any stadium in the world. The prestige achieved by such munificence would have been enormous. But permission was never given. There is something splendid about the calm confidence which the 'Take-it-or-leave-it' attitude of the Hellanodikai in this matter implies. Olympia could always command its crowds. If anyone did not like the lack of comfort, he could stay away. Discomfort there certainly was in plenty. Epictetus gives us a vivid picture of it:

'True, there are hardships and difficulties in life. Are they not to be found even at Olympia? Don't you get baked by the sun there? Don't you get crushed by the crowds? Don't you find it impossible to get a bath? Don't you get soaked whenever it rains? Don't you have an overdose of noise, of shouting and of exasperation? Yet you steel your heart and put up with it all, because you think that the spectacle makes it worth while.'

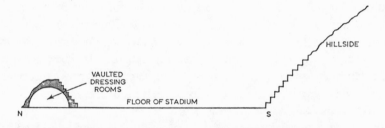

Fig. VI. Ephesus. Section through stadium. (Not to scale.)

Aelian tells us of a Chian, furious with a slave, threatening to send him not to the treadmill but to Olympia as a spectator. So in the blazing August days of the festival the spectators stood or sat on the dried-up grass on the sloping banks, and the stadium was embellished only by its statues.[6]

In strong contrast to this austere simplicity was the ingenious construction of the banking for spectators in the stadia of the Hellenistic and Roman periods, especially in Asia Minor. At Ephesus, for instance, the seats on the north side of the stadium opposite the hillside were set not on a solid bank of earth but on a long vault, divided by cross-walls into dressing-rooms and storage space (Fig. VI, Plates 27a and b). At Perga in Pamphylia a similar arrangement afforded a series of vaulted chambers opening outside the stadium, which could be used for shops or shelters (Plate 25b).

For its innumerable historical associations Olympia is supreme, but for sheer beauty the Pythian stadium at Delphi is the queen of them all (Plate 24*a*). In situation it is unparalleled, 2000 feet up on the cliffs of Parnassus, with a superb view to the south across the Gulf of Corinth to the mountains of Arcadia. Its remarkable state of preservation enables us to study its refinements of detail; the slight bulge in the middle to prevent a spectator's view from being obstructed by his neighbours; the seats of the officials in the centre of the north side; the charming recess for the fountain among the seats near the curved end, where spectators baked by the hot sun could seek refreshment. The only discordant note is the remains of the arch at the east end, a characteristic product of the vulgarity of Roman times (Plate 24*b*). But if we turn our backs on that and look west and south the radiance of Apollo and the Muses seems to haunt the place still.

It is not surprising that stadia, with their extensive space and facilities for seating large numbers, were used for other purposes at times when they were not required for athletics. Plutarch relates how Dion, the friend of Plato, after assembling Achaean mercenaries for his attempt to oust Dionysius the younger from Syracuse, gave a great banquet for them in the stadium of Zacynthus, an island near Ithaca; the occasion was marked by an eclipse of the moon, which the troops thought to be an ill omen.[7]

In Roman imperial times gladiatorial exhibitions and wild beast shows were occasionally given in the Greek half of the empire. As there were few amphitheatres specially constructed for the purpose in this part of the world, stadia and theatres were used. In the theatre at Taormina the lower seats were cut away so that the spectators should be in no danger from the animals; part of the great stone barrier which fulfilled the same function in the theatre of Thasos can still be seen. An inscription of the first century A.D. records that a gladiatorial show was given in the stadium in Ephesus, and if St. Paul did literally 'fight with beasts at Ephesus' it was in the stadium that it happened. As it is unlikely that a Roman citizen would have been condemned to do this, or, if Paul had been, that he would have escaped alive, it is probable that his words were metaphorical and referred to the riot of the silversmiths described in Acts. There are, however, remains of a cross-wall in the stadium, which may have served to cut off the curved end for some such purpose after the stadium had ceased to be used for athletics.

The famous inscription on the outside wall of the stadium at

Delphi near the entrance suggests that the stadium was used for religious ceremonies in addition to those connected with the Pythian games. It reads:

'The wine is not to be taken out of the stadium. If anyone does take it out, he must propitiate the god, whoever he may be, for whom it was mixed, and must offer sacrifice and pay a fine of five drachmas; half of this is to go to the informer.'

This law, dated by the epigraphists to the fifth century B.C., cannot refer to wine-offerings in connection with the Pythian games, which were in honour of Apollo. The indefinite 'The god, whoever he may be', would be highly inappropriate for those ceremonies. We must therefore assume other rituals, at which the congregation's share of the wine offered to the god had to be drunk on the spot, just as the part of sacrificial meat distributed among the people often had to be eaten at the place of sacrifice and not carried away.[8]

Today many of these stadia lie overgrown and hardly recognizable as what they are. This had begun to happen even in antiquity. As early as the second century A.D. many parts of the Greek mainland had fallen into poverty as wealth moved away from it to the east. Dio Chrysostom speaks of a stadium in Euboea in which crops were being grown in his day, and where the corn was so high that it almost hid the statues.[9]

An interesting later use was found for a stadium in Rhodes, where the Knights of St. John of Jerusalem settled at the beginning of the fourteenth century, after their expulsion from Cyprus. They held their jousting tournaments in the stadium, and for this purpose fitted down the middle a stone socket to hold the low wooden barrier which separated the horses of the combatants; parts of the socket can still be seen.

The Panathenaic stadium at Athens survived in a fair state of preservation until the end of the nineteenth century, when it was refashioned to make it suitable for the first modern Olympic games of 1896. The old Greek running area was made dead ground, and the seats were set back to allow a track to be laid round it; new seating in white marble, provided by a wealthy Greek expatriate from Alexandria, replaced that of Herodes Atticus. The stadium is still admirable for field events and for races up to 200 metres in length, but for any distance beyond that the bends are far too tight for modern runners, and whatever use may be found for the stadium in the future it is not likely that it will ever again witness international athletics.

When we come to the practice tracks we cannot help asking why, with the stadia available for training, there should have been so many of them. In some places the necessity is obvious. At Delphi the stadium is high above the city, and the water supply there is inadequate for baths. The advantage of the gymnasium lower down, where the water of the Castalian spring was available for baths, is evident. In a big city such as Athens there was clearly a place for training grounds in those districts remote from the stadium. But at Olympia the practice track is only 200 yards from the stadium, and in Athens one of the gymnasia, the Lyceum, was in the same quarter of the city as the stadium. The answer to the question is probably to be found in one word—shade. A stadium is completely exposed to the full glare of the sun.* Greeks were willing to endure this heat at the festivals, whether as competitors or spectators, but they were human enough to value cool shade in the intervals of training. We have to remember that when a Greek youth went to the gymnasium it was not merely for a grim training session; he was going to his club for social enjoyment as well, and much of his time there was spent in chatting with his friends. In a country as hot as Greece the inhabitants seek shade whenever possible; sun-bathing is a fashion of those who live in grey northern climes. It is small wonder then that when a gymnasium is mentioned in Greek literature there is often some reference to trees or shade. One of the most famous of these gymnasia was in the Academia at Athens. Originally this was part of the private estate of Cimon the son of Miltiades, a well-watered and well-wooded area, attractively laid out with shady walks. He presented it to the citizens of Athens for their enjoyment, and they used part of it as a training ground, just as today sports facilities are often provided in public parks. Aristophanes in the *Clouds* gives us a pleasant picture of boys enjoying themselves there:

'But then you'll excel in the games you love well, all blooming,
    athletic and fair;

* Diogenes Laertius reminds us that the great sage Thales died of sunstroke while watching games in a stadium.

Not learning to prate as your idlers debate with marvellous prickly
dispute,
Nor dragged into court day by day to make sport in some small
disagreeable suit;
But you will below to the Academe go, and under the olives contend
With your chaplet of reed in a contest of speed with some excellent
rival and friend;
All fragrant with woodbine and peaceful content, and the leaf which
the lime blossoms fling,
When the plane whispers love to the elm in the grove in the
beautiful season of Spring.'

(Tr. Rogers)[10]

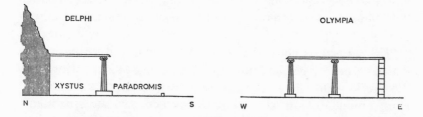

Fig. VII. Delphi and Olympia. Sections through training tracks.
(Not to scale.)

It was not only the trees which afforded shade in these gymnasia.
The practice tracks themselves were constructed with this end in
view. They were long porticos, with a wall on one side and a
colonnade on the other. It is sometimes said that the purpose of this
was to allow the athlete to train in wet weather; almost certainly
protection from the sun was an equally strong motive. At Delphi a
vertical face was cut in the cliff to take the place of the wall and the
portico was built against it. Here, as elsewhere, an open track ran
alongside the covered one. At Olympia there was a double portico;
both lengths of track appear to have been covered, allowing an
athlete to run a complete diaulos in the shade. The covered track was
called a xystus, a word later used also for the professional association
of athletes; the open track alongside was called the paradromis, and
the whole was often termed a dromos (Fig. VII, Plate 29b).

A palaestra or wrestling school was usually found near every
K

practice track. It was essentially an open court surrounded by dressing-rooms; generally there was a portico between the court and the
rooms on at least two sides, often all round, affording shade at all
times of the day to onlookers and resting athletes. The lay-out thus
resembled that of a medieval cloister. These palaestras were sometimes of considerable size; at Olympia the courtyard is 135 feet
square. In most cities there were several smaller wrestling schools,
often kept as private ventures by old athletes. We even hear of
special palaestras for old men.

In his work on architecture, written in the reign of Augustus,
Vitruvius gives full instructions for the lay-out of a palaestra and
gymnasium. No set of buildings has yet been discovered which
conforms with his plan in all its details, but the Academia or the
Lyceum at Athens or the gymnasia of some of the wealthy cities of
Asia Minor may well have been constructed to this pattern.

'The palaestra is not an Italian institution, but it has come to this
country from Greece, so I must give an account of it and show how
the Greeks plan it. In a palaestra a square or rectangular colonnaded
cloister must be constructed with a perimeter of two stades, a distance
which the Greeks call a diaulos. Three of the sides are single colonnades; the fourth, which faces south, should be double, so that when
gales occur, the rain is not blown into the inner part. In each of the
three single sides there should be a large recess with seats, on which
philosophers, littérateurs and other members of the intelligentsia
may sit and argue. In the double colonnade should be sited the
following rooms; in the middle an *ephebeum* or young men's section,
a very large recess with seats, its length one third greater than its
width; to its right the punch-ball room and next to that the powdering room; next to the powdering room, in the angle of the colonnade, a cold bath, which the Greeks call a *loutron*. To the left of the
ephebeum is the oil room and next to it the cool room of the baths;
leading from this a passage to the warm room in the angle of the
colonnade. Next to this and in line with the cold room there should
be a vaulted hot room; in one corner of this a sweating room of the
pattern already described (square or circular and domed), in the
opposite corner a warm plunge-bath. This should be the arrangement inside the palaestra.

'Outside there should be three colonnades, one of them straight in front as you leave the palaestra, the other two on each side of it, both fitted as running tracks. Of these two, the one which faces north should be double and very wide; the other should be single and made in such a way that the sides next to the wall and the columns have paths for walking not less than ten feet wide, while the middle is eighteen inches lower, with steps leading down from the side walks to this central track, which should be not less than twelve feet wide. In this way the clothes of those who are walking on the side paths will not be spoilt by the oily bodies of the athletes training on the central track. A colonnade of this kind is called by the Greeks a xystus, because athletes can exercise in winter on a covered track. Alongside the xystus and the double colonnade are laid out open-air tracks, which the Greeks call paradromides and the Romans xysta. In fine weather in winter the athletes can come out onto these for their training. They should be planned with copses and plantations of plane trees between the colonnades, and among the trees walks should be laid out with stone seats at intervals. Behind the xystus the stadium should be sited, constructed so that large crowds of spectators can watch the athletic meetings in comfort.'[11]

As this description by Vitruvius shows, facilities for bathing were normally part of these groups of buildings for athletes. We are sometimes called on to admire the hardy Greeks for taking cold baths in contrast to the effeminate Romans who preferred them hot. This theory will hardly bear examination. The Greeks took their ideals of manly conduct from Homer, who has justly been called the laureate of the hot bath. But the heating of large quantities of water for baths is neither easy nor cheap, and it was not until the Greek world became wealthy that they could indulge freely. All the evidence suggests, however, that in every period they took all the hot baths they could get. The notion that they despised them rests chiefly on a famous passage in the *Clouds*, where Aristophanes puts the defence of hot baths into the mouth of the Unjust Argument; but the defence, no matter who utters it, is unanswerable, and it is significant that the Just Argument makes no attempt to answer it. Plutarch even says that to take a cold bath after exercise is a piece of youthful ostentation.[12]

The best-known baths connected with gymnasia are those at Delphi and Olympia. At the former there was a row of basins into

which water flowed from lion-head spouts. The spouts have disappeared, but the holes through which the water came can still be
seen in the wall, together with one of the basins and the supports on
which the others rested. Near the basins is a fine circular plunge-bath,
with its steps for entering and leaving the water and the drainage hole
still to be seen (Plate 31a). At Olympia the recent German excavations have thrown much light on the bathing arrangements near the
gymnasium. The most interesting discovery has been of two sets of
small stone hip-baths, with an earthenware bowl for the athlete's feet
let into the bottom of each (Plate 31b). The first set, according to the
excavators, was constructed in the second half of the fifth century
B.C. About 400 B.C. provision for heating the water was added. A
century later a new room was built onto the bath-house to accommodate the second set of hip-baths. At the same time the first set
was cemented over, thus preserving them in the excellent condition
in which they were found; this was done probably in order to afford
cold baths under the same roof as hot. To the west of these baths was
a large rectangular plunge-bath, of which nothing is now visible;
part of it was swept away by a change in the course of the river
Cladeos and part lies under a later building. To the east are the
foundations of a building discovered in the nineteenth-century
excavations, consisting of two square rooms with a porch of four
columns in front of them. Inset in one of the rooms is a massive
circular foundation. The early German excavators, in default of anything better to call it, dubbed this building a 'Heroön' or shrine of a
demigod, and it continues to be so described in all but the most
recent guide-books and plans. The recent excavators, in view of its
proximity to the other baths, now interpret it as a 'sweat-bath'. At
both Delphi and Olympia there are remains of later baths from the
Roman period, providing the form of bathing in vogue at the time,
in which cold, warm and hot air were as important as the water.

The equipment of the smaller baths was not lavish. If an athlete
wanted a shower the attendant simply poured a bucket of water over
him. In the *Characters* of Theophrastus the Boorish Man, in order to
avoid tipping the bathman, performs the office for himself. Before
bathing the athlete scraped the oil, sweat and sand off himself with
his strigil. The elder Pliny gives us the curious piece of information
that in his day these scrapings were sold as ointment by 'Greeks
ready to make a profit out of anything'. Apollonius Rhodius and

Strabo reveal the scarcely less odd tradition that the pebbles on the island of Elba were the scrapings that fell from the strigils of the Argonauts when they visited the place in the heroic age.[13]

The gymnasium and palaestra played a very important part in the social life of the Greeks. Sometimes, as we learn from the moralists, a particular gymnasium would become the haunt of a vicious set of young men and acquire a bad name for a time, but for the most part they seem to have been for centuries a valuable institution. Their influence was by no means confined to the physical side of life; they had a contribution to make to literature and the arts. Like the stadia, they were adorned with statues of gods and famous athletes, and on their walls were pictures. These, as might be expected, were mostly of athletic scenes, but Pausanias mentions a portrait of the poetess Corinna in the gymnasium at Tanagra. At Olympia there were lists of past victors on the walls of the gymnasium. Schools often held open-air classes in gymnasia, and recitals of Homer and other poets were given in them. The members of a gymnasium would sometimes unite in a subscription for some object, the erection of a statue to a benefactor or the provision of oil or prizes at an athletic festival. At times, too, these athletic institutions had a political significance. Polycrates, the tyrant of Samos, shut down all in the island because they were liable to be centres of democratic opposition to him. When Thebes was freed from the Spartans by Epaminondas, the plot was hatched in a palaestra; and Aratus found his supporters for his revolt against Macedon in the gymnasia and palaestras of Argos.[14]

Many Greeks felt for their gymnasium the same loyalty and affection that some men today still feel for their school or university. In the *Phoenissae* of Euripides, Polyneices speaks of his longing for the familiar scenes of his native Thebes which has caused him to risk a perilous return from exile, and among the places which he mentions in this emotional outburst is 'the gymnasium in which I was brought up'. In life a Greek hated being cut off from his gymnasium; we have seen how two of Alexander's generals took their portable cover for a training track with them on the king's expedition; and Archimedes, when he designed a state galleon for Hiero of Syracuse, included a gymnasium on its upper deck. Even death did not end the loyalty completely. Inscriptions from Aphrodisias and elsewhere tell us that a man's ashes were sometimes buried in the gymnasium in which he had exercised in the days of his strength.[15]

Best of all, the gymnasia of Greece, and especially of Athens, will always be remembered for the good talk that went on in them. Socrates was a confirmed haunter of them; he knew that he would always find there someone to argue with. It was the gymnasium in the Academia which he and his admirers most favoured, and for that reason the school of Plato came to be known as the Academics, while Aristotle and his followers, who preferred the walks or peripatoi of the other big gymnasium, the Lyceum, were called the Peripatetics. There was another and older gymnasium in Athens called the Cynosarges; it was the haunt of the socially 'not quite', and for that reason, Plutarch tells us, it was patronized by Themistocles, always ostentatiously left-wing in his sympathies. Later it became the centre of the Cynics, and some said that they derived their name from it. This association of gymnasia with things of the mind as well as of the body has left its mark on language. It explains why places of higher education are called gymnasien in Teutonic countries, lycées in France and academies all over the world.[16]

VII THE MANAGEMENT OF A GREEK ATHLETIC MEETING

FOR the student of Greek athletics it is a salutary exercise to tear himself away sometimes from library and museum, to sit for a quiet hour in some ancient stadium and to ask himself how he would have run a meeting in the place 2000 years ago. If such a proceeding does nothing else it will at least bring home to him the number and extent of the gaps in our knowledge of the subject. The stadium need not be one of the most famous; indeed it is better not. We are apt to make the same mistake as the Greeks themselves and concentrate far too much attention on Olympia, forgetting the hundreds of other less spectacular but still very interesting festivals.

Greek athletic meetings, like the festivals of drama and music, were civic functions. Even where they were connected with religious celebrations this remained true, for temples and their attendant rites were normally felt to be the responsibility of the state. So the boards of officials who ran the games, the Hellanodikai at Olympia, for instance, or the Athlothetai at Athens, were elected by the state like other magistrates. The first problem of management, then as now, was, of course, finance. In a Greek city many items of public expenditure which in a modern state are met from revenue obtained by taxation were dealt with much more directly by means of the institution called the 'liturgy' or public service. Financial responsibility for certain tasks was imposed on wealthy citizens in turn, with provision for ensuring that the would-be shirker did not escape. The athletic festivals came into this category, and from time to time a rich man found himself called upon to act as 'agonothete' or giver of the games. To help him discharge this function he had, apart from the athlothetai or their equivalent, an official called the gymnasiarch. This man, elected annually in most cities, had a general responsibility for physical training in the city; he selected and organized the teams to represent the city in torch races, and at the athletic festivals it was his task among other things to arrange the supply of oil for the competitors; like the agonothete, he often dipped his hand in his own pocket to pay for materials. The social standing of a wealthy man in Greece largely depended on the way in which he discharged these public duties and on his readiness to spend money to enhance the festivals for the enjoyment of all. We have a parallel today in the large sums lavished by rich business men on professional football clubs. The agonothete, particularly in later times, could occasionally call on sources other than his own wealth in paying the bills. Many festivals were endowed either by gift, by legacy or by grant from the imperial exchequer. A problem closely connected with this, which has never been adequately discussed, is whether or not the spectators at the games paid gate-money. Gardiner declares flatly that admission was always free, but the subject is not to be dismissed as lightly as that.[1]

There is one important point to be borne in mind. For us, drama and athletics seem to have very little in common; the one is chiefly an indoor entertainment for the evening, the other an outdoor pursuit for daylight hours. In the Greek world, on the other hand, they were closely bound up with one another. Dramatic and musical performances were given in outdoor theatres, often adjacent to stadia, and often at the same festivals. The Greek word 'theatron' simply meant 'place for viewing a spectacle' and was used of the spectators' banking in the stadium as well as that in the dramatic theatre. The phrase 'the theatre of the stadium' is very well attested.* It is well established that seats in the 'theatron' were paid for; there are a few references to the practice in literature, and a large number of theatre tickets made of bronze or lead have been found. There was at Athens a 'Theoric fund', which paid among other things for seats in the 'theatron' for the poorer citizens. Modern scholarship, because of the connection of the drama with great literature, has naturally concentrated on the organization of the theatre rather than on that of the Games, and a reader of books on the drama might well suppose that the evidence for payment for seats was unmistakably

* In this book, to avoid ambiguity, the phrase has been rendered: 'The spectators' accommodation in the stadium'.

confined to the theatre; but a dispassionate re-examination of it shows that this is not so. Almost every item of evidence could equally well apply to the 'theatre of the stadium'. Certainly the Theoric fund paid the expenses of the 'Theoroi', the delegates who officially represented Athens at the Olympic, the Pythian and other great games. From the *Constitution of Athens*, once attributed to Aristotle, we learn that the term for which the managers of the Theoric fund were elected ran from one Panathenaic festival to the next; this festival was an athletic, not a dramatic one, and this suggests that the primary concern of the fund was with the athletic festivals.[2]

In addition to this evidence which is common to theatre and stadium, there is one indication which can apply only to the games. It is an inscription of about 160 B.C., recording a decree of thanks to Nicogenes for his services as agonothete for the athletic festival of the Thesea at Athens. Among other benefactions he had paid 1200 drachmas for 'kathesimon' for the Council. This word, literally 'seating', sometimes means 'fee for attending Council meeting'. Here, then, it might mean that Nicogenes had given the councillors payment for 'broken time' consequent upon their attending the games instead of the Council meeting; equally it may mean that he paid for their seats in the stadium. The question whether or not gate-money was charged in a Greek stadium must be regarded as still open, with a preponderance of probability in favour of the belief that it was. But it is clear that, as today, the gate-money by no means covered all the expenses of a meeting. Another inscription from Athens records that the discharge of his functions as agonothete in 228 B.C. cost Eurycleides seven talents. Dio Chrysostom reveals that a popularity hunter would pay as much as five talents to persuade an Olympic champion to compete at his festival.[3]

Also connected with the problem of finance when a new meeting was being organized was the decision whether it should be a 'crown' festival or one with money or other prizes. As we have seen, the chief practical difference was that in the latter the organizers put up the prize-money, while in the former the crown winner expected a more substantial cash reward from his own city. The foundation of a new crown meeting (often called 'sacred' by the Greeks) therefore demanded a series of treaties with neighbouring cities to ensure that this supplement should be forthcoming; otherwise no competitors would have entered. For this reason, most new festivals after the time

of Alexander started as 'money' games. Some of the most successful
of them were then changed to 'sacred'. At small local meetings and
school sports, trophies were sometimes given, either as sole prizes or
in addition to money awards. The recent American excavations in
Athens brought to light an oil-flask in the shape of a kneeling athlete
binding a ribbon round his head (Plate 22a). This charming little
object was almost certainly such a prize. Many centuries later, boy
victors at Side in Pamphylia received a statuette on a stand in addition
to a money prize. Xenophon tells us that when the Arcadians in
Cyrus' army held a sports meeting, the prizes were golden strigils; a
bronze strigil with obvious traces of gilding, now in the museum of
Chios, reveals what these awards probably were. An interesting
inscription from Coressus in the island of Ceos of the third century
B.C. shows that the prizes in the men's events there were weapons of
different kinds. It was laid down that these awards were not to be
sold. The stipulation was hardly necessary in the case of the prizes
for the boys' torch race, which were portions of the sacrificial meat.[4]

After finance and prizes had been settled, the next point to be
decided was the frequency of the festival, whether it was to be
celebrated annually, biennially, or, like the Olympic and Pythian
games, once every four years. Generally speaking, the more important a meeting, the less frequently it was held. Athens compromised
with her Panathenaic festival, which was celebrated annually, but
much more elaborately every fourth year, at the Great Panathenaea.
Another detail to be fixed was a suitable date. This depended on the
dates of existing meetings in the neighbourhood. Fixtures had to
allow athletes to compete without unnecessary travelling. Thus the
Asclepiaea at Epidaurus was held nine days after the Isthmian games,
an interval which allowed competitors a reasonable time to make the
journey and rest after it.[5]

The drawing up of the programme did not present much difficulty.
All over the Greek world the limited Olympic schedule of events
was for centuries the accepted standard. The only point to be decided
was the number of age-groups to be catered for. In the early days of
Greek athletics there had been two categories only, boys and men,
and to the end of its history Olympia maintained this simple
division. If the Games established at Naples in the first century A.D.
really were 'isolympian' in this particular, as an inscription found at
Olympia claims, then the Olympic definition of 'boy' was one

between his seventeenth and twentieth birthdays. About 370 B.C. we hear of a third class, of youths, between boys and men, at the Isthmian Games, and a few years later Plato is advocating the same triple division in his *Laws*. One result of this was that what constituted a 'boy' was different at Isthmia and Olympia, and this difference extended to the other 'crown' games, each of which apparently had its own definition of 'boy'. Other meetings sometimes defined their own usage by employing the terms 'Olympic boys' or 'Pythian boys' in their programmes. In the first century A.D. a festival at Cos had two boys' stade races at the same meeting, one for 'Olympic' boys and one for 'Isthmian'. In Roman times the boys at some meetings were divided into three classes: younger, middle and older; at others the youths are similarly classed. As we look through the many athletic inscriptions of the period the variations of age classification appear very confusing, but doubtless to the athletes themselves they were no more unintelligible than the categories of maiden, junior, junior-senior, senior-junior and senior are to rowing men today.[6]

When the preliminary details of a festival had been decided it had to be made known to potential competitors by proclamation in the cities of the district, and in later times by enlisting the help of the xystus, the athletes' trade union. In the days before the Greek world enjoyed the Roman peace, the herald proclaiming the games used to demand safe conduct through all territories for those attending the festival either as competitors or spectators, and invoke the anger of the god in whose honour the festival was held on any who refused to grant it. This is the origin of the so-called 'Olympic truce' which has been much misunderstood. It is sometimes suggested that in the years in which Olympiads were held a vast armistice descended on the warring cities of the Greek world. This too rosy view is based on the misinterpretation of a passage in the *Panegyricus* of Isocrates. This was a pamphlet, cast in the form of a speech to be delivered at Olympia, calling on the Greeks to lay aside their differences in face of the threat from Persia. In the course of his argument Isocrates writes: 'You have made a truce with one another and put an end to your existing enmities and come together to this place.' It is important to notice that the words purported to be addressed to an audience at Olympia, and they were true of them. At the festival, competitors and spectators alike did put aside their quarrels, even if they came from cities at war with one another, and Isocrates uses the fact as an illustration of what might be. But the words were certainly not true of the states themselves. The reader of the history of Greek wars in Thucydides or Xenophon would not detect which were the Olympic years from any diminution in the fighting. Moreover, the Olympic festival was not the only one which claimed this 'truce'. The Pythian, Isthmian, Nemean and others also demanded the same safe conduct for their patrons. When we remember that there was at least one of these festivals every year, it is obvious that, if these 'truces' had had the results sometimes attributed to the Olympic, warfare would scarcely have been possible for the Greeks at all.[7]

As the time for the meeting approached, the stadium had to be prepared for the athletes. Between festivals the running surface became overgrown with weeds and cluttered up with rubbish which had to be removed. At Olympia there was a tradition which demanded that the competitors should do this work themselves, just as not many years ago cricketers who played for a small club expected to be asked to help to roll the wicket. The vase paintings of the fifth century show us the picks with which the clearing was done and depict athletes picking up stones or collecting the refuse into large baskets (Plates 13a, 30b). Athenaeus tells a story of a citizen of Sybaris who saw a Crotoniate performing this task and asked in surprise whether so great a city as Croton could not afford slaves for the menial job. At Olympia the practice seems to have continued at least as late as the third century B.C., for Theocritus' cowman, when he goes off to compete there, takes his mattock with him. Elsewhere, however, by Theocritus' time hired labour was being employed for the work. Inscriptions recording expenditure on stadia, one from Delos belonging to the year 296 B.C. and one from Delphi of about 250 B.C., both include sums paid for this purpose. That from Delphi is particularly informative; it covers the clearing, digging and levelling of the stadium and the jumping pit, the erection of the turning posts for the races, the provision of equipment for the pentathlon and the purchase of white sand to give a final finish to the whole area. The amount of sand, 600 medimni, allows only a sprinkling about a quarter of an inch in thickness, but if it was repeated at each festival it would in time afford a good running surface of packed sand. An item in the inscription which puzzled the

French excavators of Delphi runs: 'Fencing for the Pythian stadium'; their comment is: '*Il est assez difficile d'en determiner le sens. . . . L'hypothèse la plus probable paraît être que ce mot s'applique à une clôture, mais on ne sait où elle était placée ni à quoi elle servait*'. To anyone who has stood in the stadium in Delphi it might appear that if gate-money was charged there was some reason for putting up a screen of fencing along the top edge of the stadium, as is done on many sports grounds today, to prevent non-payers from securing a free view of the proceedings from the slope above. Unhappily there is a gap in the inscription, and the sum paid for the fencing is lost, so there is no way of calculating how extensive it may have been.[8]

Alternatively the purpose of the fencing may have been to keep the spectators out of the arena, as is found necessary today in many Mediterranean football grounds. Ancient spectators of sporting events were no less excitable than modern crowds. Dio Chrysostom, it is true, congratulates the Rhodians on their orderly watching of the games and on their way of expressing appreciation of a good performance by a simple 'poppusmos', plopping or smacking of the lips; he also rallies the people of Tarsus on their use of a strange kind of snort for the same purpose. But the picture he gives of spectators at the athletic festivals in Alexandria is very different:

'When they enter the stadium, it is as if they come under the influence of drugs; they forget everything they have ever learned, and say and do the first thing that comes into their heads.'

Again, addressing the same people, he says:

'When you go to the stadium, who could describe the yelling and uproar, the frenzy, the sudden changes of expression and colour on your faces, and the terrible blasphemies you utter?'

He also gives a vivid picture of what journalists today would call a 'local derby' at Prusa in Bithynia, when spectators from neighbouring Apameia had come over to support their champions in battle with the Prusans:

'What a difference there is between the shouts of the rival factions in the stadium when they are applauding and heaping praise on their own men and those when they are expressing hatred and abuse of their rivals!'

Plutarch mentions how spectators like to run alongside a competitor to encourage him, a practice we have already encountered in the satirical epigram of Nicharcus, and one which can soon reduce any athletic meeting to chaos. Whether or not fencing was used to keep order in such crowds, there were certainly attendants, whose methods are indicated by their Greek name, 'truncheon-holders'. A régime which flogged disobedient athletes was not likely to have any compunctions about using strong-arm measures in dealing with recalcitrant spectators.[9]

But care for the crowds on the part of organizers of festivals was not confined to keeping them in order. An inscription of the second century B.C. from Parium on the Dardanelles thanks a city market official for ensuring a good supply of food for visitors to the new Panathenaea there, and also for providing a doctor to look after them. Another inscription of a century later from Priene includes a similar expression of gratitude for the provision of a doctor, in this instance more specifically for the competitors.[10]

In later times the authorities running a festival sometimes provided accommodation for the athletes competing in it. There is an interesting inscription of the second century A.D. from Corinth, in which the Roman governor of the province approves an offer by Publius Licinius Priscus Juventianus to buy the ruins of an old stoa and convert it into fifty rooms, to be allotted by the agonothete free of charge to athletes competing in the Isthmian games. This is good evidence of how by this time these prima donna performers had to be cajoled and bribed into taking part even in so senior a festival as the Isthmian. But this belongs to later times; in earlier periods athletes were less exacting. The one commodity with which they did expect to be provided, and by the quality of which they appear to have judged the efficiency of the organization of a festival, was oil. Inscriptions constantly refer to the munificence of gymnasiarchs in this respect. One from Aphrodisias speaks of an official who 'made oil run like water'. Athenaeus mentions games given at Daphne near Antioch by Antiochus Epiphanes at which the oil supplied was scented. Athens was particularly happily situated for oil supplies for her festivals. Scattered over Attica were sacred olive trees, said to be from cuttings of the tree on the Acropolis planted by Pallas Athene herself. The olives from these trees were collected by the authorities and the oil made from them was handed to the athlothetai for the use of competitors in the games. Aegina enjoyed a similar benefaction of oil from trees bequeathed to the state for the purpose by the philosopher Lycon.[11]

On the whole, however, arrangements for competitors and spectators at the festivals could safely be left to private enterprise. There were plenty of Greeks anxious to earn an honest penny by hiring out tents, huts, mules and donkeys, by selling food and drink, and by providing entertainment for the crowds at times when the games were not in progress. Spectators were not exacting about accommodation at the great games. Aelian tells us that Plato at the height of his fame shared a tent with strangers at Olympia, and they did not discover who he was until later, when he entertained them at Athens. Dio Chrysostom describes the scene at the Isthmian festival in his day:

'Then round the temple of Poseidon you could see and hear the accursed sophists shouting and abusing one another, and their so-called pupils fighting with each other, many authors giving readings of their works, which no-one listens to, many poets reciting their poems and others expressing approval of them, many conjurors performing their tricks, and many fortune-tellers interpreting omens, thousands of lawyers arguing cases, and a host of cheap-jacks selling everything under the sun.'

It is small wonder that Lucian complains of the difficulty of finding transport in which to get away from Olympia at the end of the festival.[12]

The order of events at Greek meetings appears to have been as stereotyped as the programme itself. Most surviving lists of victors at minor festivals put the prize-winners in the same order as Pausanias gives for the events at Olympia. The normal duration of the active part of a meeting, as distinct from the ceremonial, was two days. On the first the races were held in the morning and the heavyweight events started in the afternoon. On the second these events were concluded and the pentathlon was held. At Olympia the heavyweight contests were finished on the first day, and this gave time for the equestrian events as well as the pentathlon on the second. But at Olympia there were only two age-groups to be provided for, and it is clear that the number of entries was limited. At other meetings there might be as many as five age-groups in each event and the number of competitors was often considerable.[13]

The races began very early in the morning—Dio Chrysostom says 'at dawn'—giving the runners the benefit of the cool of the day. The dolichos came first, then the stade, followed by the diaulos with the armed race last. The only evidence to the contrary is in the *Laws* of Plato, who in describing the games for the ideal state he is envisaging says that the stade should come first 'as happens now'. This may mean that the heats of the stade were held first, then the long-distance race and then the final of the stade. It is probable that the races over the same distance for different age-groups were kept together, that the boys', youths' and men's diaulos, for instance, were run immediately after one another, in order to avoid unnecessary dismantling and replacement of the starting gates.[14]

In the event of a dead-heat the race was apparently re-run. Herodotus tells us that Alexander, son of Amyntas of Macedonia, ran in the stade at Olympia and dead-heated for first place. His name does not appear in the list of victors, nor is there any record of a dead-heat in the event; the only possible explanation is that Alexander was beaten in the run-off. We have seen, too, the remarkable case of Demetrius of Salamis who many centuries later dead-heated four times with Optatus and defeated him only at the fifth attempt. Judging must always have been difficult in a Greek stadium, where the width of the track and consequent length of the finishing line made the use of anything like a tape impossible, and it may well be that judges then were more disposed than those of today to give a verdict of dead-heat. The lot of judges is never a very happy one, and in Greek times, if we can believe an odd story told by Pausanias, they were exposed to even greater risks than today. In 396 B.C. Eupolemos of Elis defeated Leon of Ambracia in the stade at Olympia in a very close finish; of the three judges two gave Eupolemos as the winner, while the other gave Leon. Leon thereupon arraigned the two who had favoured his opponent before the Olympic Council and was awarded damages against them. But in spite of this the result of the race was not upset, and Eupolemos remains the winner to this day, duly attested by four authorities.

Even today the decisions of governing bodies in the world of sport are often incomprehensible to the ordinary mortal.[15]

In addition to the judges at the finish, umpires were required at the turning posts in the diaulos and dolichos to ensure that runners did not take a short cut. On a vase now at Würzburg an umpire can be seen seated near the kampter to discharge this function (Plate 4b).[16]

The races for the various age-groups must have occupied the greater part of the morning. When they had finished, the heavyweight events began; this meant that they took place during the hottest hours of the day. Wrestling came first, then boxing, and the pankration last of all. At Olympia in 212 B.C. there was an exception. Pausanias tells us that in that year Cleitomachus of Thebes entered for boxing and the pankration and Caprus of Elis for wrestling and the pankration. Caprus won the wrestling. Cleitomachus then asked the Hellanodikai to hold the pankration next, on the ground that he was less likely to be injured in that event than in boxing. They granted his request, but although this meant that Caprus had to fight the pankration without a rest after his victory in wrestling, he defeated Cleitomachus. Cleitomachus, however, went on to win the boxing. This modification in the usual programme did not set a precedent. Inscriptions from Athens and Thebes in the second century B.C. and from Aphrodisias in the Roman period show that the old order of events was maintained, wrestling, boxing, pankration.[17]

In attempting to describe the organization of these events we are faced with an unfortunate ambiguity in the meaning of the English words 'round' and 'draw'. If we say of a man in a tennis tournament, 'He was knocked out in the second round', the meaning is unmistakable, but if we say the same of a boxer in the modern Olympic games the words can signify two completely different things. They may mean, as in tennis, that he was dismissed from the competition by being defeated in the second of the eliminating stages on the way to the final, or that he was knocked senseless during the second of the periods into which a match is divided by time. As there were no such time divisions in Greek boxing, wrestling or pankration, the word 'round' in Greek athletics always means 'eliminating stage of a competition'. Unfortunately, 'draw' cannot be so easily dismissed. It may refer to the process of drawing lots, by which competitors are matched against one another—'The draw for the second round'—

L

or it may mean the result of a contest which neither side wins, corresponding to a dead-heat in a race. Greek used different words for the two senses. English, unhappily, has no convenient synonym for 'draw' in either meaning. Only the context can decide. At least this affords a useful warning against being too dogmatic about the meaning of Greek technical terms of athletics; a similar ambiguity may often be concealed there.

We are fortunate enough to have a detailed description of the draw for the heavyweight events at Olympia in one of the dialogues of Lucian, who claims that it is an eyewitness' account:

'A silver vessel, consecrated to the god, stands in front of them. Into it are thrown small lots, about the size of a bean, with letters written on them. Two have Alpha, two Beta, two others Gamma, and so on in the same way if there are more competitors, but always with two lots having the same letter. Then each of the competitors comes forward, recites a prayer to Zeus, puts his hand into the vessel and takes out one of the lots. Then the next man does the same. An attendant* stands by and seizes each man's hand to prevent him from seeing which letter he has drawn. When all have drawn, the Chief of Police, I think, or one of the Hellanodikai—I have forgotten which it is—goes round the competitors as they stand in a circle and examines their lots. In this way he pairs the one with an Alpha and the one who has drawn the other Alpha in the wrestling or pankration. In the same way he puts together the two Betas and the others with the same letter. This is what happens if the number of competitors is even, eight, four or twelve for instance; but if the number is odd, an extra lot is thrown in with the others, marked with a letter which has no corresponding duplicate. The man who draws this has a bye, and waits until the others have finished the round, for there is no letter to pair with his. This is a considerable stroke of luck for the athlete, for he will still be fresh when he has to meet opponents already exhausted.'[18]

Lucian's account shows that the Greeks were well aware of the injustice that may be caused when a competitor draws a bye. It is curious that they should never have taken the simple steps necessary to reduce the inevitable unfairness as far as possible. The number of

* The Greek word literally means 'whip-holder'.

competitors can always be expressed in the formula 2^n+x, and the modern practice is to hold a preliminary round of x matches to reduce the number to 2^n, after which there are no more byes and all is fair and straightforward. But the Greeks never did this. Whatever the number of entrants, they simply paired them, with a bye if the number was odd, as Lucian relates, and went on doing this until the final, with the result that there might be a bye in every round. For instance, with seventeen competitors the modern method would be to hold a preliminary round of one match; 15 entrants would be exempt from this round, but thereafter there would be no byes. The Greeks had a first round of eight matches with one bye, a second of four plus a bye, a third of two plus one bye, a fourth of one match and a bye and then the final.* The man with the bye was called 'ephedros', 'sitting by'. The luck of the draw might cause a competitor to be ephedros in several rounds, thus giving him a very great advantage indeed. This is no doubt what Pindar had in mind when he complained that Alcidamas of Aegina, who won the boys' wrestling at Nemea, was deprived of victory at Olympia by the 'reckless draw'. It is because of the advantage which the draw could confer that a victor in his list of successes sometimes claims as an additional merit that he won 'anephedros', without drawing a bye in any round.[19]

As the bye was of such importance in athletics, it is not surprising that it figures too in metaphors in literature. In the *Frogs* of Aristophanes, Dionysus goes down to the Underworld to bring back to life the greatest poet of the past to save Athens in her hour of need, and he holds a contest to decide which one was the greatest. For dramatic simplicity Aristophanes wanted a straight fight between Aeschylus and Euripides, but he knew that his audience would want to know what was the position in this struggle of the third great Athenian tragic poet, Sophocles. Accordingly he represented Sophocles as the ephedros in the contest, and trusted that at the climax of the play the audience would forget about him. In the *Rhesus* of Euripides, when Hector is anxious to mount an attack on the Greeks outside Troy, Aeneas restrains him by reminding him that even if he should win this battle he will have to face an ephedros, Achilles, who, sulking in

* Before we plume ourselves too much on modern superiority we might remember that the first English Golf Championship arrived at the penultimate stage with three competitors, one of whom then had a bye into the final.

his tent, will take no part in the first fight. Partly because English has no single noun for 'A man who has drawn a bye', and partly because of a certain vagueness in the minds of many classical scholars about what an ephedros really was, the word has been translated in such passages in several very misleading ways: 'supporter', 'reserve', 'substitute' and even 'second'.[20]

In addition to this elaborate machinery for pairing competitors in the games by drawing lots, the Greeks had a simple method of giving priority of choice to one or other of two contestants under circumstances where we should toss a coin and call 'Heads' or 'Tails'. The Greeks spun a fragment of a broken pot, black on one side and white on the other, and called 'Night' or 'Day'. The device is attested chiefly for children's games, but there is no reason why it should not have been more widely used.[21]

One interesting question is the number of competitors at Greek meetings. Most of our evidence comes from inscriptions, but Lucian's description of the Olympic draw is of some value. It is significant that the biggest number of entrants he mentions is twelve; this bears out the evidence of the inscriptions, for no Olympic victor in the heavyweight contests claims to have defeated more than four opponents. Four rounds allow a maximum of sixteen entrants. At Olympia the fear of ridicule after a poor performance would tend to keep entries down, while on the other hand the prestige value of having even competed there would tend to swell the numbers. We have to remember that would-be competitors at Olympia had to put in a month's compulsory training at Elis before the festival. Pausanias tells us that at Elis there was a gymnasium 'in which the Hellanodikai match the wrestlers according to age and skill', the only mention in our records of any such classification. The purpose of this was probably to eliminate unworthy entrants and so save time at the festival itself.[22]

Elsewhere the numbers of competitors were much higher. Two inscriptions from Antioch in Pisidia record wrestlers who survived seven rounds to win, and one from Xanthus in Lycia claims that a wrestler won after nine rounds. Seven rounds are necessary only if the number of entrants exceeds sixty-four; nine if the number exceeds 256. No doubt in the early rounds the matches went on simultaneously, but, allowing a minimum 'ring' of ten yards by ten for each contest, a stadium could not have held more than sixty fights at the same time. Even if some of them had been held in gymnasia in other parts of the city, there would have been the problem of finding competent umpires or referees for so large a number of matches. It looks as if these competitions at Antioch and Xanthus must have been local affairs, spread over several weeks.[23]

Gardiner makes the strange mistake of asserting that the heavy-weight events at Olympia were held not in the stadium but in the Altis. He bases this belief on the statement of Xenophon that when the army of Elis burst into Olympia during the festival of 364 B.C., the wrestling of the pentathlon was going on in the Altis. But, as we have seen, there is no reason for believing that this was anything but an emergency measure, made necessary by pressure of time because the stadium was otherwise engaged. All the other evidence speaks of boxers, wrestlers and pankratiasts in the stadium. Later writers in particular make it clear that these heavyweight fights were the most popular part of the programme with spectators, and it is incredible that they should have been conducted in a place where few could watch them.[24]

The pentathlon was held on the second day of a meeting. The reason for this was probably bound up with a question which seems never to have been asked by modern writers on the subject; where was the long-jump pit? A glance at a plan of the stadium at Olympia or Delphi will show that there was no place for it between the starting lines which would not interfere with the lanes for the runners in the stade race. The space between the outside runners' lanes and the spectators' seats is not wide enough to accommodate a permanent pit which would give the watching crowds a reasonable view of the jumpers. Equally there was no room for it between the starting sills and the ends of the stadium, especially if, as we have seen was prob-able, the pit had to be prepared for a leap of fifty feet or more. The only possible solution seems to be that the pit was dug somewhere in the middle of the stadium, perhaps rather nearer to the curved end, after the races had been held. If the first three events of the pentathlon did not produce a clear winner and the contest had to continue with the stade race, the loss of a couple of lanes would not be disastrous. Before the next festival there would be plenty of time for the dis-turbed soil of the pit to consolidate itself sufficiently not to handicap the runners in the lanes affected; the process could be helped by the use of the roller, an implement which the Greeks used in the stadium.

Although the same Greek word 'skamma' is used both for the jumpers' pit and for the heavyweights' ring, it is hardly conceivable that the events were held in the same place. For the jumpers the soil must have been loosened to a considerable depth; boxers, wrestlers and pankratiasts required a firm foothold, with only a sufficient layer of soft sand on the hard surface to prevent a fall from being dangerous. This could have been put down quickly anywhere in the stadium.

One problem on ancient sports grounds as on modern was thieving from dressing-rooms. How seriously this was regarded at Athens we may judge from a chance remark of Demosthenes. He reveals that at the beginning of the sixth century B.C. Solon, although in his reforms he lessened the severity of many of the punishments in the Draconian code, left untouched the death penalty for the theft from any gymnasium of an article valued at more than ten drachmas.[25]

The great enemy of the organizers of any athletics meeting is time. When the duration of each event can be predicted, as it can with any race, a programme can be planned, but even then it is not easy to drive competitors into adhering to it. There are many indications that Greek athletes were as highly strung and temperamental as our own. A Greek verb derived from 'Agon', athletic contest, means 'to be in an agony of nervousness'. Pausanias records that in A.D. 13 a pankratiast, Sarapion of Alexandria, ran away from Olympia on the day before the contest. He was fined for cowardice, but a man who had reached Olympic standard in the pankration would hardly have suffered from that defect; the cause was probably sheer panic. They were incurably superstitious, too. Plutarch describes how an athlete would become convinced that his success was bound up with a particular strigil or oil-flask, and would go into a frenzy of fury if he lost it. Philostratus tells us of their recourse to wizards and magicians in the belief that they could guarantee victory; a papyrus has preserved a gnostic charm of about A.D. 300, designed to secure success in the stadium for one Sarapammon in the name of a mysterious deity Sylicusesus. Appeals to oracles were frequent. The astrologers were prepared to let athletes know what the stars foretold for them on the basis of their horoscopes. Ptolemy in his *Tetrabiblos* lays it down that 'if Venus rules action and Jupiter testifies, her subjects will be crown-winning athletes, men considered worthy of honours, and'—rather oddly for athletes—'men who owe their success to women.' He also states that if Mercury and Mars together rule action, they make men wrestlers, but as the same combination also makes men sculptors, armourers, doctors, adulterers, evil-doers and forgers, the support of these planets would appear to be a mixed blessing.[26]

Athletes subject to these influences cannot have been easy material for the organizers of a festival to handle. No doubt the presence of attendants armed with whips and ready to flog any unruly competitor prevented those displays of temperament which modern spectators have to endure, but there is a limit to what the strictest discipline can do, and it cannot have been easy to keep to a time schedule even in the races. With events whose duration cannot possibly be foretold, such as the heavyweight fights under Greek rules, the difficulties are far greater. At Olympia the arrangement of the programme did allow a certain latitude; there was no reason why athletics should not continue all through the second day, even if the equestrian events had already started in the hippodrome. Smaller meetings without horse and chariot races lacked this safety valve. But sometimes even at Olympia time ran out and one of the heavyweight contests had to be abandoned as a draw. When this happened in early times at a 'crown' meeting the prize was not awarded but was apparently dedicated to the god of the festival and called 'sacred'. This word became the technical term for a drawn contest and it continued to be so used when in later times the competitors in a draw were crowned jointly or the money prize was divided between them.[27]

The earliest-known draw at Olympia occurred in the pankration at the end of the first or beginning of the second century B.C., probably the former. The inscription recording it is a charming example of lapidary language at its most effusive:

'DECREE OF THE PEOPLE OF ELIS

Marcus Vetilenus Laetus has given information that Tiberius Claudius Rufus, a pankratiast, came to the Olympic festival and passed the prescribed time in the city with due propriety, so that he was approved by all for his seemly conduct both public and private. He performed attentively the exercises under the observation of the Hellanodikai in accordance with the ancestral custom of the Games, so that he had clear hopes of winning the most sacred of all crowns. When he appeared in the stadium, he exhibited a great and remarkable performance, as was proper, in a way worthy of Olympian Zeus, of his own skill and training, and of the universal esteem in which he was held, hoping to place on his brows the Olympic wreath. He fought through every round, matched against the most illustrious opponents, without ever drawing a bye. He came to such a climax of manliness and courage that in the final, fighting a man who had drawn a bye, he placed his hopes of the crown above his own life and held out until nightfall so that the stars overtook him, driven to exert himself to the utmost by his hope of victory, so that he roused the admiration both of our own citizens and of the spectators who had assembled from all parts of the world for the most sacred Olympic festival. Accordingly it has been decided to decree honours to him, inasmuch as he has magnified and glorified the festival, and to allow him to erect a statue at Olympia, with an inscription setting forth his victories at other festivals and giving details of his drawn contest, which he alone of men of all time secured.'

The word 'alone' seems strangely unjust to his unknown opponent in the final; a single pankratiast can hardly make a draw.[28]

As time went on, draws became much more frequent. A century after Claudius Rufus, a wrestler from Magnesia on the Sipylus, Marcus Aurelius Hermagoras, records in his inscription that he won twenty-nine crowns and 127 firsts in games with money prizes, and that he drew at Olympia and on eighteen other occasions. Allowing for a few defeats—with an Olympic finalist they would presumably not be many—this gives a proportion of well over 10 per cent of drawn matches. Where a money prize was at stake, finalists sometimes came to an agreement before the match to make it a draw and divide the prize. At least one pankratiast in his inscription claims never to have done this. But the reason for the increasing number of drawn matches was not always as venal as this. Victory, in games as in war, is gained only by taking risks. The professional athlete whose livelihood depends on his escaping injury avoids risks as far as possible. In any of the heavyweight events a bout in which neither contestant is willing to take the slightest risk can go on interminably.[29]

At 'crown' festivals, as in the modern Olympics, the trophy was awarded immediately after each event. Vase paintings suggest that the wreath was handed to the victor who then placed it on his head. How money prizes were given to the winners we do not know. When the last event was completed the herald brought the Games to a close with his farewell: 'The festival, bestower of noble prizes, is ended; Time bids us delay no longer.'

But after the spectators had departed there was still one ceremony left. Like the chorus and actors at a dramatic festival, athletes and officials expected to be invited to a banquet. To provide this entertainment was the final privilege of the agonothete.[30]

VIII TRAINING FOR GREEK ATHLETICS

THE urge to give advice is one of the strongest temptations to which mankind is exposed, and the temptation is rarely resisted. Here is the basis of most training in sport. Homer's Nestor is the precursor of every coach who ever admonished team, crew or individual player. Advice is the great exception to the rule that in this life 'You don't get owt for nowt'. Everyone is only too willing to give it. Anyone embarking on any activity, from growing a nasturtium in a pot to pole jumping, is sure to be assailed with a mass of exhortation and warning, most of it bad. It is remarkable then that advice is so often paid for. The only possible explanation is that other anfractuosity of the human mind which leads men to believe that whatever costs nothing is valueless, and that the mere act of paying for something in itself confers some excellence on what is bought.

There are three sides to training for most sports. There is the acquisition of skill in the technique of the game, the mastery and co-ordination of the muscular movements which experience has shown to be most likely to produce victory. Then there is the preparation of the body generally to face the stress of competition by making it accustomed to enduring fatigue. Finally there is mental preparation, which tries to produce the right degree of self-confidence and to ensure that the contestants shall not fail of their best through nervousness or panic on the great day. In our own language we think of the man responsible for the first and third of these objects as the coach, and the man who looks after the second as the trainer, but the two terms are, of course, neither exact nor exclusive of each other. In football a wealthy club may employ both: a coach to

170

instruct the team in ball control and in the strategy and tactics of the game, and a trainer to ensure that the men shall be at their fittest on the day of an important match by arranging a programme of exercise for them and by tending their minor ailments. In rowing, on the other hand, the coach is expected to cover the whole field, to instruct the individual oarsmen in the details of rowing technique and to plan a training programme which will bring the crew to their race at the peak of their potential. If we remember this lack of precise meaning in our own terms we shall beware of ascribing too hard and fast a meaning to the three Greek words for trainer, paidotribēs, aleiptēs and gymnastēs. Philostratus and Galen both make it clear that the function of the gymnastes included that of the paidotribes or aleiptes but was much wider; he therefore corresponds roughly to our coach. The literal meaning of paidotribes, 'boy-rubber', and aleiptes, 'anointer', suggests that massage was an important part of their duties.[1]

The giving of advice to athletes goes back to Homer. Training as a profession also goes far back in Greek history, because physical exercise was always a fundamental part of Greek education. It is only within living memory that specialist teachers of physical training have become a commonplace in our schools; the paidotribes was always an essential part of a Greek school. It is not surprising then that trainers appear early in the story of Greek athletics. By the fifth century B.C. it seems to have become normal for every athlete of any pretensions to be trained by a professional. Pindar several times ascribes the success of his victors to the excellence of their trainers. The story of Callipateira, the daughter of Diagoras of Rhodes, reminds us that at the end of the century there was at Olympia a special enclosure for trainers. Much of the efforts of these men must have been devoted to coaching their charges in technique. Running is a natural activity, but jumping, throwing and especially the heavyweight events involve skills which must be acquired and in which the experienced exponent can help the beginner a great deal. We have already seen a description of a coach putting boys through wrestling exercises and instructing each in the appropriate move and counter-move. But most of the meagre information we have about Greek trainers is concerned with the other side of their work, their care for the athlete's fitness and particularly for his diet.[2]

Pausanias tells us that the first athlete to train on a meat diet was Dromeus of Stymphalus, twice winner of the dolichos at Olympia about 480 B.C., and adds that previously the chief food of athletes had been cheese. Another tradition attributes the first victory on meat to Eurymenes of Samos, winner of a heavyweight event at Olympia some forty years before Dromeus, and ascribes the innovation to his trainer, the philosopher Pythagoras. In view of the later Pythagoreans' insistence on vegetarianism this may seem strange, but it may well be that, as often happens in such cases, the Pythagoreans were more Pythagorean than Pythagoras himself. Africanus records that Charmis of Sparta, victor in 668 B.C., trained on a diet of dried figs. We have to remember that meat was not such a normal part of everyday meals in Greece as it is in northern countries today. Until their country escaped from poverty most Greeks probably ate meat only at a religious celebration, when parts of the sacrificial animal not offered to the god were distributed among the participants. Their usual diet consisted of thick soup—made chiefly from vegetables—cheese and fruit, fish both fresh and dried, bread and a variety of cakes made with honey. It is noteworthy that while the fish market appears frequently in fifth-century literature, the first mention of a butcher's shop does not occur until the Hellenistic period. Probably, then, the moralists' denunciations of the supposedly excessive diet of athletes were partly at least the outcome of envy. They start with Euripides, who calls athletes the slaves of their jaws and the victims of their bellies, and thereafter become a commonplace. Athenaeus collects several pages of variations on the theme from the works of Greek poets. Yet Epictetus warns would-be Olympic champions that among the hardships they must face is a strict and plain diet.[3]

There are, of course, reasons why an athlete must be careful about his food. Xenophon hints at one when he says that the man in training should avoid bread. Clearly the Greeks knew the danger of too much starch. But by the second century A.D. concentration on details of diet had become farcical. Philostratus says that in his day trainers solemnly discussed the relative merits for a training diet of deep-sea and inshore fish, basing their arguments on the kind of seaweed each was likely to have eaten, and that they rejected pork from pigs pastured near rivers or the sea and demanded that meat for their charges should come from pigs fed only on cornel berries and acorns.[4]

Along with the theory that athletes ate and slept too much went an equally well-worn jest that they were all beef-witted. Plutarch ascribes to trainers and coaches a belief that intelligent conversation at meals spoils the food and gives the diners a headache. He also records a remark of Antiphon: 'Training makes athletes as golden-gleaming as the columns in the palaestra—and as solid stone.'*5

In the early centuries training appears to have been directed largely by rule of thumb. Athletes simply practised beforehand the skills which they would use in competition. For general fitness there were the exercises done in school or palaestra under the eye of the paido-tribes. Even in adults' gymnasia these were often done in groups or classes, as Plato informs us. The hardy life of the farmer was regarded as athletic training, lifting heavy weights, working at the forge, pulling the plough, grinding corn and catching hares by running them down. Philostratus mentions some other unconventional methods of training in early times. A great boxer, Tisander of Naxos in Sicily, who won four crowns in the Olympic and four in the Pythian games, used to keep himself fit by long-distance swimming in the sea, a routine which would scarcely be approved today. We learn from the same source of runners being paced by men on horse-back; this is born out by a vase painting in the Bibliothèque Nationale in Paris of a runner between two horses with riders and by a similar vase painting in the British Museum of a rider between two runners.[6]

Before the end of the fourth century B.C., training was becoming stereotyped. Aristotle, who, as we have seen, was a keen devotee of athletics and who was certainly not given to loose statement, says in the *Nicomachean Ethics*: 'We argue about the navigation of ships more than about the training of athletes, because it has been less well organized as a science.' This is a remarkable assertion in view of the long Greek history of seafaring. But if there was little debate about training in Aristotle's day there was certainly plenty of it some centuries later, and the book from which most of our knowledge of Greek athletic training is derived, the *Gymnastic* of Philostratus, was itself a contribution to the discussion. From its muddled and rambling pages we can at least catch a few glimpses of the athletic scene in the second century A.D. In its essence the book is an attack on contemporary training and a plea for a return to earlier methods. Yet

* Philostratus makes it clear that the golden gleam of Greek athletes' bodies, like the tan of some modern sun-bathers, was not due entirely to nature. He recommends the athlete to be careful in his choice of a yellow powder and to apply it not by throwing it on his body but by dusting himself with a supple wrist and with fingers widely spaced. This will ensure a bloom like that on peaches or plums.

the author cannot conceal his pride in the scientific outlook of his
day, which has, he obviously thinks, given training a sound theoreti-
cal basis in physiology. Athletes could now be 'typed' accurately and
treated accordingly. This physiology was based on the conception
of the two pairs of opposing principles, hot and cold, wet and dry,
combining in the four humours of the human body, the blood, hot
and wet, the bile (cholē), hot and dry, the phlegm, cold and dry, and
the black bile (melaina cholē), cold and wet. The health and character
of the individual depended on the proper mixture or 'temperament'
of these humours in the body, but normally in everyone one or other
of them was in slight excess and produced its characteristic temperament, sanguine, choleric, phlegmatic or melancholic. Together with
the belief in the four elements, similarly based on the conflicting
principles, earth, cold and dry—air, hot and wet—fire, hot and dry—
and water, cold and wet, the theory appeared to give a coherent
picture of the nature of the whole external world. It dominated the
field of thought until early modern times; the language of Chaucer
and Shakespeare is shot through and through with it.[7]

Philostratus passes in review the athletes of these different temperaments. The choleric are as unproductive of victory as hot and dry
sand is of crops for the farmer. Their one merit in competition is that
they are quick to take decisions. The phlegmatic are too slow because
of their coldness. They need to be driven hard in training, while the
choleric need to be prevented from trying to train too quickly; the
former demand the spur, the latter the rein. The melancholic he does
not trouble to consider for athletics; they are too much compounded
of mud and slime. His ideal type is the sanguine. Able to face hard
work, with a healthy appetite, seldom ill and recovering quickly
when he does fall sick, easy to train and accepting instruction readily,
the sanguine man is to the trainer what a block of perfect marble is
to the sculptor.[8]

Though scientific circles might regard the human body in this way,
athletes themselves had long had their own nicknames for the
different shapes of humanity encountered in the gymnasium, and we
meet these too in the pages of Philostratus. There was the 'Lion',
with great chest and arms but 'inferior behind' with narrow hips and
feeble buttocks. The 'Eagle', with equally powerful torso, had his
legs slung from wider hips and consequently showed an open fork
like a standing eagle. Both these types were reckless, vigorous and

aggressive, but apt to be easily abashed by failure. The 'Lath' and the 'Piece of string' are both tall with long arms and legs, but whereas the former is stiff with clear-cut lines and well split up, the 'String' is loose-jointed, supple and pliant in twisting. 'Laths' are more head-strong in grappling, but 'Pieces of string' are slippery customers. 'Bears' are thick-set, supple, fleshy, less well articulated, hard to throw, evasive and tenacious. Their breathing appears to be tearing them to pieces, like that of bears when they run.[9]

The feature of contemporary training methods which most arouses Philostratus to anger is the system of the tetrad or four-day training cycle, which has obvious affinities with the 'interval' training fashionable today. He outlines the routine of the four days: Preparation, Concentration, Relaxation and Moderation. Preparation consists of a number of short, brisk exercises, designed to arouse the athlete and make him keen for the next day's exertions. The day of Concentration is one of all-out effort, aimed at showing what the energy stored up in the constitution of the athlete can effect and exhausting him completely. Relaxation gives him the chance to recover from this, while the day of Moderation is devoted to technical exercises in the athlete's own particular event. Philostratus's objection to the system is that its rigidity prevents due consideration being given to the psychology of the individual—the author has all the jargon. He gives an extreme example of the harm done by this rigidity. Gerenus, a wrestler from Naucratis in Egypt, crowned a long career of successes with a victory at Olympia. On the last day of the festival he was entertained at the official banquet given by the authorities, and next day he gave a party for his friends in celebration of his victory. Next morning, not surprisingly, he was not feeling at his best, but he reported for training as usual. His coach was furious with him for having broken training. It was apparently the second day of the tetrad, and the trainer insisted on Gerenus going through the full routine for that day, with the result that in the middle of the exercises he collapsed and died.*[10]

* Gerenus' coach was not the supreme example of a martinet in the history of Greek athletics. There was a trainer at Olympia who, because he thought that his man had not done his best in the contest, stabbed him with a strigil and killed him. Oddly enough, Philostratus seems rather to approve of the action. 'Let the strigil be used as a sword on worthless athletes', he writes, 'and let the trainer at Olympia have greater power than the Hellanodikai'.

Philostratus reveals that the authorities at Olympia, true to their intense conservatism, would have nothing to do with the tetrad system. Would-be competitors at the festival still had to put in the compulsory month's training before the games, and this passage makes it clear that the exercises during that period were prescribed in detail by the Hellanodikai. So the athlete, no matter how dependent he had become on the routine of the tetrad, had to forget about it when he arrived in Elis, and acquiesce in the training methods of a past age. Perhaps the Hellanodikai were wise. Fashions come and go. We learn from Epictetus that in the first century A.D. weight-lifting was as popular a form of training for all forms of athletics as it is today. A century later Philostratus never mentions it.[11]

For us the most interesting part of the *Gymnastic* is not the main thesis but the chance remarks dropped accidentally here and there which bring to life what went on in stadium or gymnasium. We learn, for instance, that whereas wrestlers trained, as we should expect, by wrestling with one another, boxers did not fight with sparring partners in training but only engaged in shadow boxing or used the punch-ball. Philostratus also tells us that pankratiasts used a heavier punch-ball than boxers, and he gives the strange advice that they should allow the ball to hit them on the head to accustom them to receiving the opponent's attack. He does not always succeed in expressing himself clearly. One of his statements about boxing appears thus in the only published English translation:

'The best kind of a belly is one which recedes, for such men are nimble and have good wind. Still, a boxer derives some advantage from a belly, for it wards off blows from the face when it projects into the path of the opponent's thrust.'

At first glance this looks like caricature, an upper cut delivered from knee height and prevented from reaching its mark by what Mr. Mantalini might well have called 'a demned outline'. Yet in fact Philostratus is writing sound sense. As a boxer faces his opponent he is normally leaning forward with his stomach tucked in. When a blow is aimed at his face, one counter-move open to him is to draw back his head in order to ride the punch if it lands. If he has to do this without moving his feet, as may well happen, he will inevitably hollow his back, and this thrusts his stomach violently forward. So if we emend the translation to 'It is a defence against blows at the face, if it is thrust forward as the opponent strikes', the passage makes sense. It is, of course, not the forward thrust of the stomach that is important but the drawing back of the head, which forms part of the same movement. Philostratus has put it badly, but he knows what he is talking about.[12]

Another interesting recommendation in the Gymnastic is that all exercises should be performed with jumping-weights used as dumbbells. Galen, a medical writer of the previous century, supplements this advice with details of an exercise which we all know for making the waist supple:

'Place jumping-weights in front of you about six feet apart and stand between them; bend over and pick up the weight on the left with the right hand and the weight on the right with the left hand. Replace and repeat, keeping the feet firmly fixed.'[13]

Every palaestra had a number of young men hanging round it prepared to engage in a wrestling bout with any wealthy athlete who wished to hire them for the purpose. Such a sparring partner was properly called a prosgymnastes, but was colloquially known as a 'statue'. Epictetus preserves a delightful phrase for training with a partner of this kind—'embracing a statue'. Demosthenes, in a passage of virulent abuse of his rival Aeschines, says: 'Your mother brought you up to be a fine "statue" and a first-rate ham actor', from which we may deduce that the profession of sparring partner was not held in high esteem. Coaches, on the other hand, were men of some position in the community. To undertake the training of others afforded a useful sphere of activity for the athlete when his days of competition were past. Some of the few whose names we know had been notable performers in their day. Iccus of Tarentum, honourably mentioned by Plato, had won the pentathlon at Olympia. Melesias, trainer of two athletes celebrated by Pindar, had certainly won at Nemea and Isthmia, and may have been an Olympic victor as well. Hippomachus of Elis, winner of the boys' boxing at Olympia about 300 B.C., later in life took to training. His aim for his charges was general physical excellence rather than mere success in competition, and he claimed that those he trained could be recognized at a distance as his pupils, even when they were shopping in the market. Evidently he

M

was a stern disciplinarian, for he once struck an athlete he was coaching, for showing off to the spectators at a training session.[14]

But not all trainers were first-class performers themselves. Lampon of Aegina coached two of his sons to victories at the Isthmian games. Pindar wrote odes to commemorate these successes, and in one of them he calls Lampon the 'Naxian whetstone' of his sons. As Chaucer's Pandarus says:

> 'A whetston is no kerving instrument,
> And yet it maketh sharpe kerving tolis.'

We may be sure that had Lampon been a 'kerving instrument', Pindar would not have failed to tell us of his successes.[15]

Perhaps the greatest of all trainers was Herodicus of Megara, who appears to have emigrated to the Megarian colony of Selymbria on the Sea of Marmora. It is not for his work as a trainer that we remember him best but because he was a doctor too, and it was from him that Hippocrates of Cos learned the rudiments of that art which was to make him the father of modern medicine.[16]

IX WOMEN IN GREEK ATHLETICS

IF THE evidence for men's athletics in ancient Greece is scanty, that for women's is even scantier, and the little that does exist raises most tantalizing problems. Substantially the whole of our knowledge depends on three pieces of positive information.

Pausanias, describing the temple of Hera at Olympia, writes:

'Once every four years the women of the Committee of Sixteen weave a robe for the statue of Hera, and they also arrange the Heraean festival. This consists of races for unmarried girls. They are not all of the same age; the youngest run first, then those of the second age group and finally the oldest girls. This is how they compete; their hair hangs loose, and they wear a tunic reaching to a little above the knee, with the right shoulder bare as far as the breast. Like the men, they have the Olympic stadium reserved to them for these Games, but the stade is shortened for their races by about a sixth. To the victors they give olive wreaths and a share of the beef sacrificed to Hera, and they are allowed to erect statues of themselves with inscriptions. The attendants who help the Sixteen to run these Games are women. As with the Olympic festival, they trace back these girls' Games to antiquity, declaring that Hippodameia in gratitude to Hera for her marriage to Pelops established the Committee of Sixteen and with their help inaugurated the Heraean festival.'

It is disappointing that Pausanias gives us no idea how long these games had been going on before his day. The 'tracing back to antiquity' we need not take seriously. The invention of such aetiological myths was a commonplace of his time. The dress of the girl runners which he describes is that in which the goddess Artemis appears in ancient art when she is depicted in her capacity as huntress.[1]

No inscription relating to a woman athlete has been found at Olympia, though three have been discovered recording women who entered winning chariots for the equestrian events there. Nor among the many statues of athletic victors at Olympia which Pausanias mentions does he include any of a woman. The only surviving base of this kind comes from Delphi. On it must have stood three statues of young women, and the inscription reads:

'Hermesianax son of Dionysius, citizen of Caesarea Tralles and also of Corinth, erected these statues of his daughters who themselves also hold the same citizenships.

'Tryphosa won the stade at the Pythian Games held by the agono-thetes Antigonus and Cleomachidas, and the stade at the ensuing Isthmian Games held by the agonothete Juventius Proclus, the first girl ever to do so.

'Hedea won the race for war chariots at the Isthmian Games held by the agonothete Cornelius Pulcher, the stade at the Nemean Games held by the agonothete Antigonus, and the stade at the games in Sicyon held by the agonothete Menoetas; she won also the competition for girl harpists at the Sebasteia at Athens held by the agonothete Novius, son of Philinus. She was the first girl ever to be made a citizen of [*Name lost*].

'Dionysia won the [*Event and name of festival lost*] held by the agonothete Antigonus, and the stade at the Asclepeia in sacred Epidaurus held by the agonothete Nicoteles.

Dedicated to Pythian Apollo.'

From the names of the agonothetes this inscription can be dated to the middle of the first century A.D. It is a most astonishing document. From it we learn that early in the Christian era there were well-established meetings for women athletes at the chief centres of men's athletics on the Greek mainland—Delphi, Isthmia, Nemea, Sicyon and Epidaurus—in addition to the games at Olympia described by Pausanias, and that they attracted these girls from Asia Minor to cross the Aegean year after year to compete in them. Yet our knowledge of these festivals rests on this one stone alone.[2]

There is one further piece of epigraphic evidence. An inscription is recorded from Patrae on the Gulf of Corinth:

'I, Nicophilus, erected this statue of Parian marble to my beloved sister Nicegora, victor in the girls' race.'

The stone has disappeared and so we have no means of judging its date, but there is no reason to doubt the authenticity of the transcript of the inscription. It does not reveal where the victory was achieved, whether at a meeting in Patrae or at one of the more famous festivals. As Nicophilus would almost certainly have mentioned the latter had it been possible to do so, the local meeting seems more probable.[3]

In the inscription of Hermesianax it is not clear whether Tryphosa won twice at the Pythian games or once at a festival at which Antigonus and Cleomachidas were joint agonothetes. She claims to have been the first girl ever to have won at the Pythian and at the next Isthmian games. In men's athletics this was not at all an unusual achievement, and Tryphosa's claim suggests that the women's festivals had not long been in existence.

If we go back to the fifth and fourth centuries B.C. the scene is different. Women already took part in athletics at Sparta, performing naked before men. The custom was attributed to Lycurgus, the traditional founder of the Spartan constitution, who prescribed physical training for women to fit them to become the mothers of Spartan soldiers. But it is clear from Plato's *Republic*, where he proposes to introduce similar training for the women of the Guardian class in his ideal state, that the practice was foreign to the Athenians. He expects his proposals to be met with ridicule. We have to remember that the Greek word for athletics was 'gymnastic', meaning literally 'exercises performed naked'. We have to remember, too, that the most important event for the Greeks was not running but wrestling, a sport in which, even if clothing is worn, it is liable to be torn off. Hence for the ordinary Greek the proposal of athletics or 'gymnastic' for women involved nakedness, and outside Sparta the Greeks did not care for the idea. It is noteworthy that when in the later *Laws* Plato repeats his demand for physical training for women he rejects wrestling and the pankration for them in favour of fencing—apparently women never boxed anywhere in Greece. Apart from this he limits their athletic programme to running, and suggests that for this girls over thirteen years of age should wear 'appropriate dress'.[4]

It is possible that in these proposals in the *Laws* Plato is reflecting an existing custom, and that while girls in the rest of Greece did not wrestle as in Sparta, they did run races. There is a lonely line of Sappho, preserved by a grammarian only because the girl's name in it shows an unusual form of the accusative case: 'Hero of Gyara, that fleet-footed maiden, was a pupil of mine.' Torn as the line is from its context, we cannot say whether or not Sappho is claiming to have trained Hero in running. The only thing of which we can be certain is that the word 'fleet-footed' enshrined a memorable quality in the girl. Sappho was not one to pepper her poems with elegant epithets for metrical convenience like a schoolboy trying to imitate Ovid. Whatever else the imaginative may deduce from the line, even the most sceptical must concede the minimal conclusion that in the island of Lesbos in the sixth century B.C. girls ran.[5]

The programme of races for girls proposed by Plato in the *Laws* is a severe one, with the stade, diaulos, dolichos, and one which he calls the 'ephippios'; as he puts it between the diaulos and the dolichos, it is probable that he means the half-mile, the race which at Nemea was called the 'hippios'. It is curious that while he suggests that for youths the distances should be two-thirds of those of the corresponding men's races and for boys one half, he proposes no concessions of any kind for women; he may have taken the shorter distances for granted. Except in Pausanias there is no mention of shorter courses for women, but in the stadium at Epidaurus, which we know from Dionysia's victory to have been the scene of women's races, there are pairs of small columns at regular intervals along the sides (Plate 30*a*). It has been conjectured that these may have marked the starting places for boys' and women's races. In Pausanias and in the inscription of Hermesianax there is no mention of any race longer than a stade, but clearly, with the evidence so inadequate, we cannot state dogmatically that Greek women never raced over a greater distance.

It would then be in accordance with the small evidence at our command to believe that for centuries Greek girls, dressed in tunics, ran races in school sports and local meetings, and that at the beginning of the Christian era more formal meetings were organized at some of the great centres of men's athletics. The evidence of Olympia suggests, and it is probable on other grounds, that while the stadia used were the same as the men's, the women's events were held at different festivals.

Wrestling for women seems never to have spread far from Sparta. It is true that there is a much-quoted statement in Athenaeus, who wrote at the beginning of the third century A.D., that in the island of Chios girls could be seen wrestling with boys, and there are whispers in Suetonius and Juvenal of the same thing happening in Italy in the first century, but these should probably be regarded as belonging to the scandal of café society rather than to the serious history of women's athletics. Athenaeus has one other remark which may be relevant. Into the middle of his descriptions of men athletes who were great eaters he injects the solitary statement: 'Heracleitus in *The Entertainer* says that a woman named Helen ate enormous quantities.' He does not say explicitly that Helen was an athlete, but in the context it can hardly be otherwise; we are left in tantalizing ignorance of the results of this imitation of male training methods.[6]

With the exception of the priestess of Demeter at Olympia, women were strictly excluded from men's athletic meetings. The statement in Pausanias, 'They do not prevent unmarried women from watching', is certainly one of the many corrupt passages in the text of that author. It flatly contradicts Pausanias's own statement that any woman caught at the games or even on the opposite side of the Alpheus on the relevant days would be thrown down the cliffs of Mount Typaeum. Suetonius tells us that when Nero established games on the Greek pattern in Rome he invited the Vestal Virgins to be present because of the precedent of the priestess of Demeter at Olympia. This gesture would have been meaningless if all virgins had been admitted at Olympia. The probable explanation of the corruption in Pausanias is that a scholiast's note referring to the girls' races has made its way into the text. There seems to have been some laxity over women spectators at the Greek games given in Italy by Roman emperors, but it did not go unchecked. We learn from Suetonius that on one occasion, as a wrestling match was about to begin, the emperor Augustus, who was particular about these matters, noticed that there were women present among the spectators. At once he stopped the proceedings, postponed the boxing to the next morning and let it be known that he would be displeased if women came to the theatre before the boxing was over.[7]

Inscriptions reveal that in imperial times women sometimes held the office of gymnasiarch in Greek cities, particularly in Asia Minor. Such officials are recorded in Pamphylia, Caria, the island of Paros and Athens. We might expect that these women would concern themselves chiefly with the physical training of girls, but so far as the inscriptions reveal anything of their activities in their official capacity there is nothing to distinguish them from men. The most informative inscription is from Aphrodisias; it records a decree in honour of Tata, daughter of Diodorus and wife of Attalus, life-long priestess of Hera and Mother of the City:

'When priestess of the Emperors for the second time, she twice made the oil flow like a river in the baths regardless of expense even for the greater part of the night.'

Almost identical words are used in another inscription of the same period to describe the bounty of a male gymnasiarch of Aphrodisias, Adrastus.[8]

The question of women's athletics in Greece in relation to men's is, of course, only a very small part of the much wider problem of the place of women and their activities in Greek life as a whole, the proper consideration of which is obviously far beyond the scope of this book. In so far as the little we know of women's athletics contributes at all to the broader study, it suggests that in the Hellenistic and Roman periods the position of women came more and more to resemble what it is in the Western world today. It is when we go back to the classic age of the sixth to the fourth centuries B.C. that the difficulty of the problem is felt most acutely. That the position of women in society at that time differed considerably from that to which we are accustomed is clear enough, but the difference has probably been exaggerated because of our ignorance of the facts. The reason for this ignorance is revealed by the famous dictum of Pericles in the *Funeral Speech* that the greatest glory of a woman is not to be talked about by men, either for praise or blame. Greek men certainly seem to have done their best to help women to achieve this glory. A Greek kept his public and his private life well apart. His women-folk belonged to his private life, and there appears to have been a convention that men did not talk about this side of their affairs in ordinary conversation, a convention like that which not long ago used to operate at undergraduate dining tables and in officers'

WOMEN IN GREEK ATHLETICS

messes. One result of this is that the Greek women whose names spring at once to mind, Helen, Clytemnestra, Electra, Antigone, all belong to the heroic age; if we start to draw up a similar list for the classical period we soon find ourselves running out of material.[9]

Thanks partly to the excellence of the climate, a Greek man spent a larger proportion of his life away from his home than we do. Apart from the work by which he earned his living, there was the political life of the city and his leisure time in palaestra and gymnasium. His women shared none of these with him. When a woman married, the home became the centre of her life. She went out less than a man, and less than most women do today. One particular custom contributed largely to this; it was the man of the house who did the daily shopping for food, or, if he was wealthy, he sent a slave to do it.

Our ignorance of the home life of the Greeks is increased by the fact that their literature, splendid and many-sided as it is, belonged almost wholly to the public part of their lives. Because contemporary women figure so little in this glittering literature it is sometimes assumed that they must have been dull, uneducated and illiterate creatures, a view for which there is no justification whatever.* There was one department of Greek literature which did touch on private life—lyric poetry. The remains of this which have come down to us are pitifully small, but it is noteworthy that some of the best of what has survived is the work of women, Anyte, Sappho, Erinna, Nossis and Moero. Equally significant is the fact that Greek men nowhere express surprise at these achievements, as they must surely have done had most women been illiterate. We must beware of attaching too much importance to a few famous descriptions of symposia or banquets, in which only men appear. It would be equally misleading to take descriptions of football club dinners or regimental reunions as representative of the everyday life of the modern male. If we wish to know what a Greek home was like, we must turn to the handful of works of literature which lift a corner of the curtain that covers it, Xenophon's *Oeconomicus*, a few scenes of comedy and one or two speeches in private lawsuits, or better still to the arts which do

* The summit of absurdity in this matter is reached in the suggestion that respectable Greek women were all so brainless that their husbands were driven to seek intelligent companionship with cultivated courtesans such as Pericles's Aspasia. It requires a singular degree of naïveté to suppose that these relaxations of statesmen are selected for their cultural or intellectual qualities.

concern themselves with private life, vase painting and funerary monuments. We shall then catch glimpses of a home life which, even if it occupied a smaller portion of a man's time than it does with us, did not differ fundamentally from that which we know today.

This, then, is the woman's existence into which we have to try to place the little that we know or can conjecture about girls' physical training in these centuries. It fits well enough; the exercises and races at school and possibly between school and marriage in those girls' societies of which we see something in the fragments of Sappho, and which were probably not as peculiar to the island of Lesbos as is often supposed; then came marriage, usually at about eighteen years of age, and it is clear that in every period of the Greek world, that put an end to all athletic activity. The mother-of-three winning an Olympic victory is not a Hellenic figure.

X CONCLUSION

THE study of Greek athletics is, of course, not very important in the great sum of things. If it has any value it is that it helps to fill in the total picture of the life of the Greek world of antiquity which forms a considerable part of our cultural ancestry, and so enables us to understand our own world better and to enjoy it more. We all accept that it is essential both for the individual and for society to achieve a proper balance of the different sides of life, to assign to the physical its due share in the interests and activities which go to make up a rounded whole. It is generally believed, and it is probably true, that some of the Greeks at some periods of their history came nearer to achieving this balance than any other people of whom we know. But the tendency to idealize the Greeks can easily be carried too far. Particularly in the nineteenth century, classical scholars were apt to write as if an Athenian of the age of Pericles could do little wrong compared with a man of any other time or place, and this rosy view is sometimes taken of the athletics of the Greeks as well as of the other departments of their life. This will not do. Even Gardiner could write of the modern discus: 'It is a thick clumsy object, the product of modern imagination, utterly unlike and inferior to the specimens which we have in our museums.' *De gustibus non est disputandum*, but today few people who have thrown a discus would dispute that the modern missile is far better adapted to its purpose than any ancient discus so far discovered, and that if it is well thrown its flight has real elegance.

Another misconception which we must remove from our minds is the unconscious belief, largely the result of the teaching of ancient history in our schools and universities, that the Greeks suddenly left off with the death of Alexander in 323 B.C., and the Romans then began. For the Greek man in the street there was no abrupt change in daily life either at the death of Alexander or when the Greek world became part of the Roman empire. Certainly when we are considering the place of sport organized as entertainment in the life of the community, the Roman imperial period of Greek society has more to say to us than the classical age of the sixth to the fourth centuries B.C. It has been one of the aims of this book to remove these two misapprehensions, to bring a more critical attitude to bear on the so-called 'golden age' of Greek athletics, and to broaden our view of the Greek world to include the later developments of Greek civilization when it had spread far beyond the bounds of Greece itself.

Most people would admit the value of sport and games to the mental and physical well-being of individual or society. Certainly no one who has ever played games in however undistinguished a capacity would doubt the former, and today politicians and industrialists are discovering the importance of well-organized sport for the avoidance of political and industrial unrest. Few people, on the other hand, can be entirely happy about some developments in the world of sport, which are often thought to be modern, though as we have seen they were as evident in Greece as they are today. It is easier to see that something is wrong than to suggest a remedy. No doubt all would agree that ideally there is one simple rule for all sport; during the few seconds, minutes or hours while the game is in progress, nothing should be so important to the participants as to win it by fair means; once the game is finished, nothing should matter less than who did win. At the less eminent levels of amateur sport this ideal is often attained today; perhaps there have been times when it was approached at the highest levels, in Britain in the nineteenth century and in Greece in the sixth and fifth centuries. But a considerable price was paid for this; both these periods were times of great social and economic inequality, and almost all the athletes and games players were members of a privileged wealthy class, in Greece a class supported by slave labour. Much as we may admire the sporting scene of those times, we must recognize that it is part of a state of affairs which no one would wish to recall. It might have been hoped that with the increase of wealth and its more equal distribution, amateurism in its best sense would have continued to dominate the

CONCLUSION 189

world of games, drawing its exponents from an ever-widening field. Unhappily, in the most popular games this has not happened; the reason is to be found in another development.

Not only are games pleasant to play but many of them afford great enjoyment to spectators; all the problems of modern sport spring from this simple fact. In logical language the essence of sport is the enjoyment of the players; the pleasure of spectators is an accident. We may laugh at the medieval schoolmen for their addiction to these distinctions, but in any department of life we disregard the difference between essence and accident at our peril. So long as a sport is true to itself, the only purpose of the organization of it is the enjoyment of the players; as soon as the interests of the spectators are allowed to become predominant, corruption has set in and the essence of the game has been lost. In other words, sport can be an entertainment for spectators, but what is primarily entertainment for spectators can never be sport in the true sense of the term.

We must beware of adopting a high moral attitude over this. The desire of spectators to be entertained by games is perfectly legitimate, and so is the willingness of professional players to satisfy the demand for sport at the highest levels of skill. To entertain by playing football is no more discreditable than to entertain by playing the piano. The difference is that to play the piano for money has no effect on music, whereas to play football for money changes the whole character of football. For when sport is treated in this way, when the accident becomes the essence, inevitably a change takes place in the sport itself, and its philosophy and highest ideals can no longer be maintained. It would be pitifully naïve to suggest to a professional player that the result of a game does not matter once the game has finished; his standard of living for years ahead often depends on it. If the second part of our definition of the true philosophy of sport has to go, the first half only too often goes with it. 'Nothing is so important as to win by fair means' becomes 'Nothing is so important as not to lose'. A perverted logic is brought to bear; it is taken for granted that to avoid defeat is a necessary step on the road to victory. The way to avoid defeat in a game is to take no risks. But games, like wars, are never won without taking risks. The professional player is only too ready to avoid risks of all kinds. He has a wife and family to think of. If he takes risks which result in defeat he is not likely to be popular with his fellows, deprived of the cash bonus for a win, or with his employers. So the stultifying aim, 'At all costs avoid losing', lays its deadly hand on much modern sport, and unfortunately it is not confined to the professional field. Boys naturally imitate their heroes, the highly skilled professional stars, and so the rot spreads. Worse follows. Nothing is more calculated to make a game boring to spectators than this negative policy of risking nothing. Gates fall off, and in an attempt to lure the crowds back the governing authorities of the game start tinkering with the rules. These efforts are always futile. The source of the trouble is not in the rules but in the attitude of mind of the players, and this is no more altered by fiddling with the rules than men are made moral by Act of Parliament. The result is more likely to be the spoiling of a fine game. Rugby football has already been ruined in this way, and cricket is in some danger of suffering the same fate.

Greek athletics underwent the same decline for the same reasons. We have seen the growth of professionalism in the Hellenistic and Roman periods, bringing with it the inevitable mental attitudes. In a race, of course, it is hardly possible for the will to win to be replaced by a will not to lose. It is true that sometimes in a long-distance race none of the competitors wants to set the pace because all happen to be runners of the kind who like to come from behind to win. For the instructed spectator this can produce an absorbing spectacle. Modern crowds, obsessed with the belief that the sole aim of athletics is to break records, often protest when a race is run in this way, but to the connoisseur of tactics a five-minute mile can be just as thrilling as a four-minute one. Given well-matched competitors, a race can hardly fail to be exciting, because there is no place for the negative aim of avoiding defeat. It was in the heavyweight events of the Greek athletic programme that the professional's desire to avoid taking risks and to escape defeat at all costs showed its deadly results. We have seen the great increase in the number of drawn matches in these events as time went on, and the situation reaches the height of absurdity in the ability of the boxer Melancomas to go on skipping round his opponent for two days without exchanging a blow. We might be surprised at the way in which huge crowds continued to flock to the stadia of the Greek world to witness these tedious exhibitions, were we not confronted by the same readiness of crowds today to conform with fashion by packing our own arenas for displays which are often equally meaningless. In one respect alone the Greeks were our superiors in this matter. So far as we know, they made no attempt to improve the state of affairs by tinkering with the rules. Greek conservatism and the prestige of Olympia prevailed. Olympia made no concessions, and so no one else could.

The Greek philosophy of sport and its place in the life of the individual and of the community does not appear to have differed much from our own. We recognize its value for both mental and physical health. Probably we lay more stress on the latter than did the Greeks, because modern industrialized society with its greater nervous strain needs more mental relaxation than was demanded by the daily life of the Greeks. But there are signs that the Greeks were well aware of the mental relief obtained by concentrating on the requirements of a game as a distraction from other preoccupations. The supreme example of this occurs in the crises of wartime, as anyone who has played games under such anxieties can testify. Greek history affords its parallel to the story of Sir Francis Drake and his game of bowls, but it is a story with a less happy ending for the central figure. In 391 B.C. Thibron of Sparta was in command of forces in contact with the enemy at Ephesus. One morning after breakfast he went outside his camp with a flute player named Thersander to practise throwing the discus. The enemy seized their opportunity, mounted a surprise attack and killed him.[1]

But naturally enough it is the contribution that athletics can make to a sense of physical well-being that Greek writers stress most. It is true that later medical writers complain that athletes were often lethargic and slow-moving, but we must remember that by 'athletes' these writers mean boxers and wrestlers rather than runners. The many palaestras and baths scattered among the cities of the Greek world show how widely the ordinary Greek felt the desire for the physical euphoria attained and maintained by regular exercise, and Greek literature of all ages produces an impression of a people who enjoyed a better balance of life in this respect than the members of any subsequent civilization. Here lies the chief superiority of Greek athleticism over our own.

The reason for this advantage is probably that physical training was better integrated into Greek education than it is into ours. The Greeks lived nearer to the time when the survival of an individual or of a community depended on physical fitness. Training for hunting or war is the earliest form of education. As civilization developed,

military training lost some of its most warlike aspects and among the
Greeks gave rise to athletics. To it were added the necessary elements
of intellectual education, first 'grammar' or the ability to read and
write, and then what the Greeks called 'music', which covered all
the subjects over which the Muses presided, among them poetry,
history, mathematics, astronomy, dancing and drama. But the
intellectual and the aesthetic remained an addition to the physical; at
no time was there any danger that they would oust 'gymnastic' from
the curriculum. Greek education was in origin and remained a well-
balanced combination of the three elements. The climate helped. For
a great part of the year the Greek is not driven indoors by the
weather, and much of the instruction in 'grammar' and 'music' was
given in a gymnasium or palaestra.

Two surviving inscriptions throw an interesting light on the
organization of Greek education in the Hellenistic period. One of
them, dating from 199 B.C., records a benefaction to found a school
at Miletus. It provided for four teachers and four paidotribai or
physical training instructors. The former were to be paid forty
drachmas a month, the latter thirty; the intellectual side of education
had by this time established this slight superiority, or more likely the
law of supply and demand dictated the salaries. An interesting
provision of the benefaction is that a paidotribes might take any of
his pupils to compete at a 'crown' athletic festival, but must provide
and pay a substitute to do his duties during his absence. A similar
endowment of a school on the island of Teos is recorded in another
inscription of about the same period. This provided three teachers
for boys and girls at salaries of 600, 550 and 500 drachmas a year, and
two paidotribai at 500 a year each. There was also provision for a
teacher of music (in our sense of the term) and for two visiting
specialists in military training. It was laid down that the demon-
stration lessons required of the teachers of 'grammar' before the
appointments were made should be given in the gymnasium.[2]

Such, then, was the framework of Greek education. Perhaps a
Greek boy, listening to Homer being read to him and his friends in
the palaestra and then studying geometry with the help of figures
drawn in the sand on which they had just been wrestling, was receiving an integrated preparation for life of a quality which could not be
matched anywhere in the world today.

The balance of our education is far less happy. Here we are the victims of history. After the collapse of the Roman empire of the west, such culture as survived was almost entirely in the hands of the Christian Church, and while Christianity may have theoretically rejected the Manichaean heresy, the Christian life in practice has always tended to be corrupted by the Manichaean distrust of the physical. The education given by the priests and monks of the middle ages was exclusively literary. The laity, who had to furnish the fighting men, kept alive military training, and there was often an unfortunate rift between the two, the scholar despising the soldier while the warrior showed an equal contempt for the clerk. This deplorable dichotomy has haunted our education ever since. It might have been expected that the Renaissance would transform the system, but although some Renaissance writers on education call attention to the importance of the care of the body as well as of the mind, the practical effect on the schools was small. There the chief result of the Renaissance was the addition of some arid Greek to the arid Latin already taught in them. Schoolboys, of course, played games, as they always will, but no one seriously thought of the games as part of the preparation for life. When Byron played cricket for Harrow against Eton the game was not numbered among the official activities of either school. There seems to be no reason to doubt the tradition which ascribes to Arnold of Rugby the credit for being the first headmaster to encourage games as a proper element in school life, and Arnold was a great Greek scholar. The assistant masters trained by him at Rugby, when they became heads of the new schools which were founded as a result of Victorian prosperity and enthusiasm for education, took the Rugby code of football rules with them and planted them in these new foundations. The other long-established schools followed suit in the encouragement of games, and physical activity became a normal part of the official life of all boarding schools.

Much has been written in recent years in criticism of British public schools, and no doubt some of it is justified, especially of those cut-price establishments which sprang up in imitation of the older and generally sounder foundations. What is not justifiable is the way in which the credit side of the account is often entirely disregarded by the critics. If we lay aside the social and political prejudices which envy produces, it is difficult to point to anything that has made a greater contribution to educational progress than the British public

N

schools of the nineteenth century. We are not concerned here with
their high intellectual standards. What is interesting from our point
of view is that now, for the first time since ancient Greece, physical
well-being attained through sport was regarded as an essential part
of a complete education. From these schools boys went to Oxford
and Cambridge, to the Services and into the countryside, and there
organized the games which they had come to look on as a necessary
part of the good life. The result was the great Victorian upsurge of
interest in sport, which has spread through all sections of society and
into all parts of the world. It might all have happened without
Arnold and his enthusiasm for the Greeks: it probably would, but in
a different way, and there are still some features in the world-wide
sporting scene which can be traced to their origin in the public
schools of nineteenth-century Britain and of which Britain can
legitimately be proud.

Naturally enough, in the successive stages of the spread of
secondary and higher education under state auspices during the
present century more and more attention has been devoted to the
physical side, and today the provision of facilities is often lavish. Yet
no one could be very well satisfied with the results. Admittedly,
difficulties are much greater in day schools than in boarding schools.*
Time is restricted; pressure on the time-table grows with an ever-
widening curriculum, and the claims of physical training are too
often felt to be the least urgent. If a boy's trigonometry is weak he is
excused physical training so that he can have extra coaching. There
are several reasons for this attitude. One is that too many teachers are
not interested; they have never themselves experienced the satisfaction of a body thoroughly fit through proper training, and they
simply do not know what is involved. An even more potent cause is
that the physical training periods produce no obvious results in the
General Certificate of Education, which is by no means a certificate
of general education. Yet nothing would be simpler than to include
in the Certificate a statement of a candidate's performance in physical
tests. It is far easier to evaluate a person's achievement against
absolute standards in the quarter mile or the long jump than it is, for
example, in English Literature. Yet at the present moment, when
almost any subject of study under the sun can be offered by a school
as a 'special' in the General Certificate, the only one connected in any

* Yet except in Sparta the Greeks had no boarding schools.

way with man's physical well-being appears to be cookery, disguised as domestic science.

It would be foolish to decry the great amount of fine work that is being done in the organization of school games. Indeed, the judicious spectator in search of real enjoyment will often prefer to watch a school match rather than an international. But schools cannot be expected to be exempt from the general attitudes and scales of value of the society of which they are part. In schools, as elsewhere, there is a tendency to concentrate on the potentially good performer and to neglect the mass who can never hope to excel. There is nothing new about this. In 257 B.C. a trainer in Egypt wrote to the wealthy father of one of his pupils: 'You wrote to me about Pyrrhus, instructing me, if I was certain that he would win victories, to train him, but if not, that I should avoid incurring useless expense and taking him away from his literary studies.' So today the games master or mistress is tempted to concentrate on those boys and girls who may hope to reach the school's first teams. At the other end of the scale wonderful work is done for the physically handicapped. What is needed is stimulus, encouragement and opportunity for the great mediocre mass, who will never be first-rate, but who at least are not in wheeled chairs. The object to be achieved is clear enough. Browning put it admirably:

> 'To man, propose this test—
> Thy body at its best,
> How far can that project thy soul on its lone way?'

A Greek of Plato's time would have understood and sympathized with this, though he would probably have phrased the last line rather differently. It does not matter very much what a man's physical potential is. What is important is that he should come as near to it as possible at all stages of his life. Here we feel that the Greeks did better than we are doing. It is sometimes forgotten that except for the elation of victory the reward for the ordinary performer is as great as for the outstanding. The boy who trains and practises hard to achieve five feet at the high jump will have as much satisfaction from a sense of physical well-being as the jumper who can exceed six feet. The Amateur Athletic Association used to acknowledge the validity of this point of view by awarding medals at their championships to all athletes who attained a set standard in an event, whether or not they won. A similar attempt in schools some forty years ago to encourage all pupils to aim at achieving quite mediocre standards in as many events as possible appears to have died out. The problem still awaits solution.[3]

The difficulties are, of course, far greater for us than they were for the Greeks. They had an education in which physical training was fundamental right from the beginning. We have inherited a system in which physical education has still to achieve its proper position against the pressure of many vested interests trying to keep it out. Moreover, the Greek concentration on the limited field of Olympic athletic events made uniformity of practice simple, whether in a single school or in the Greek world as a whole. We on the other hand enjoy a great variety of games and sports, all of them appealing to a body of enthusiasts. It is obviously impossible for any school to cater for all of them. Yet there is a basic mastery of physical skills and controls which is essential to enjoyment of all these sports and games as well as to general health, and it is legitimate to ask of any educational system that it shall ensure that all who pass through it shall have their ability in this sphere, no less than their intellectual capabilities, developed to the limit of their possibility.

The modern variety of sport is of immense value. It makes it possible for everyone to find a form of physical activity suited to his age, ability and temperament. It also enables us to divide the world of sport into two halves. In the more publicized section the spectators' gate-money is of paramount importance, and the whole organization of the entertainment is based on this, with some platitudinous lip-service paid to 'sport' in its proper significance. In these games even so-called 'amateurs' are apt to ask themselves how much they can make out of the game by their skill. This attitude goes very far down; it is whispered that in some areas even school football matches are not taken very seriously unless a talent scout from a professional club is rumoured to be present. But we may easily overlook the many games and sports which attract few paying spectators and in which the participants are consequently amateurs perforce. So far from hoping to make any money out of their game, they know that it will cost them a good deal. It is here that the sporting ideal is most nearly approached. For the most part the players are whole-hearted about the game while it is in progress; they are certainly light-hearted enough about it when it is over. The contrast with the first group is painful. There too often the matches are lukewarm affairs, half-heartedly conducted by hack performers. Yet the results are endlessly discussed in the Press and elsewhere with owlish solemnity.

And so we are back at the paradox that sport must be treated at the same time seriously and not seriously. Perhaps even when we are throwing ourselves whole-heartedly into a game we are deceiving ourselves about its momentary importance. If that is so, then surely, in view of its undeniable value to humanity, the deception is what Plato called a 'noble lie'. To resolve the paradox is no easy task. The young, the active participants in sport, cannot be expected to have the maturity of judgement necessary for so subtle a reconciliation of values. When we are old, and seeking to recapture something of youth by watching the games of today or recalling those of yesterday, our judgement is equally likely to be warped by emotion. The Greeks, as we have seen, found it no easier than we do to solve the problem. Yet the last word may perhaps be left with the painter of the two sides of a vase now in Würzburg (Plate 32). At least there was one Greek who did not take the victor with his crown and palm too seriously.

NOTES

THE abbreviations used for the names of authors, periodicals, etc., are those given in the Introduction to the latest edition of Liddell and Scott's *Greek Lexicon*, with the following additions:
AAW = *Athletics of the Ancient World*, by E. N. Gardiner.
IAG = *Iscrizioni Agonistiche Greche*, by L. Moretti.

CHAPTER I

1 D. Chrys. xxxiv. 12.

2 For the traditional dates of the first inclusion of each event in the programme of the Olympic Games, see Pausanias, V. viii. 5 ff. They are: Stade, 776 B.C.; Diaulos, 724 B.C.; Wrestling and Pentathlon, 708 B.C.; Boxing, 688 B.C.; Pankration, 648 B.C.; Boys' running and wrestling, 632 B.C.; Boys' boxing, 616 B.C.; Race in Armour, 520 B.C.; Boys' pankration, 200 B.C. A Boys' pentathlon was held in 628 B.C. but immediately discontinued. There is no evidence that the events were not held earlier. Philostratus (Gym. 12) adds the information that the dolichos was introduced in 720 B.C.

3 Unwritten rules; Aristotle (EN. 1180B) says that it would seem to make no difference whether the rules of athletics are written or unwritten.

4 D.L. V. 26.   Thanks at Delphi; Syll³. 275.   Protagoras etc.; Plato, Sph. 232E. D.L. IX. 55. Authors known to have written works on athletics, now lost, include Euphorion, Dicaearchus, Ctesicleides and Aristippus.   Philostratus; there appear to have been at least two writers of this name belonging to the Lemnian family; they are

indistinguishable in style, and it does not matter for our purpose which of them wrote the *Gymnastic*.

5 Javelin throwing; Lucian. Anach. 27. εἰς μῆκος ἁμιλλωνται.

6 A pair of bronze plates with pear-shaped holes in the middle, now in the British Museum, were once thought to be discuses. They are probably the weights of a 'bolas' lasso.

7 Delphi accounts; Inscr. Inv. 3862. See BCH xxiii p. 566 ff.

8 Even so sound a critic as Gardiner placed too much reliance on the vases. In his early writings he reconstructed techniques for Greek jumping and discus throwing, working into his sequences of movements the postures of the jumpers and throwers in every known vase painting. (JHS. XXIV. p. 189 ff. XXVII. p. 24 ff.). The results are comic. By the time he came to write AAW he had largely abandoned these theories.

9 For an attempt by a sculptor to depict athletes in action see Plate 14b. Other examples include the celebrated but much restored group of pankratiasts in the Uffizzi in Florence (for illustration see Gardiner AAW Fig. 199) and some small bronze groups in the British Museum (AAW 197, 198). There is evidence that boxers and pankratiasts were sometimes represented in an appropriate pose in their victor statues; e.g. D. Chrys. xxxi. 156. IAG 33 = Inscr. Ol. 174, ὧδε στάς of a boxer. IAG 36 = IG 2470, τοίας ἐκ προβολᾶς of a pankratiast. Dio Chrysostom (xxxvii. 10) also writes of statues of runners in motion, but none appears to have survived.

CHAPTER II

1 Hyacinthus; Philostr. Im. I. 24. 2. Ovid, Met. X. 162.   Acrisius; Paus. II. xvi. 2.   Phocus; Schol. Pind. Nem. V. 25.   Penelope; Paus. III. xii. 1. Strabo (XV. i. 66) records that among Indians brides were given as prizes for boxing. Atalanta; Apollod. III. 9. Endymion. Paus. V. 1. 4.

2 Androgeos; D.S. IV. 60. 4. Plato (Rep. V. 452c) says that gymnastic exercises originated with the Cretans.

3 Games in Elis; Hom. Il. xi. 698.   Later funeral games; Paus. III, xiv. 1. Hdt. VI. 38. Isoc. IX. 1. Demosth. LX. 13.   Brasidas; Thuc. V. xi.

Anyone who can bring himself to believe that athletic sports originated in fertility rites will find the various theories fully expounded in *Der Ursprung der Olympischem Spiele* by Ludwig Drees. (Stuttgart. 1962.)

4 Crowns; Pind. Ol. VII 77 ff. Isth. IV. 69. I. 65 and schol. ad loc. Thebes; Pind. Isth. IV. 69.   Oak crowns at Rome; IAG 71. Stat. Silv. V. 3. 231. Juv. VI. 387.   Prizes; Pind. Nem. IX. 51. X. 23. Isth. I. 19.   Pellene; Pind. Ol. IX. 98 and schol. Strab. VIII. vii. 5. Aristoph. Birds 1421 and schol.   Panathenaia; Pind. Nem. X. 35. AP. XIII. 19. Schol. Aristoph. Plut. 584. Syll³. 1055.   Others; AP. XIII. 8. IAG. 84.   Caria; Hdt. I. 144.

5 Plut. Solon, xxiii. 3.

6 Expense of competing; Pind. Isth. V. 57. Aeschines (Emb. 148) says that his father Atrometus was an athlete before he lost his money. Coroebus; Ath. IX. 382B.   Glaucus; Paus. VI. x. 1. Philostr. Gym. 20.   Fish porter; Ar. Rh. I. 7. 1365a.   Aegon; Theocr. IV. Philammon; Themist. Or. XXI. 249.   Argos chariot; Pap. Ox. 222.

7 Plato; D.L. III. 4.   Theogenes, Milo, Phaÿllus, Dorieus; see below ch. 5.   Antiochus; Xen. Hell. VII. i. 33.

8 Xen. Mem. III. v. 15, 18.

9 Alexander; Plut. Alex. iv. 5. Mor. 179d, 471e. Plato, Prot. 335e. Last words; Arr. Anab. VII. 26.   Perdiccas; Ath. XII 539C. Ael. VH. IX. 3.   India; Str. XV. i. 67. Philostr. Vit. Ap. Ty. II. 27. Jerusalem; 2 Mac. iv. 8 ff.

10 Amorgos; Syll³. 390.   Magnesia; Syll³. 557/62.

11 'Talent' games; IAG 69. 86.   Aphrodisias; CIG 2758.

12 Augustus; Suet. Aug. xxxix.   Nero; Suet. Ner. xii. 4. xl. 4. xlv. 1.   Domitian; Suet. Dom. iv. 4. v.

13 Rescript; P. Lond. 137. For a full treatment of these associations see C. A. Forbes, 'Ancient Athletic Guilds', *Class. Phil.* L. No. 4, Oct. 1955.

14 Herminus; P. Lond. 1178.

NOTES TO PAGES 36–63

15 Pliny Ep. X. 34, 35.

16 Xystus; B Mus. Inscr. 615. CIG 2811 B.   Aphrodisias; CIG 2758.

17 Pliny, Ep. X. 118, 119.   The theory on the meaning of 'eiselastic' put forward by L. Robert in Reg. LXXIV 149/150, no. 221 is untenable.

18 Oppian, Hal. I. 197.

19 Xenophanes and Euripides; ap. Ath. X. 413. Plato; Ll. 729d. Diogenes; D.L. VI passim. Many more examples of this critical attitude towards athletics are given by B. Biliński in *L'agonistica sportiva nella Grecia antica* (Rome; Signorelli. 1960).   Exaenetus; D.S. XIII. 82.   City walls; Plut. Mor. 639e. Suet. Ner. xxv. 1.   Maecenas; Dio Cass. LII. 30.   Boy wrestler; Philostr. Gym. 45.   Rescript of Diocletian; Codex Justin. X. 54. 1.

CHAPTER III

1 Tydeus; Hom. Il. iv. 387.

2 Phaeacian games; Od. VIII. 83 ff.

3 Funeral games; Il. XXIII. 262 ff.

4 Ap. Rhod. II. 1 ff.   Theocr. XXII 54 ff. This rendering of the fight in modern terms owes much to A. S. F. Gow's translation in his edition of Theocritus.

5 Virg. Aen. V. 104 ff.

6 Stat. Theb. VI. 255 ff.

7 Quint. Smyrn. IV. 171 ff.

8 Sponges; in an inscription recording expenditure on Games at Delos in 269 B.C., there is an item 'sponges' next to olive oil. BCH XIV. p. 389 ff.

9 Nonnus. XXXVII. 103 ff.

10 Milton, P.L. II. 528.

CHAPTER IV

1 Lucian, Anach. 27.

2 Thuc. I. 6.   Orrhippus; CIG 1050. Paus. I. xliv. 1.   Hippomenes; Isid. Orig. XVIII. 17. 2. The innovation of running naked is also ascribed by Julius Africanus to Acanthus of Sparta, who won the dolichos at Olympia in 720 B.C., the year in which Orrhippus won the stade.   Xen. Ages. I. 28.

3 Distance of dolichos; Schol. Soph. El. 687. Schol. Aristoph. Birds, 291. AP IX. 319. Philostr. Gym. 11.   Hippios; Bacchyl. IX. 25. Plut. Solon xxiii. 5. Eur. El. 826. Paus. VI. xvi. 4. IAG 44, 53 (=IG IV. 1136), 56.   Hermogenes; Paus. VI. xiii. 3.

4 Philostr. Gym. 32. Arist. IA 705a 17. Pr. 881b 6.

5 πόνος; Pind. Ol. V. 16, XI. 4. Nem. VI. 24. Isth. I. 42, V. 25, VI. 11. Xen. Hipparch. VIII 5. 6. Cyn. I. 7. Demosth. LXI. 23. Plato, Laches 182A. Soph. El. 945.

6 Heats; Paus. VI. xiii. 4. Gardiner (AAW p. 136) says: 'There were preliminary heats, apparently of four runners, only the winners running in the final.' This is hardly possible. Olympia would not have provided for twenty starters, if only four had been allowed to start in each heat. For heats in races see also Plato, Polit. 266c.   Aristoph. Ach. 488. Kn. 1161.   Soph. El. 711. Trumpeters; IAG 38. 70. 90. AP. VI. 350.   Ath. X. 415a. Herodorus, the hero of this anecdote, was periodonikes ten times in trumpeters' competitions in the fourth century B.C.

7 Spikes; Str. XI. v. 6. For a discussion of the whole problem of the start see my article, 'Stadia and starting grooves', in *Greece and Rome*, Second Series, Vol. VII. No. 1. March 1960.

8 Tension at start; Plut. Mor. 224f.   Themistocles; Hdt. VIII. 59.   'Beat the gun'; προεκπηδᾶν, προανίστασθαι. Strattis ap. Pollux III. 3.   ὕσπληξ; Aristoph. Lys. 1000. AP. VI. 259. Lucian, Cat. 4.   Fall; Plut. Mor. 732d.   Noise; AP. XI. 86.

9 Gardiner. AAW. p. 137.

10 Plato, Phaedr. 254e. ὥσπερ ἀπὸ ὕσπληγος ἀναπεσών.

11 Inscr. Delos 1400. 1409.

12 Epidaurus; Syll³. 1075 = IG IV. 1508.

13 καμπτήρ of life; Eur. Hipp. 87. El. 955. Herodas Fr. XII.   Base of
    post; Homer's turning post for the chariot race is a dead tree propped
    up by white stones on each side (Il. xxiii. 327). A Lucanian painting of
    a chariot race, now in the museum at Paestum, shows a base of the
    same kind.   Chariot crashes at turn; e.g. Call. Aet. Fr. 195.

14 Gift of Eudoxus; Syll³. 419. An epigram in the Anthology (AP. VI.
    259) in which a boy victor claims to have defeated nine other runners
    at Isthmia and Nemea suggests that it may have become the general
    practice in the diaulos also to use only the right half of the starting
    line.

15 Aesch. Ag. 788. μήθ'ὑπεράρας μήθ' ὑποκάμψας καιρὸν χάριτος; The
    metaphor is generally assumed to be from javelin throwing, but
    ὑποκάμψας is completely unsuited to this. This 'cutting in' may be
    the explanation of ὑποθεῖν οὐκ ἐῶ in Aristoph. Kn. 1162.

16 Greek terms; διώκειν; ἐπιδιώκειν, προδοσία Poll. III 3.   'Respice
    finem'; Eur. El. 954. Plut. Phil. 18. 2. id. Demetr. 19. 2. D.L. V. 20.
    Soph. El. 735.   Motion; Arist. N.E. X. 1174a.   'Boys' dolichos';
    Lucian, Hist. Conser. 30.

17 Oppian. Hal. IV. 101 ff.

18 Pind. Ol. VIII. 67. Pyth. VIII. 84.   Eutychides; AP. XI. 208.   Er-
    asistratus; AP. XI. 83.   Charmus; AP. XI. 82.   Marcus; AP.
    XI. 85.

19 Distance of armed race; Aristoph. Birds 291. Paus. II. xi. 8. Poll. III.
    6. Armour worn; Paus. VI. x. 4. Pausanias (V. xii. 8) says that twenty-
    five shields for the race were kept at Olympia, a curious contrast to the
    ten at Delphi. Plato (Lg. 833a) would have all races run in armour.

20 Some examples of combinations from IAG.; 10, Aeschylus, stade and
    armed. 44, Demetrius, stade, dolichos, hippios. 45, An Achaean runner,
    stade, diaulos, armed. 50, Onasiteles, stade, diaulos, armed, dolichos,

torch. 53, Socrates of Epidaurus, hippios, diaulos, armed. 56, Draconto-
menes, diaulos, hippios, dolichos. 60, A Coan, stade, pentathlon,
pankration. 61, Another Coan, stade, diaulos, pentathlon.   Leonidas; Paus. VI. xiii. 4.   Polites; Paus. VI. xiii. 3.   Metrobius;
IAG 66 = CIG 2682.

21 Eleutheria; Paus. IX. ii. 6. Plut. Aristeid. xxi. i. Str. IX. ii. 31. Philostr.
Gym. 8.

22 Torch; Aristoph. Frogs 129 ff., 1087 ff. Wasps 1204. Fr. 442. Inscr. Delos
1950, 1956 (= IAG 57), 1958 etc. Syll³. 667, 671, 958, 1068.   On
horseback; Plato Rep. I. 328a. cf. Coin of Tarentum C3 B.C. in
Gardiner AAW Pl. 35(i).   Dedication of torch; AP. VI. 100.

23 Marathon; Hdt. VI. 105. Plut. Mor. 347c.   Lucian (Laps. 3.)
attributes both parts of the story to Pheidippides.

24 For the pentathlon see G. E. Bean, 'Victory in the Pentathlon', AJA
LX (1956) p. 361, where earlier discussions are excellently summarized.
An even fuller treatment is in Zum Pentathlon der Antike by J.
Ebert (Berlin, 1963), which reached me too late for more than a passing
reference.   Second rate; Pl. Amat. 135e.   All-rounder; D.L.
IX. 37.   Origin; Philostr. Gym. 3.   Second prizes; Syll³. 958,
1055. CIG 2360.   Time; in 472 B.C. the pentathlon went on
too long and upset the programme at Olympia; Paus. V. ix. 3.

25 Plut. Mor. 738a, τοῖς τρισὶν ὥσπερ οἱ πένταθλοι νικᾷ (sc. τὸ ἄλφα).
Schol. Aristeid. Panath. III. 339d.   πρώτῃ τρειάδι; IAG 82 = IGR
1761. Poll. III. 6 s.v. ἀποτρίαξαι. Schol. Aesch. Ag. 171 s.v. τριακτήρ.
Pindar's statement (Nem. VII. 72) that the javelin 'released neck and
muscle from the sweat of wrestling' bears out this view of how the
pentathlon was decided.

26 Tisamenus; Hdt. IX. 33. Paus. III. xi. 6.   Automedes; Bacchyl.
VIII. 27.   Ephesian; IAG 75 = Ephesos II No. 72.

27 Xen. Hell. VII. iv. 29.

28 Inscription from Rhodes published by Carratelli in Annuario 30/32
(1952/4) p. 289 No. 65. See article by Moretti in Rivista di Filologia
(1956) p. 55, and Bean op. cit.   Discuses; Paus. VI. xix. 4.

29 For jump and discus see my article 'An Olympic Epigram; the athletic
feats of Phaÿllus' in Greece and Rome, Second Series, Vol. VII. No. 1,
March 1960.   Weights; Philostr. Gym. 55. Lucian, Anach. 27.

Arist. IA. 705a 17. Pausanias (V. xxvi. 3.) records at Olympia a statue of an allegorical figure carrying halteres, which he describes thus: 'They are semi-circular or rather semi-elliptical, made so that the fingers fit through them as they do through the handles of a shield'. The statue belongs to the fifth century B.C. As Pausanias finds it worth while to describe the shape, it was obviously obsolete in his day. An Attic red-figured column crater in the Villa Giulia at Rome depicts two jumpers, one with weights of the pattern described by Pausanias, the other with the telephone hand-piece shape. This suggests that the change in fashion occurred during the fifth century B.C. (CVA Italy, Rome, Villa Giulia, II. Inv. 1044). For some modern experiments in jumping with weights, see E. Lindner, *Die Benutznung der Halteren im Weitsprung der Antike*, in Archaeol. Anzeiger, 1956, p. 129.

30 Phaÿllus; see p. 133 ff.   Chionis; Johann. Antioch. Fr. 1. 27.

31 Flute; Philostr. Gym. 55. Paus. V. vii. 10, V. xvii. 10, VI. xiv. 10.

32 Themistius; ed. Schenkl in Comm. in Arist. Graeca, V. pt. ii. p. 26.   βατήρ; Seleuchus and Symmachus in Lexica Segueriana, Cod. Coislinianus 345. Bekker, Anec. 224.   Righthandedness; Plato. Lg. 794d.

33 βατήρ = τέλος, τέρμα. Poll. III. 3. As most Greek races started and finished at the same line, 'finishing line' in Pollux is identical with 'starting line'.

34 Philostr. Gym. 55.   Rhodian Inscr.; see note 28 above.

35 Lucian, Anach. 4.

36 Medical writers; e.g. Galen, De San. Tu. viii. l., xi. 3.

37 Aristoph. Clouds 144.

38 Hom. Il. VII. 264. Lucian, Anach. 32.

39 Bronze discus; Lucian, Anach. 27.   Stone; Pind. Ol. X. 72 and schol. ad loc., Isth. I. 25.   Shape; Plut. Mor. 288b. Moon at half-full is φακοειδὲς καὶ δισκοειδές. See also Empedocles ap. D.L. VIII. 77. The museum at Cagliari has an ingot of almost exactly the same size as a modern discus.

40 For list of known discuses see Gardiner AAW p. 156.   Paus. I xxxv. 5.

41 Whirling; Il. xxiii. 840.   Myron's cow; AP. IX. 713–742.

42 Philostr. Im. I. 24. 2. For a discussion of this passage see my note in CR New Series, vol. XI, No. 1, March 1961.

43 Stat. Theb. VI. 711.

44 Philostr. Her. II. 3.

45 For a discussion of the problems see my article, 'Greek Javelin Throwing', in *Greece and Rome*, Second Series, Vol. X, No. 1, March 1963.   Throwing at a mark; Antiphon's Second Tetralogy deals with the hypothetical case of a boy accidentally killed in a gymnasium while picking up javelins thrown at a mark.   Throwing for distance; Hom. Od. viii. 229, Il. xxiii. 637. Lucian, Anach. 27.

46 Elder; Bacchyl. VIII. 33.   Cornel; Xen. Cyr. VII. i. 2. Str. XII. vii. 3.   Bronze-cheeked; Pind. Pyth. I. 43. Nem. VII. 70.   Ferrules; for illustrations see E. Curtius, *Die Ausgrabungen zu Olympia* (Berlin, 1875–81), Vol. IV. Nos. 1061, 1062. Two vases in the British Museum, F84 and F169, clearly show athletic javelins with points.

47 Gardiner. JHS XXVII (1907) p. 258.

48 Stat. Theb. VI. 353.   Olbia inscr.; IAG 32.   Strabo XIV. i. 23.

49 Kicking; Lucian, Anach. 3, where ὀρθοστάδην suggests boxing rather than the pankration. Philostr. Gym. 11, 34. Eusebius, Praep. Ev.V. 34. Herodas (Mime I) says that Gryllus won five prizes as a boxer οὐδὲ κάρφος ἐκ τῆς γῆς κινέων. It is not clear whether this means that he did not kick, or that he did not find it necessary to use the normal footwork of a boxer.   Grappling; Plut. Mor. 638f.   Onomastus; Philostr. Gym. 12.   Pythagoras; D.L. VIII. 47.

50 Boxing gloves; ἱμάντες Paus. VIII. xl. 3. Philostr. Gym. 10. Plut. Mor. 80b. σφαῖραι Plato, Lg. VIII. 830a, 830e. Plut. Mor. 825e. Pausanias (VI. xxiii. 4) uses ἱμάντων τῶν μαλακωτέρων in this sense. Philetaerus (Edmunds, Gr. Com. Fr. 423) preserves another word for boxing gloves, πυξίδας οὐκ ἔλεγον ἀλλ' ἱμάντας. (πυξίς in this sense is not in LSJ).   μύρμηκες; Schol. Pind. Nem. V. 49. Poll. III. 5. AP II. 225.   Sheepskin; κωδία Philostr. Her. II. 6.   Ear-guards; ἀμφωτίδες Plut. Mor. 38b, 706c.   Cauliflower ears; Plato, Gorg.

515e, Prot. 342b. D.L. V. 67. Philostr. Her. III. 3.   Punch-ball;
κώρυκος Lucian, Lex. 5. Philostr. Gym. 57. Dionysius Chalcus ap.
Ath. 668a.   Shadow-boxing; Paus. VI. x. 3. Plut. Mor. 130e.
D. Chrys. XXXII. 44.   Onasander (Strat. X. 4) advocates the use of
ἱμάντες by soldiers in mock battles.

51 Melancomas; D. Chrys. XXVIII.   Cleomedes; Paus. VI. ix.
6.   Damoxenus; Paus. VIII. xl. 3.

52 Cicero, Ep. Att. XIII. 21.

53 Downward blow; e.g. Ap. Rhod. II. 90. Theocr. XXII. 104. Stat.
Theb. VI. 776.

54 Olympicus; AP. XI. 75, 76.   Apis; AP. XI. 80.   Cleombrotus;
AP. XI. 79.

55 Oppian, Cyn. IV. 200.

56 Plut. Mor. 638d.   Plato, Symp. 217c.

57 Three falls; Plato, Euthd. 277c, Phdr. 256b. Aesch. Eu. 592 and schol. ad
loc. D. Chrys. XIII. 25.   AP. XI. 316 suggests that victory was by the
best of five falls.   Fair fall; Aesch. Suppl. 91, πίπτει δ᾽ἀσφαλὲς οὐδ᾽
ἐπὶ νώτῳ.   Powdering; AP. XVI. 25 (This epigram makes clear
the distinction between ψάμμος, the sand of the stadium, and κόνις,
the wrestler's body-powder). Plut. Mor. 52b.   Aristoph. Kn.
572. Philippus; AP. XVI. 25.

58 Lucian, Anach. 2.   Aristoph. Kn. 490.

59 Technical terms with possible meanings: ἀγκυρίζειν, hook opponent's
leg. Eupolis, Fr. 262. λαβὴν παρέχειν, afford opponent a hold. Pl. Rep.
544. Plut. Alcib. vii. 2. μέσον λαμβάνειν, grasp round waist. Aristoph.
Cl. 1047, Eccl. 260. ἐξαγκωνίζειν, thrust with elbow. Aristoph. Eccl.
259. ὑποσκελίζειν, sweep opponent's legs from under him. Pl.
Euthyd. 278b. Lucian, Char. 8. τραχηλίζειν, grasp by the neck. Pl.
Erast. 132c. Plut. Ant. 33. λυγίζεσθαι, twist. Lucian, Lex. 5. πλέκειν,
σύμπλεκειν, Come to close quarters. Poll. III. 4. ἐρείδειν, Aesch. Ag.
63 or ἀντερείδειν τὸν ὦμον, thrust the shoulder under opponent.
Philostr. Vit. Soph. 526. Poll. III. 4. ἕδραν στρέφειν, change one's
stance. Theophr. Char. XXVII. 14. cf. Theocr. XXIV. 111. ἄφη, grip.

D.H. Dem. 18. (Later) powder. Epict. III. 15. 4. ἀλέξημα, evasive move. Plut. Mor. 977f. ἀγκαλίζεσθαι, get opponent's head in crook of elbow, 'in chancery'. Plut. Mor. 638f. ἐμβολή, παρεμβολή, thrusting leg between or alongside opponent's. σύστασις, closing. παράθεσις, placing body alongside opponent's. All in Plut. Mor. 638f. προδεικνύειν καὶ σκιάζειν, feint. Onas. Strat. xlii. 6. In Plato, Euthyd. VII, 277c, βαπτιζόμενον is obviously a continuation of the preceding metaphor from wrestling, and indicates the position of a wrestler on the ground with his opponent on top of him. ἀκροχειρισμός; Lucian, Lex. 5. Ar. N.E. 1111a. Paus. VI. iv. 3. Suidas s.v. ἀκροχειρίζεσθαι contrasted with προσπαλαίειν; Plato, Alcib I. 107e.

60 Pap. Ox. 466. Text in Jüthner's edition of Philostr. Gym. p. 26.

61 Two rings; Philostr. Gym. 53. Lucian, Anach. 1. Plut. Mor. 638c, 790f. Pliny N.H. XXVIII. 13. XXXV. 2 and 47. Sen. Ep. LVII. 1. Mart. XIV. 50.   Eur. Bacch. 455.

62 Telemachus; IAG 29 = Syll³. 274.

63 Pindar's pankratiasts; Nem. II, III, V. Isth. IV, V, VI, VII, VIII.   M. Aur. XI. 2.

64 'Halter'; Philostr. Her. II. 6.

65 Kicking in pankration; Theocr. XXII. 66. Epict. III. xiv. 14 (where a pankratiast prides himself on his kicking).   Biting; Lucian, Dem. 49.   Gouging; Epict. III. xv. 4. Aristoph. Birds 442.

66 Sostratus; Paus. VI. iv. 2. IAG 25.

67 Paus. VIII. xI. 1. Philostr. Im. II. 6.

68 Aristoph. Wasps, 1191, 1382. 'Iron chest' is Rogers' brave attempt to reproduce a play on two meanings of the Greek word θώραξ, 'chest' and 'bronze breastplate'.   Prizes at Aphrodisias; see above p. 42.   Melancomas; see above p. 99.

CHAPTER V

1 Milo; chief authorities. Paus. VI. xiv. 5. D.S. IV. 24. 7, XII. 9. Philostr. Ap. Ty. IV. 28. Ar. NE. 1106b. Ath. X. 412f. AP. XI. 316,

XVI. 24. Lucian, Charon 8. Hdt. III. 137. D.L. VIII. 39. Str. VI. 1. 12.
Simon. Fr. 185. Ael. V.H. II. 24, IV. 17, XII. 22. Aul. Gell. XV.
16.   Seven Crotoniates; Str. VI. 1. 12.   Philippus; Hdt. V. 47.

2 Pythagoras' interest in athletics; Lucian, Somn. 8. See also below, p.
172. The athletic metaphor in the anonymous 'Hymn of Pythagoras'
(Collectanea Alexandrina, ed. J. U. Powell) may be significant; καί
μοι πρῶτον μὲν ψυχά/ὀρθὰν βαίνοι πρὸς γραμμάν/ἀψευδοῦς γλώσσης
ῥύμῃ.   Democedes; Hdt. III. 125 ff.

3 Phaÿllus; chief authorities. Hdt. VIII. 47. IAG 11 = IG I². 655 = Tod
21. Plu. Alex. 34. Paus. X. ix. 2. Aristoph. Ach. 214, Wasps 1206.

4 The ancient evidence for Theogenes is excellently set out in J. Pouilloux, Recherches sur l'histoire et les cultes de Thasos, (Paris. 1954), Vol. I,
Ch. 2, but Pouilloux goes beyond the evidence in some of his interpretation. The chief sources are: IAG 21 = Syll.³ 36. Paus. VI. vi. 5, VI.
xi. 4. Lucian, Deor. Conc. 12. Euseb. Praep. Ev. V. 34. 6. D. Chrys.
XXXI. 95. Plut. Mor. 811. Ath. X. 4121 Inscr. Thasos Inv. 645, 718,
722, 1033.   Euthymus; Paus. VI. vi. 4. Str. VI. i. 5. Pliny NH. VII.
152. Ael. V.H. VIII. 18. IAG 13 = Inscr. Ol. 144. See also Gianelli,
Culti e miti della Magna Grecia (Milan, 1928).

5 Cleomedes; Paus. VI. ix. 6. Plut. Rom. 28.

6 Polydamas; Paus. VI. v. 1, VII. xxvii. 6. Plato, Rep. I. 338c and schol.
ad loc. D.S. IX. 15. Lucian, Hist. Conscr. 35, Herod. 8, Pr. Im. 19,
Conc. Deor. 12. D. Chrys. LXXVII. 20. Philostr. Gym. 22.

7 Chaeron; Paus. VII. xxvii. 7. Ath. XI. 509b.

8 Eubatas; Paus. VI. viii. 3. (where name appears as Eubotas). D.S.
XIII. 68. Ael. V.H. X. 2. Xen. Hell. I. 2. 1.   Cleitomachus; Paus.
VI. xv. 3. Ael. V.H. III. 30. Plut. Rom. 28. Polyb. XXVII. 7. AP. IX.
588. Plut. Mor. 710d.

9 Dioxippus; D.S. XVII. 100. 2. Ael. V.H. XII. 58. Ath. VI. 251a.
Hypereides, Pap. Ox. Vol. XIII. 1607. In Minor Attic Orators (Loeb)
Vol. II. p. 397.

10 Diagoras and family; Pind. Ol. VII and schol. Paus. VI. vii. 2. Ael
V.H. X. 1. Cic. Tusc. I. 46. 111. D.S. XIII. 45. Thuc. III. 8. Xen. Hell.
o

I. 1. D. Chrys. XXXI. 126. AP. XIII. 11. Possibly IAG 23 = Syll³.
82 = CIG 1715.

11 Xenophon; Pind. Ol. XIII and schol. Fr. 122 (107). Ap. Athen. xiii,
573E. D.S. XI. 70. Paux. IV. xxiv. 5. Ath. XIII. 573f.

12 Amesinas; Afric. sub ann.   Philostr. Gym. 43.   Echeclous; Aul.
Gell. V. 9. Val. Max. I. 8. 4.   Eurydamas; Ael. V.H. X. 19.

13 Demetrius; IAG 86. M. R. E. Gough in *Anatolian Studies* 2 (1952)
p. 127.

14 Milesian runner; IAG 59. For records in Greek athletics see M. N. Tod,
'Greek record-keeping and record-breaking', CQ xliii (1949).

15 Asclepiades; IAG 79 = IG XIV. 1102 = IGR I. 153.

16 Phil. iv. 1.   1. Thess. ii. 19.

17 1 Cor. ix. 24 ff.   Phil. iii. 13.   2 Tim. ii. 5.   1 Tim. iv. 7.

18 Epictetus; e.g. I. 6. 26, 18. 21. II. 8. 12, 18. 22, III. 12. 2, 12. 10, 15. 4,
20. 10, 21. 3, 22. 51, 24. 52, 25. 2, 25. 4, IV. 1. 106, 4. 11, 4. 24, 4. 30,
9. 15.   2 Tim. iv. 7.

19 δέρειν = to flog; Aristoph. Clouds 442, Wasps 485.   ὑπωπιάζω;
Luke xviii. 5.

20 Gal. ii. 2.   Phil. ii. 16.   Eph. vi. 12.

21 Col. ii. 18. καταβραβεύω. The word occurs in witnesses' evidence cited
in Demosthenes, In Meidiam 93, and in a scholium on Hom. Il. I. 399.
παραβραβεύω is found in the same sense in Africanus sub ann. A.D. 149,
and in Plutarch and Polybius.

22 Letter of Claudius; P. Lond. 1912. Text in Select Papyri, Vol. II (Loeb)
No. 212. p. 86.   Catacombs; H. J. Leon, *Jews of Ancient Rome*
(Philadelphia, 1960) p. 203, Fig. 14.   For the position of Jews in
Hellenistic society see V. Tcherikover, *Hellenistic Civilization and the
Jews* (Philadelphia, 1961).

23 Tarsus; Str. XIV. v. 12 ff.   Festivals; IAG 78, 81, 85 = CIG
4472 = IGR III. 1012. CIG 2810. B. Mus. Inscr. 611.   Repairs to
stadium; CIG 4437.   2 Cor. xi. 23.

24 Socrates at Isthmia; Plato, Crito 52d. Most MSS of Plato omit this, but see Ath. V. 216b.

25 Lystra; Acts, xiv. 12.   Finish the course; Acts xx. 24. 2 Tim. iv. 7.

CHAPTER VI

1 Suet. Aug. xliii. 1.

2 Eudemus; Syll³. 288.   Nicaea; Pliny, Ep. X. 39, 40.   Aegina; Paus. II. xxix. 11.   Eleusis; Syll³. 970.

3 Athens. Lycurgus; Syll³. 326. Heraclitus; Syll³. 401. Herodes; Paus. I. xix. 6. Philostr. Vit. Soph. 550.   Delphi; Paus. X. xxxii. 1. Philostr. Vit. Soph. 551.   Exedra; Philostr. Vit. Soph. 551. Lucian, Peregr. 19.

4 Isthmia; Paus. II. i. 7.

5 The recent excavations at Olympia are conveniently summarized by Emil Kunze in *Neue Ausgrabungen in Olympia* (Berlin).   Tomb; Schol. Pind. Ol. I. 149.

6 Epict. I. vi. 26.   Ael. V.H. XIV. 18.

7 Plut. Dion xxiii. 3. In his life of Philopoemen (xi. 1), Plutarch mentions a military tattoo given in the stadium at Nemea in 205 B.C.

8 St. Paul; 1 Cor. xv. 32. Acts xix. 24.   Delphi Inscr.; Schwyzer DGE 321. L. H. Jeffrey, *Local scripts of Archaic Greece* 104.

9 D. Chrys. VII. 38.

10 Thales; D.L. I. 39. AP. VII. 85.   Shade; Vitruv. V. 11. Syll³. 463. D. Chrys. XXXII. 20. Philostr. Ap. Ty. IV. 3. Anticleides ap. Ath. XIII. 609d. Plut. Mor. 148b. D.L. III. 7. Eupolis Fr. 32.   Academia; Plut. Cim. xiii. 8. Aristoph. Clouds 1002 ff.

11 Palaestras for old; Aristoph. Fr. 715.   Gymnasium; Vitruv. V. 11.

12 Aristoph. Clouds 1043 ff.   Plut. Mor. 131b.

o*

13 Shower-bath; Plato, Rep. I. 344d. Theophr. Char. IX. 8. Pliny NH. XXVIII. 13. Ap. Rhod. IV. 655. Str. V. ii. 6.

14 Vice; Aristoph. Cl. 417, 991, Peace 762, Wasps 1025. Lucian, Nav. 2. P. Flor. 332 (Loeb Sel. Pap. I. p. 309). Pictures etc.; Paus. II. x. 7, VI. vi. 3, X. xxxvi. 9. D.L. IX. 62. Xen. Anab. VII. viii. 1. Pliny NH. XXXV. 2. Corinna; Paus. IX. xxii. 3. Homer; P. Ox. 1025 (Loeb Sel. Pap. I. p. 438). Subscriptions; B. Mus. Inscr. 969. BSA Annual 1961, p. 18, No. 46. Polycrates; Ath. XIII. 602d. Epaminondas; Plut. Mor. 594c. Aratus; Plut. Ar. vi. 4.

15 Polyneices; Eur. Phoen. 368. Generals; Ath. XII. 539c. Ael. V.H. IX. 3. Archimedes; Ath. V. 207d. Burial; MAMA VIII. 406. IGR IV. 1302/10 (Cyme) SGDI 3502/9 (Cnidos).

16 Talk; Plato, Charm. 153a, Theaet. 144c. Plut. Mor. 513c, 749c. Academia; D.L. III. 7. Lyceum; D.L. V. 2. Cynics; D.L. VI. 13. Themistocles; Plut. Them. i. 2.

CHAPTER VII

1 Hellanodikai; Paus. V. ix. 4. Philostr. Ap. Ty. III. 30. Athens; (Arist.) Ath. Pol. 62. 2. At Athens in the fifth century the expenses of the Panathenaea were partly met from the funds of the Delian League. Syll³. 94. 1. 57. Gymnasiarch; Isques, Men. 42, Philost. 60, Apoll. 36.

2 τὸ θέατρον τὸ ἐπὶ τοῦ σταδίου; Syll³. 970. cf. θέατρον παναθηναικόν, Syll³. 288. For a discussion of entrance money in theatres see A. W. Pickard-Cambridge, *The Dramatic Festivals of Athens*, Ch. VI, 3. p. 270 ff., with illustrations of entrance tickets. Theoric fund; (Arist.) Ath. Pol. 43. 1.

3 Nicogenes; Syll³. 667. Eurycleides; Syll³. 497. D. Chrys. LXVI. 11.

4 Money games becoming sacred; IAG 84 = IGR IV. 1519 has five examples νῦν ἱερός. Syll³. 557. Prize at Side; CIG 4352. Xen. Anab. I. ii. 10. στλεγγίδες χρυσαῖ. στλεγγίς in an athletic context usually means 'strigil'; another meaning is 'headdress'. Coressus; Syll³. 958.

5 Asclepiaea; Schol. Pind. Nem. III. 145.

6 Naples; Inscr. Ol. 56.   ἀγένειοι at Isthmia; IAG 22 = IG II. 1301.   Plato, Lg. VIII. 833c.   Olympic boys; IAG 61. Pythian boys; IAG 60, 75. SEG III. 335. Isthmian; IAG 60, 61. SEG III. 335.   Cos; IAG 61.   Three classes of boys; Syll³. 667. Of youths; Syll³. 959.   IAG 68 of the second century A.D. has παῖδες ᾿Ακτιακοί.

7 Olympic truce; Isoc. IV (Paneg.) 43. Plut. Lycurg. I. 1. Aeschin. Emb. 12. Thuc. V. 49. Pausanias (V. xx. 1.) records that the truce was inscribed on the discus of Iphitus, a legendary founder of the Olympic festival; the discus was preserved in the temple of Hera. Other truces; Pythian; Plut. Mor. 413d. Isthmian; Paus. V. ii. 1. Nemean; Plut. Arat. xxviii. 3. Eleusinian; Aeschin. Emb. 133.

8 Clearing stadium; Ath. XII. 518d. Theocr. IV. 10.   Delos; BCH XIV. p. 389 ff. Delphi; BCH XXIII. p. 566. Inv. 3862.   Athlete with basket; Gardiner AAW Fig. 56. CVA Brussels III. l. c.

9 Rhodians; D. Chrys. XXXI. 163.   Tarsus; D. Chrys. XXXIII. 36.   Alexandria; D. Chrys. XXXII. 74.   Prusa; D. Chrys. XL. 29.   Plut. Mor. 593d. συμπαραθέουσιν.   Nicharchus; AP. XI. 82.   ῥαβδοῦχοι; Plato, Prot. 338a.

10 Parium; Syll³. 596.   Priene; Inscr. Priene. No. 111. line 176.

11 Corinth; see L. Robert in Hellenica, I. vii and O. Broneer in Hesperia VIII (1939) p. 187. Oil; Syll³. 691, 714, 717. Aphrodisias; MAMA VIII. 484.   Daphne; Ath. 210f.   Sacred olives μορίαι; (Arist.) Ath. Pol. 60. 1.   Lucian, Anach. 9. Lysias VII.   Aegina; D.L. V. 71.

12 Plato; Ael. V.H. IV. 9.   Isthmia; D. Chrys. VIII. 9.   Transport; Lucian, Peregr. 35.

13 Order of events at Olympia; Paus. V. ix. 3, VI. xiii. 3, VI. xv. 5.

14 Dawn; D. Chrys. XXVII. 5. ἐξ ἑωθινοῦ.   Plato, Lg. 833a.

15 For a discussion of draws and dead-heats see my Notes on three Athletic Inscriptions in JHS LXXXII (1962) p. 9.   Alexander; Hdt. V. 22.   Demetrius; IAG 86 = SEG XII. 512.   Eupolemos; Paus. VI. iii. 7, VIII. xlv. 4. P. Ox. 2381. D.S. XIV. 54. Afric. Ol. 96.

16 In Homer's chariot race Phoenix is sent to be umpire at the turn; Il. XXIII. 359.

17 Cleitomachus; Paus. VI. xv. 5.   Order. Athens; Syll³. 667. Thebes;
   CIG 1590. 1591. Aphrodisias; CIG 2758.

18 Draw; Lucian, Herm. 40.

19 Luck of draw; Pind. Nem. VI. 63. Pausanias (VI. i. 2.) says that he will
   not enumerate all Olympic winners, because some won by the luck of
   the draw and not by merit.   ἀνέφεδρος; Inscr. Ol. 54, 225, 227.

20 Aristoph. Frogs, 790 ff. Eur. Rhes. 119. Soph. Aj. 610.   In
   Coephoroi 865,

   τοιάνδε πάλην μόνος ὢν ἔφεδρος
   δισσοῖς μέλλει θεῖος 'Ορέστης
   ἄψειν. εἴη δ'ἐπὶ νίκῃ,

   Aeschylus must have written ἀνέφεδρος or μόνος οὐκ ἔφεδρος. The
   ἔφεδρος of the received text, in spite of all the efforts of generations of
   editors to explain it, makes nonsense.

21 'Night or Day'; Plato Comicus, Fr. 153.

22 Number of entrants. Olympia; Inscr. Ol. 164 = IAG 20 (4 opponents
   beaten). Inscr. Ol. 174 = IAG 33 (4). Inscr. Ol. 225 (3 beaten
   ἀνέφεδρος). Paus. V. xii. 6 (3 beaten in boys' boxing). Pind. Ol. VIII.
   68 (4 in boys' wrestling).   Elsewhere; IAG 48 (3). Pind. Pyth.
   VIII. 82 (4 at Delphi).   Prestige of competing at Olympia; Newton
   Halicarnassos II. 774, 59.

23 Antioch; JRS III (1913) p. 267 ff.   Xanthus; IGR 623.

24 Gardiner, *Olympia*, p. 308.   Xen. Hell. VII. iv. 29.

25 Thefts; Dem. XXIV (Timocr.) 114.

26 Sarapion; Paus. V. xxi. 18.   Superstitions; Plut. Mor. 461e.
   Philostr. Ap. Ty. VII. 37.   Charm; P. Ox. 1478 (Loeb. Sel. Pap. I.
   p. 443).   Astrology; Ptol. Tetr. IV. iv. 179, 180.

27 ἱερός e.g. IAG 71 = Inscr. Magnesia 180, 181. IAG 72, 77 = IG XIV.
   739 = IGR I. 144. IAG 79 = IG XIV. 1102 = IGR I. 153. SEG XI. 61.
   I. Ol. 56. SIG 1073. 48. Polyb. XXXIX. 8, 9.

28 Ti. Claudius Rufus; Syll³. 1073 = I. Ol. 54.

29 Hermagoras; IAG 77 = IG XIV. 739 = IGR I. 444.   Pankratiast;
   M. Aurelius Asclepiades; see above, Ch. V. p. 127.

30 Farewell; Lucian, Dem. 65.   Julian (Loeb. Lyra Graeca III. p. 528)
   gives the herald's opening summons: 'The festival, bestower of noble
   prizes, is beginning; Time bids us delay no longer. When you hear my
   summoning cry, set foot alongside foot on the starting line. Victory
   shall be in the hand of Zeus'.   Feast; e.g. Syll³. 691. At Olympia;
   Paus. V. xv. 12. P. Ox. VII. 1015 (Loeb. Sel. Pap. III. p. 526) has an
   anonymous poem in praise of Theon, a gymnasiarch, for providing oil
   and buns, δώρων Δημήτερος ἀγνῆς, for boys.

CHAPTER VIII

1 Function; Philostr. Gym. 14. Galen, San. Tuend. II. viii. 25.   Massage: Ar. N.E. 1118b. Galen (VI. 4). speaks of 'many varieties of
   massage', unfortunately without describing them.

2 Pind. Ol. VIII. 53. X. 19. Nem. IV. 93, V. 47, Isth. IV. 71.   Callipateira; Paus. V. vi. 8. The same story is told by Philostratus (Gym. 17.)
   of Callipateira's sister Pherenice.

3 Dromeus; Paus. VI. vii. 10.   Eurymenes; D.L. VIII. 12. Porph. Vit.
   Pythag. 15.   Charmis; Afric. sub ann. 668.   Butcher's shop;
   Theophr. Char. IX. 4.   Euripides and others; ap. Ath. 413c ff. Cf.
   Xen. Mem. I. ii. 4. Plut. Arat. 3, Mor. 995e.   Oversleeping; Plut.
   Phil. 3, Mor. 274d. D. Chrys. VIII. 29.   Epict. III. 15. εὐτακτεῖν,
   ἀναγκοφαγεῖν, ἀπέχεσθαι πεμμάτων.

4 Bread; Xen. Mem. III. xiv. 3.   Trainers on subject of diet; Philostr.
   Gym. 44.

5 Plut. Mor. 133b.   Antiphon; Plut. loc. cit.   Yellow powder;
   Philostr. Gym. 56.

6 Training classes; Pl. Pol. 294d.   Farming as training; Philostr.
   Gym. 43. Xen. Oec. v. 8. D.L. I. 81. Ael. V.H. VII. 4. Tisander;
   Philostr. Gym. 43. Paus. VI. xiii. 8.   Vases; CVA France vol. X.
   Paris, B.N. II. 67. No. 350. British Museum B.F. Lekuthos, B578.

7 Aristotle N.E. 1112b. Isocrates (XV. 183.) says, 'Trainers teach their

pupils first the moves (σχήματα) which have been found by experience to be useful in competition.'

8 Temperaments; Philostr. Gym. 42.

9 Lion etc.; Philostr. Gym. 37 ff.

10 Tetrad; Philostr. Gym. 47.   Gerenus; id. 54.   'Stabbed with a strigil'; id. 18.

11 Tetrad at Olympia; Philostr. Gym. 54.   Month's training; Philostr. Ap. Ty. V. 43. Paus. VI. xxiii. 1 ff. Syll³. 1073.   Weight-lifting; Epict. III. xii. 9, xx. 10.

12 Shadow-boxing; Philostr. Gym. 11. Pl. Lg. 830c. Xen. Symp. ii. 18. Paus. VI. x. 3. Lucian, Herm. 33.   Boxer's belly; Philostr. Gym. 34. Tr. R. S. Robinson.   Punch-ball (κώρυκος); Ar. Rhet. III. 11. 13. Philostr. Gym. 57. Lucian, Lex. 5. Plautus, Rudens 722.

13 Halteres as dumb-bells; Philostr. Gym. 55. Galen, San. Tuend. II. 11. 3.

14 Sparring partner; Inscr. Priene 111. (προσγυμναστής). Xen. Symp. ii. 17, Lac. Pol. ix. 4. (συγγυμναστής). Isoc. I. 12. (ἀνταγωνιστής). Epict. III. xx. 9 (προσγυμναζόμενος), I. xxiv. 1, I. xxix. 34, IV. iv. 11 (νεανισκός). Seneca Ep. LXXXIII. 4. (progymnastes). The comic poet Timocles (C. 4 B.C. ap. Ath. VI. 246f) speaks of parasites and hangers-on of the wealthy, who offer themselves as sparring-partners and allow their patrons to use them as punch-balls (ἀντὶ κωρύκων).   Statue; ἀνδριάς. Epict. III. xii, 10, Ench. 47. Dem. XVIII. (De Cor.) 129. ἡ μήτηρ —— τὸν καλὸν ἀνδριάντα καὶ τριταγωνιστὴν ἄκρον ἐξέθρεψέ σε. The usual rendering, 'pretty darling', based on Bekker, Anecd. 394, 29, is far too feeble for the passage in Demosthenes.   Iccus; Paus. VI. x. 5. Lucian, Hist. Conscr. 35. Plato, Prot. 316d and schol. ad loc., Lg. VIII. 840a.   Melesias; Pind. Ol. VIII. 54 and schol. ad loc., Nem. IV. 93.   Hippomachus; Paus. VI. xii. 6. Ael. V.H. II. 6. Plut. Dio 2. Ath. XIII. 584c. Aeschines (Tim. 189) also says, 'We can recognize an athlete by his general air of well-being (εὐεξία) without visiting the gymnasium'.

15 Lampon; Pind. Isth. VI. 73.

16 Herodicus; Plut. Mor. 554c. Schol. Pl. Prot. 316e, Rep. 406a. Lucian, Hist. Conscr. 35.

CHAPTER IX

1 Paus. V. xvi. 1.

2 IAG 63 = Syll³. 802.

3 Nicegora; Fr. Spiro in Fest. Vahlen. (Berlin. 1900) p. 137. See Moretti, IAG p. 168.

4 Sparta; Paus. III. xiii. 7. Plut. Lyc. xiv. 2, Mor. 227d. Eur. And. 597.   Plato; Rep. 452 ff., Lg. VII. 804e, VIII. 833c.

5 Sappho; Fr. 73 (Loeb. Lyra Graeca I), 71 (Bergk). Ἥρων ἐξεδίδαξ' ἐγ Γυάρων τὰν ἀννόδρομον.

6 Chios; Ath. XIII. 566e.   Italy; Schol. ad Juv. IV. 53. Suet. Dom. IV. 4.   Helen; Ath. X. 414d.

7 Priestess and unmarried women; Paus. VI. xx. 9.   Typaeum; Paus. V. vi. 7.   Nero; Suet. Ner. XII. 4.   Augustus; Suet. Aug. XLIV. 3.

8 Women gymnasiarchs; SEG XIV. 575 (Pamphylia). CIG 267 (Athens), 2384 (Paros), 3953 (c).   Tata; MAMA VIII. 492 = CIG 2820. Adrastus; MAMA VIII. 484.

9 Pericles; Thuc. II. 45.

CHAPTER X

1 Thibron; Xen. Hell. IV. viii. 18.

2 School at Miletus; Syll³. 577.   At Teos; Syll³. 578.

3 Egyptian trainer; P. Cairo Zen. 59060. (Loeb. Select Papyri, I.88). Browning; Rabbi Ben Ezra.

A NOTE ON BOOKS

MOST of the Greek and Latin authors quoted or referred to in this book are available in the Loeb edition, with English translation opposite the original text. Where athletic details are concerned the translations are sometimes unreliable, and I have tried to supply more accurate versions. The most important literary work on the subject not published in Loeb is the *Gymnastic* of Philostratus; for this there is Jüthner's excellent edition (Leipzig, 1909), with introduction and notes in German. To celebrate the Paris Olympiad of 1924, an *Anthologie des Textes Sportifs de l'Antiquité* in a French translation by M. Berger and E. Moussat was published in 1927 (Grasset, Paris.). The task has been much better performed in English by Mrs. R. S. Robinson in *Sources for the History of Greek Athletics* (University of Illinois, 1955). This book is particularly valuable because it includes all the most important parts of Philostratus's *Gymnastic*. Two other indispensable works for those who wish to refer to the original sources are *Iscrizioni Agonistiche Greche* (Rome, 1953) and *Olympionikai* (Rome, 1957), both by L. Moretti. The former is a selection of 90 inscriptions representing all periods, with a sane and scholarly commentary on each in Italian. The second is a list of all known Olympic victors, also with notes in Italian; it renders obsolete the earlier works on the subject by Förster, Klee, Knab and Mezö.

Of general treatments of Greek athletics, E. Norman Gardiner's *Athletics of the Ancient World* (Oxford, 1930) is incomparable. It incorporates the best of his earlier *Greek Athletic Sports and Festivals* (London, 1910) and of his articles in the *Journal of Hellenic Studies* from 1903 to 1907 which were the beginning of the intelligent modern treatment of the subject. It also embodies all that was worth keeping in the work of Krause, Jüthner and Schröder.

For Olympia and its monuments there is the official report of the German excavations, *Die Ausgrabungen zu Olympia* (5 vols. Berlin, 1876–81) and the complete publication of the results by F. Adler, E.

Curtius, W. Dörpfeld and others, *Olympia; die Ergebnisse der von dem Deutschen Reich veranstalteten Ausgrabung* (5 vols. Berlin, 1890–7), but these are for the specialist. The ordinary reader will find all he wants in E. N. Gardiner's *History and Remains of Olympia* (Oxford, 1925). This now needs to be supplemented by an account of the recent excavations. Here again there are the official reports, *Berichte über die Ausgrabungen in Olympia* (6 vols. Berlin, 1937–58) and the complete account by E. Kunze and H. Schlief, *Olympische Forschungen* (4 vols. Berlin, 1944–59) for the specialist, conveniently summarized by E. Kunze in *Neue Ausgrabungen in Olympia* (Berlin, 1960).

The subject of Athletics in Greek Art still awaits full modern treatment. The quality of the reproductions in such works as Furtwängler's *Die Bedeutung der Gymnastik in der Griechischen Kunst* (Leipzig, 1905) and Brauchitsch's *Die Panathenäischen Preisamphoren* (Leipzig, 1919) renders them inadequate today, and the same is true of W. W. Hyde's *Olympic Victor Monuments and Greek Athletic Art* (Washington, 1921), valuable as the book is in other respects. Gardiner's *Athletics of the Ancient World* is excellently illustrated. The *Corpus Vasorum Antiquorum* includes all athletic vase paintings in the museums it has so far covered, but the standard of reproduction, especially in the early volumes, is not high. *Lo Sport nell'Arte* by R. Carità (Bergamo, 1960) has some good reproductions of Greek work in its early pages, and most books on Greek vase-painting include a few athletic subjects in their plates. When the Olympic Games were held in Berlin in 1936, an exhibition of vase paintings and small objects depicting the athletics of antiquity was arranged, and the illustrated catalogue by C. Blümel, *Sport der Hellenen*, with notes in German, remains the best volume of illustrations of Greek Athletics, but naturally the material is drawn chiefly from German museums. As an act of academic piety to celebrate the same Olympiad, an essay, *Olympia*, by the eminent nineteenth-century German scholar E. Curtius, was republished (Berlin, 1935), together with German translations of some passages from Pindar, Pausanias and Lucian. The essay is of some little value as showing the romantic nineteenth-century view of Greek athletics, but the most interesting feature of the book is that it is illustrated with some of the early work of the photographer Martin Hürlimann.

Other books and articles dealing with particular parts of the subject have been mentioned in the notes. Bibliographies including older works on Greek athletics will be found in the books of Gardiner, Moretti, Robinson and Kunze mentioned above, and there is an excellent bibliography in J. Ebert's *Zum Pentathlon der Antike*.

MAP I

SHOWING ORIGIN OF ATHLETES KNOWN TO HAVE WON AT OLYMPIA. 776–600 B.C.

Athens	7
Cleonae	1
Corinth	2
Croton	1
Dyspontium	1
Elis	3
Epidaurus	3
Hyperesia	1
Messenia	8
Pisa	1
Sicyon	1
Smyrna	1
Sparta	33
Sybaris	1
Syracuse	1
Thebes	1

The numbers are of victories, not of victors.

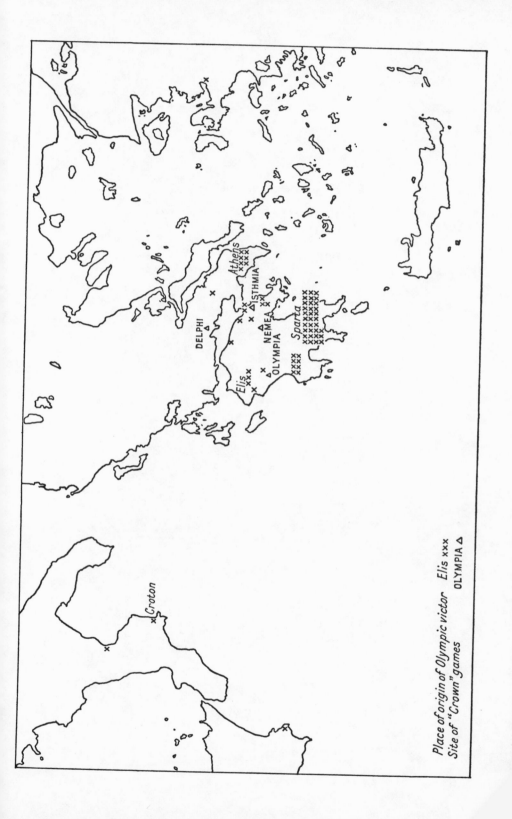

Place of origin of Olympic victor Elis ×××
Site of "Crown" games OLYMPIA △

MAP 2

SHOWING ORIGIN OF ATHLETES KNOWN TO HAVE WON AT OLYMPIA, 596–300 B.C.

Place	No.	Place	No.	Place	No.	Place	No.
Aegeion	1	Corcyra	6	Magnesia on Meander	5	Pheneus	1
Aegina	5	Corinth	6	Malis	1	Phigaleia	4
Akragas	3	Cos	1	Mantinea	6	Posidonia	2
(Agrigento)		Crete	4	Maronea	1	Rhodes	9
Ambracia	1	Croton	20	Messana	4	Samos	5
Amphipolis	1	Cyrene	5	(Sicily)		Scotussa	1
Andros	1	Delphi	2	Messene	4	(Thessaly)	
Anthedon		Dipea	1	Methydrion	2	Sicyon	4
(Boeotia)		(Arcadia)		(Arcadia)		Sparta	13
Apollonia	1	Elis	27	Miletus	7	Stratos	1
(Illyria)		Ephesus	4	Naxos	4	Stymphalus	2
Argos	9	Epidamnus	1	(Sicily)		Syracuse	9
Astypalaea	1	Epidaurus	2	Opus	4	Taras	9
Athens	14	Halicarnassus	1	Orcomenos	1	(Tarentum)	
Barce	1	Heraea	10	Orestasius	1	Tegea	1
Camarina	1	(Arcadia)		(Arcadia)		Thasos	2
Carystus	1	Himera	6	Parrhasia	2	Thebes	2
Caulonia	1	Larissa	3	Patrae	2	Thespiae	2
Ceos	3	Lemnos	1	Pelinna	4	Thessaly	5
Chalcis	2	Lepreum	8	(Thessaly)		Thurii	3
Cleitor	3	Locri Epiz.	6	Pellene	10	Tiryns	1
Cleonae	1	Macedonia	1	Peparethus	1	Troezen	1
Colophon	1	Maenalus	7	Pharsalus	3		

The numbers are those of victories, not victors.

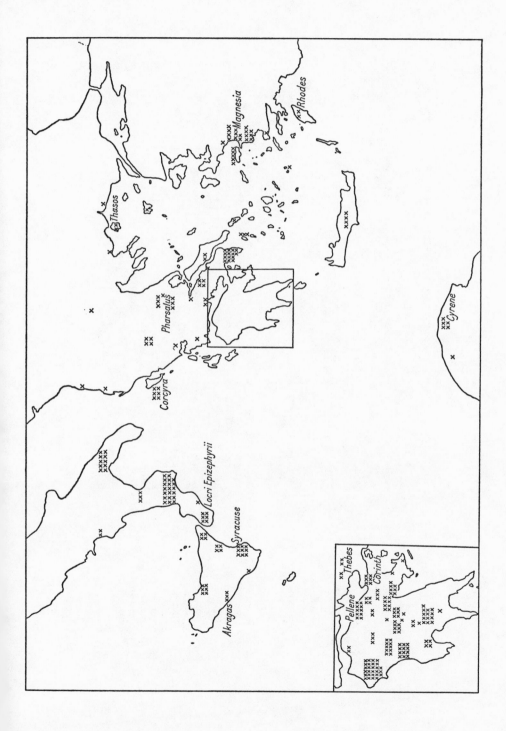

Magnesia
Rhodes
Thasos
Pharsalus
Cyrene
Corcyra
Locri Epizephyrii
Syracuse
Akragas
Pellene
Thebes
Corinth

MAP 3

SHOWING ORIGIN OF KNOWN OLYMPIC VICTORS, 296 B.C.–369 A.D.

Place	No.	Place	No.	Place	No.	Place	No.
Acreae	5	Cappadocia	1	Laodicea (Phrygia)	1	Salamis (Cyprus)	7
Adana	2	Caria	1	Larissa	1	Samos	2
Adramyttium	1	Ceramus (Caria)	3	Lesbos	3	Sardis	3
Aegeira	4	Chios	3	Lindos	1	Seleucia (Orontes)	2
Aegina	1	Clazomenae	1	Macedonia	2	Seleucia (Tigris)	1
Aeolis	1	Colophon	2	Magnesia (Meander)	10	Sicyon	11
Aetolia	2	Corcyra	2	Magnesia (Sipilus)	1	Side	2
Alexandria (Egypt)	43	Corinth	1	Mantinea	1	Sidon	2
Alexandria (Troas)	2	Cos	5	Megalopolis	1	Smyrna	7
Ambracia	1	Cumæ (Aeolis)	1	Megara	1	Sparta	7
Amphissa	1	Cydonia (Crete)	1	Messene	4	Stratonicea (Meander)	3
Anthedon (Boeotia)	1	Cyparissa	2	Miletus	10	Syracuse	2
Anticyra (Phocis)	1	Cyrene	3	Naucratis	1	Tarsus	1
Antioch (Syria)	6	Cyzicus	4	Neapolis (Italy)	1	Tauromenium	1
Apamaea (Bithynia)	2	Delphi	1	Nicaea (Bithynia)	2	Tegea	2
Arcadia	1	Elatea	2	Nysa (Caria)	1	Tenedos	1
Argos	4	Elis	17	Patrae	1	Tenos	1
Armenia	1	Ephesus	11	Pergamum	2	Thebes	2
Aspendos	1	Epidaurus	1	Petra (Macedonia)	1	Thelphusa	1
Assos	1	Epirus	1	Pharsalus	1	Thurii	2
Athens	2	Eritrea	2	Philadelphia (Lydia)	8	Thyateira (Lydia)	2
Bargylia (Caria)	1	Gortyna (Crete)	1	Phoenicia	2	Tralles	3
Bithynia	3	Halicarnassus	1	Prusa	1	Tritea	1
Boeotia	2	Hypaepa (Lydia)	1	Rhodes	19	Tyana	1
		Iasus (Caria)	1			Xanthus	8
						Zacynthus	1

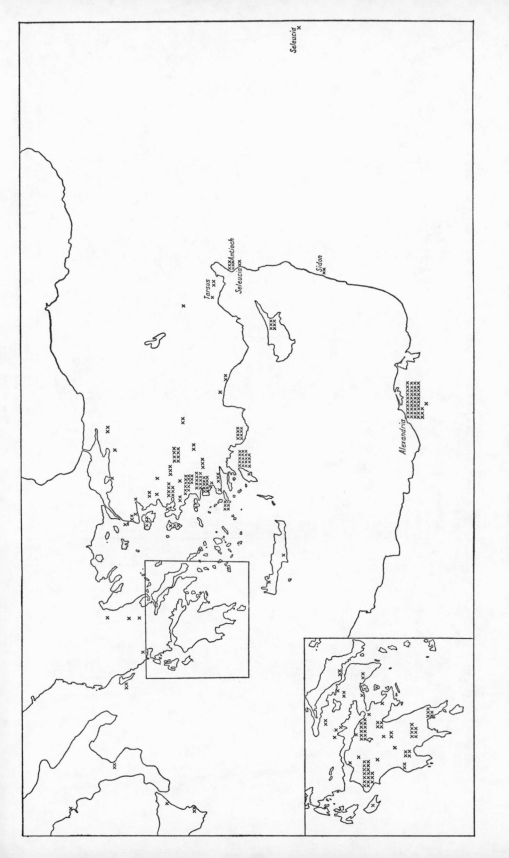

Seleucia

Tarsus
Antioch
Seleucia
Sidon

Alexandria

MAP 4

Cities of the Greek world in which athletics meetings are known to have been held. Where more than one festival is known, the number is indicated in brackets. Some of these meetings were annual, some biennial, and some were held once every four years.

Adana
Adramyttium
Aegae (Cilicia)
Aegae (Macedonia)
Aegium (Achaea)
Alexandria (Egypt) (7)
Anazarbus (5)
Ancyra (6)
Antinoopolis (Egypt)
Antioch (Pisidia)
Antioch (Syria)
Apamea
Aphrodisias (3)
Apollonia (Galatia)
Apollonia (Illyria)
Argos (3)
Ascalon
Aspendos
Athens (8)
Balbura
Beroea (Macedonia) (3)
Beroea (Syria)
Berytus
Brundisium
Byzantium
Caesarea Panias
Caesarea Stratonis (2)
Castabala
Caunus
Cedreae
Cephallene
Chalcedon
Chalcis (Euboea) (2)
Chalcis (Syria)
Chios
Cibyra
Citium

Claudiopolis (Bithynia)
Cleitor
Cnidos
Colophon
Corcyra
Coronea
Cos (4)
Cyzicus (4)
Damascus (3)
Delos (3)
Delphi (3)
Demetrias
Dion
Dodona
Eleusis
Ephesus (8)
Epidaurus (2)
Gaza
Gortyna
Hadrianea (Bithynia)
Halicarnassus (3)
Heraclea (Pontus)
Hieropolis (Phrygia) (4)
Hieropolis (Syria)
Histiaea
Iasos
Iconium
Isthmia (3)
Laodicea (Phrygia) (5)
Laodicea (Syria)
Larissa (2)
Lebadea (2)
Leucas
Lusi (Arcadia)
Magnesia (2)
Mantinea (2)
Marathon

Massalia
Mazaca (2)
Megara
Mesembria
Metropolis
Miletus (4)
Mitylene
Mopsuestia
Myndus
Neapolis (Italy)
Neapolis (Samaria)
Nemea
Neocaesarea (2)
Nicaea (Bithynia) (5)
Nicomedea (3)
Nicopolis (Alexandria)
Nicopolis (Epirus)
Nysa (Caria)
Odessus
Oenoande
Olbia
Olympia
Opus
Oropus
Patrae
Pella
Pellene
Pergamum (7)
Perga
Perinthus
Pessinus
Pheneus
Philadelphia (Arabia)
Philadelphia (Lydia) (2)
Philippopolis (2)
Phthia
Plataea

Prusias (3)
Puteoli
Rhion
Rhodes (5)
Rome (4)
Sagalassus
Salamis (Cyprus)
Sardis (5)
Scythopolis
Sicyon (3)
Side
Sidon
Smyrna (4)
Sparta (12)
Stratonicea
Tarentum
Tarsus (4)
Tavium
Tegea
Teos
Termessus
Thebes
Thermus
Thespiae
Thessalonica
Thyateira
Tlos
Tralles (2)
Tripolis (Phrygia)
Tripolis (Syria)
Troas
Tuessus
Tyre (4)
Xanthus
Zeugma

All these festivals are attested by the inscriptions of athletes who won victories at them or of the agonothetai who arranged them. It is a reasonable assumption that most of the cities which produced Olympic victors (Maps 1, 2 and 3) held their own athletic meetings, and that those of them which do not appear in the list above should be added to it. It is hardly conceivable, for instance, that Croton, Syracuse and Akragas (Agrigentum) did not hold such festivals in their great days. The existence of a stadium, as at Cyrene, is also adequate evidence of meetings having been held.

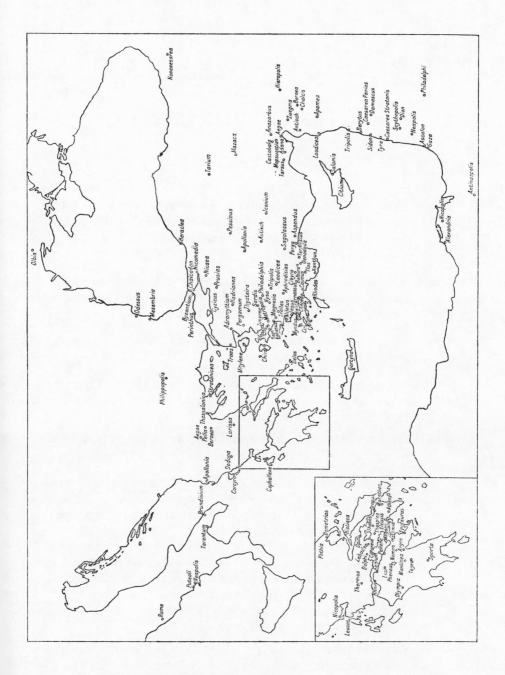

Naucaesarea

Olbia

Odessus

Mesembria

Heraclea

Byzantium Chalcedon Nicomedia
Perinthus Nicaea
Cyzicus Prusias
Adramyttium Hadrianea
Troas Pergamum Thyateira
Mytilene Sardis Philadelphia
Chios Smyrna Tralles Laodicea
Teos Magnesia Aphrodisias
Ephesus Nysa
Delos Miletus Cnidus Caunus Oenanda
Myndus Halicarnassus Telmessus
Cos Panthus
Rhodes

Tavium

Mazaca

Castabala Anazarbus
Mopsuestia Sidena
Tarsus Aegae
Laodicea
Calamis Seleucia

Hieropolis

Zeugma Beroea
Antioch Chalcis
Apamea

Caesarea Panias
Berytus Damascus
Sidon Caesarea Stratonis
Tyre Scythopolis
Neapolis
Ascalon Philadelphi
Gaza

Philippopolis

Aegae Thessalonica
Pella
Beraea
Dodona Larissa

Apollonia
Corcyra
Cephallene

Brundisium
Tarentum

Puteoli
Nicopolis

Rome

Pessinus
Apollonia
Antioch Iconium
Sagalassus
Perga Aspendus
Pamphylia Side
Perge
Xanthus

Gortyna

Antinoopolis

Nicopolis
Alexandria

Pthia Demetrias
Thermus
Leucas Opus Thespiae Chalcis
Delphi Thebes Tanagra
Lusso Plataea Megara
Olympia Mantinea Argos Epidaurus
Tegea

Nicopolis
Leucas

Sporta

NOTES ON THE PLATES

1(*a*) The pose of the discus thrower obviously owes more to the dance than to the stadium. Yet it suggests two features of the genuine throw: the reversal of the feet and the swing of the upper part of the body from the hips.

2 It is curious to note that these boxers of *c*. 1600 B.C. are wearing ear-guards. The only other evidence for these in antiquity is the statement of Plutarch seventeen centuries later (p. 99).

3 The runners are depicted in an impossible position, with left arm and left leg advanced together.

4(*a*) The runners show the same mistake as those in Plate 3. The shorts of the runners were not on the vase originally, but are the result of over-painting in modern times.

(*b*) From the same vase as (*a*). The turning post can be faintly detected behind the left leg of the last runner.

5(*a*) This small bronze statue is described on the museum label as 'Jumper landing', which is certainly wrong. With more probability it has been interpreted as a diver, but to this there are two objections: a diver's feet are usually level, and he generally looks down at the point on the surface of the water which he hopes to hit with his dive. The feet of the statue are in the position suggested by the grooves in the starting sills of several stadia, and the pose corresponds exactly with Plato's description of the runner at the start resembling a charioteer reining in his horses.
Height: 5¾ inches. Fifth century B.C.

(*b*) Allowing for the shape of the space to be filled, the stance of the athlete corresponds closely to that of the bronze in (*a*).

6 Left: wrestlers. Right: a jumper landing. Behind him stands an athlete holding two javelins; in front of him, an umpire with a measuring-rod. The jumper is using weights of the earlier pattern; the wrestlers and the javelin thrower appear to be wearing caps. The three vertical lines below the jumper obviously represent pegs at the side of the pit to mark the efforts of other competitors; a German scholar suggested that they were spikes set in the pit itself to discourage jumping short. End of sixth century B.C.

7 Jumper landing. His effort is accompanied by music on the double flute.

8 Jumper in mid-air. His weights are of the later 'telephone hand-piece' pattern. The figure on the right holds a measuring-rod.

9(a) The origin of the discus. It is clear why the Greeks called the discus 'lentil-shaped' or 'moon-shaped'. The weight of this ingot is 24 pounds.

(b) The thrower is in mid-turn, and the effort he is expending is well suggested. To the left is a pickaxe of the kind used by athletes for clearing the stadium; to the right, the athlete's oil-flask and sponge or towel.

10 Small bronze statue of an athlete of the second century B.C. in the pose of Myron's Discobolos. This probably comes nearer to the original than do the large marble and plaster copies and casts in our museums. The right foot and discus are restored. Height: 9½ inches.

11(b) Discus thrower at forward point of rest in his preliminary swing. The left hand comes up to steady the discus and to prevent the muscles of the throwing arm from tightening. The thrower is wearing a cap. As recently as 1959, an English translation of a German work included a picture of a thrower in this position, with the caption 'Athlete preparing to throw the discus with both hands'. The javelin thrower is pressing back the javelin with his left hand to keep the loop taut. Above: pair of jumping-weights. Behind: pickaxe.

12(a) The moment before the throw. The thrower's forefinger is extended to hold the loop; the javelin is pointed. The pillar is probably the turning post in the middle of the starting line; it is noteworthy that it is stepped at the base.

(b) The javelin thrower is running up to the line, the discus thrower is taking up position, holding the discus in his left hand and flexing

P

the muscles of his throwing arm; both are accompanied on the double flute. Right: a boxer is adjusting the himas on his left hand.

(c) The thrower is tightening the thong of the javelin loop by holding it under his left foot and pulling. Behind him hang his sponge and oil-flask.

13 (a) Palaestra scene. Left: wrestlers using akrocheirismos technique. Centre: umpire with wand of office and forked stick for punishing offenders. Athlete with pickaxe. Right: boxer preparing to put on himas.

(b) Two pairs of wrestlers closely engaged. Between them a water-jug and towel. The clothed figure on the left is probably an umpire; he holds his rod with his first and second fingers extended as if for throwing a javelin. The object in his left hand may be a flower he is smelling or a powder-puff for the bodies of the wrestlers.

14 (a) The middle of a throw in wrestling. Left: umpire.

(b) Small bronze group. The hold which the older athlete has secured on the younger seems designed to force the surrender in the pankration rather than to lead to a throw in wrestling. This is a copy made in Roman imperial times of an earlier Greek original. Height: 6½ inches.

15   Boxers in action. Umpire with forked stick.

16   The end of a boxing match. The competitor on the right holds up his hand in acknowledgement of defeat. The artist has not depicted boxing gloves on the fighters' hands, but there is no reason to believe that this is a pankration contest. Right: athlete holding himas. Left: umpire with forked stick.

17   A pankratiast is biting the left forearm of his opponent, who is retaliating with his right fist. The umpire, partly seen on the right, is about to intervene.

18   This may depict either wrestling or the pankration, probably the latter. It looks as if the athlete on the right has tried to kick, as he was allowed to do in the pankration, but has been outwitted.

19 (a) Boxers in action. The extended forefinger of the boxer to the right is not easy to explain.

(b) If Plutarch's statement that grappling was not allowed in boxing is correct, this must be the pankration; the absence of himantes supports this. The athlete on the right is bleeding from the nose.

(c) Boxers in action. If the athlete on the left is not parrying with his left, he is hitting with the heel of the hand. Left: umpire. Right: boxer holding himantes.

20   Left: boxers. Centre: pankratiasts; each is trying to gouge his opponent's eye, and the umpire is about to flog them apart. Above them hangs a discus in the sling which was used to carry it.

21   These are obviously pankratiasts, although the artist has depicted them wearing gloves.

22(a) This elegant little figure, found in the agora at Athens, was probably a prize at some athletics meeting. The boy is binding the ribbon of victory on his head. The ribbon is modern.

(b) The inscription on this bronze cauldron reads: 'I was put up as a prize at the games of Onomastus son of Pheidileus'. The bowl, which belongs to the sixth century B.C., was found at Cyme in Italy.

(c) This relief is from a base on which once stood a statue of an athlete, Alexander of Rhamnus. It shows some of the trophies which he won. From left to right: the amphora of olive oil from the Panathenaic games at Athens, the wreath of pine from the Isthmian games, the shield from the Heraea at Argos, and the wreath of wild celery from the Nemean games. It belongs to the Hellenistic period.

23(a) This shows the stadium at Olympia in the spring of 1963, restored after the recent excavations.

(b) This eastern boundary wall of an earlier stadium was revealed in the excavations. It lay across the later stadium, 60 yards west of the starting line seen in the foreground of (a). The photograph was taken in the autumn of 1961. The foundations were covered when the surface of the stadium was restored in 1962.

(c) Stone supports for seats in the small stand for the use of officials at Olympia.

24(a) The elaboration of this marble seating at Delphi is in strong contrast to the simplicity of the spectators' accommodation at Olympia. Much of the wall supporting the seats on the south side has fallen away, taking the seats with it. The slight barrel-shaped widening of the stadium in the middle is clearly seen.

(b) The bases on the right belong to an ornamental arch of Roman times. The stones between these bases and the starting line are archaeologists' dumpings. The distance between sill and arch is so small that it is obvious that no race could have finished at this end of the stadium.

25   The stadium at Perga is a good example of the elaborate Greek buildings in the new Hellenistic cities of Asia Minor which arose after the time of Alexander the Great. The apsidal rooms on the outside of the supporting wall (b) probably served as shops or shelters.

26   The arrangements for the husplex at Isthmia, revealed by the excavations of Professor O. Broneer. Each groove for cords is crossed by bronze staples at the end near the post socket and at the point where it reaches the starter's pit.

27(a) The stadium at Ephesus had an elaborate façade adorned with columns standing on bases. In front of these was another row of bases which held statues. Behind these can be seen the vaulted banking for spectators' seats. A breach in it allows the vault to be seen.

(b) In the foreground, one of the cross-walls which divided the long vault into separate rooms. These were lighted by openings (right) among the spectators' seats.

28(a) The careful cutting of the grooves in this starting sill at Olympia can be seen, with a steep back wall to give a secure grip to the runner's toes, and a chamfered front wall to prevent tripping him up on the first stride. The cutting of the second socket so near the first at the bottom of the picture may have been connected with the necessity to have the exactly correct position for the turning post in the diaulos.

(b) These pairs of holes in the starting line at Corinth show the same careful cutting as the grooves at Olympia. The gap in the centre reveals a similar but earlier sill, at an angle to the later one. The change was probably made necessary by new buildings encroaching on the first track.

29(a) This isolated groove and socket, near the practice track in the gymnasium at Delphi, can have had no conceivable purpose except for practising starts with the husplex.

(b) The practice track (gymnasium) at Olympia was a stade in length and was roofed from the wall on the left to the outer row of columns, so that both legs of the track were covered. The similar track at Delphi had one leg roofed and one open.

30(*a*) The stadium at Epidaurus had stone seats at the finishing end only. The sill across the track in the foreground has grooves and sockets for the husplex. The stone pillars lying in front of it may be connected with another form of starting gate. There is an entrance for athletes through the embankment on the right in the middle of the seats.

(*b*) The athlete is carrying away the larger stones from the surface of the stadium before clearing the weeds with a pickaxe.

31(*a*) The holes in the back wall were concealed behind stone lions' heads, through whose mouths water poured into basins supported on the blocks below; one of the basins can still be seen to the right. In the left foreground is the large circular plunge bath.

(*b*) These 'sit baths' were discovered in the recent excavations. Each has an earthenware bowl for the athlete's feet set in the bottom of the bath at the lower end. The baths are arranged in groups.

GENERAL INDEX

234

INDEX OF GREEK AND LATIN
AUTHORS